IMAGES of America

CUMBERLAND COUNTY

IMAGES
of America

CUMBERLAND COUNTY

Joey Powell

ARCADIA
PUBLISHING

ISBN 978-0-7385-0270-0

Published by Arcadia Publishing
Charleston, South Carolina

Printed in the United States of America

Library of Congress Catalog Card Number: Applied for.

For all general information contact Arcadia Publishing at:
Telephone 843-853-2070
Fax 843-853-0044
E-Mail sales@arcadiapublishing.com
For customer service and orders:
Toll-Free 1-888-313-2665

Visit us on the Internet at www.arcadiapublishing.com

Contents

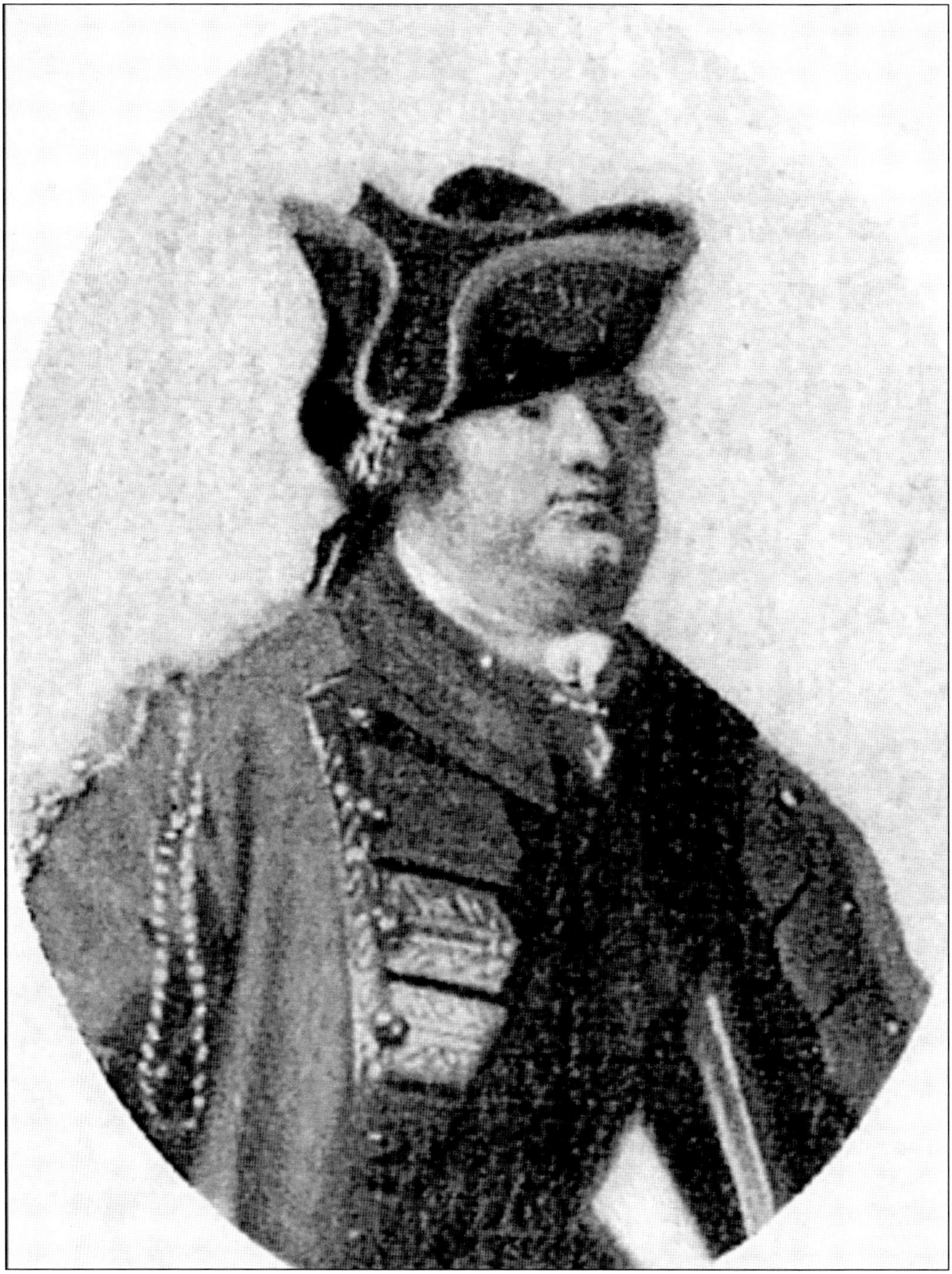

Pictured here is William Augustus, the Duke of Cumberland, son of King George II of Great Britain. He led the victorious British troops against the Scottish Jacobites at the Battle of Culloden on April 6, 1746.

INTRODUCTION

Cumberland County was established in 1754. Prior to its formation it was part of Bladen County. Bladen, which was formed in 1734, originally extended westward to the Mississippi River. Half of North Carolina's counties, and all of the state of Tennessee, originated in Bladen County.

Throughout the history of North Carolina, counties have been formed at the discretion of the legislature. Since laws governing the creation of new counties were not covered in the state constitution, they were formed as the need arose due to increases in population and the resulting need for increases in services provided.

The first influx of people to settle in what is now Cumberland was the Argyll Colony, a large group from Scotland that landed at Brunswick along the lower Cape Fear River in 1739. Upon landing, many of these immigrants moved up the Cape Fear in search of good, unclaimed land. These journeys brought many settlers to what is now Cumberland County.

A second mass migration of Scots to present-day Cumberland occurred after the Battle of Culloden Moor in Scotland in 1746. The defeat of the Scots at the hands of the English resulted in harsh measures placed upon them by the English government. As the earlier Argyll Colony did, many of them moved up the Cape Fear looking for good land on which to settle. With many of these Scots settling in northern Bladen County, it was apparent that a new county was needed, thus the creation of Cumberland County in 1754.

The new county was named in honor of William Augustus, the Duke of Cumberland, son of King George II of England. He had served as the commanding English officer at the Battle of Culloden. It is ironic that the new county, settled mostly by immigrants from Scotland, was named for their enemy in that earlier battle.

Cumberland's first county seat was called Choeffington. It was located on a bluff overlooking the confluence of Lower Little River with the Cape Fear, near the present village of Linden in northern Cumberland. Choeffington was a thriving village, complete with taverns, businesses, and a horse-racing track.

In 1763 the county seat moved to Campbellton, a village that was established in 1762, and later merged with Cross Creek to become Upper and Lower Campbellton. In 1783, the name was changed to Fayetteville in honor of Revolutionary War hero Marquis de Lafayette.

As the population of North Carolina grew, the need for new counties continued. In 1784, Cumberland was split into two counties named Fayette and Moore. Fayette County was short lived; five months later the legislature changed its name back to Cumberland.

Today, Cumberland is the fourth most populous county in North Carolina with an approximate population of 300,000. It contains 661 square miles, ranking it 18th in the state in that category.

Fayetteville is Cumberland's largest city and is the county seat. It is a major commercial center of southeastern North Carolina. Other Cumberland communities include Hope Mills, Spring Lake, Stedman, Vander, Godwin, Wade, Falcon, Eastover, Gray's Creek, and Linden. Cumberland is also the home of Fort Bragg and Pope Air Force Base.

One

Roadways, Railways, and Waterways

Transportation has been of vital importance to the people of Cumberland County since it was first settled in the early 1730s. Cumberland's original highway was the Cape Fear River. Once the Tuscarora threat of the early 1700s had ended, the Cape Fear valley was considered safe for settlement. The establishment of the thriving communities of Brunswick and Wilmington on the lower Cape Fear opened the door for settlement in what is now Cumberland. Throughout the 1730s, settlers left Wilmington and traveled upstream in search of land on which to build their homes. The number of people settling in Cumberland greatly increased when a large group of Scottish immigrants known as the Argyll Colony arrived via the Cape Fear in 1739.

Early settlers turned Native American trails and animal paths into roads of their own. The famed Fayetteville and Western Plank Road followed an old buffalo path that ran along high ridges throughout the county. Roads were laid out to such distant western North Carolina locales as Morganton and the Yadkin River. Modern roads following these earlier roadways in Fayetteville are appropriately named Morganton Road and Yadkin Road.

One of the first railroads in the United States was constructed in Fayetteville. Built in 1828, this wooden railed experimental railroad ran from old Campbellton to the Market House, but did not succeed. Railroads later came to Cumberland to stay; the Atlantic Coast Line, a major north-south connection, arrived in the late 1880s. Its downtown Fayetteville station remains in use as people ride Amtrak to destinations along the eastern seaboard.

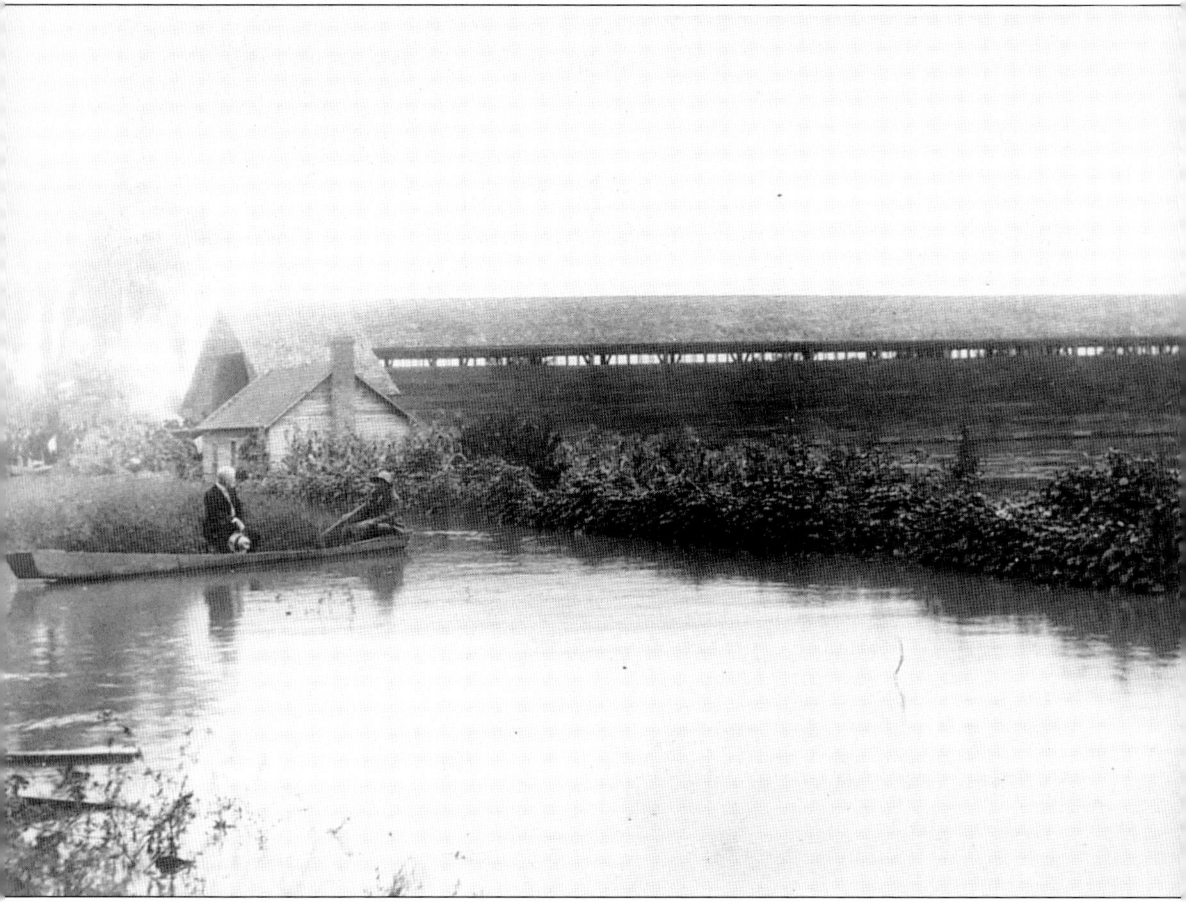

The Clarendon Bridge, spanning the Cape Fear River, is pictured during the flood of 1908. Damaged by the flood, the bridge was destroyed shortly afterward when a farmer burning an adjacent cornfield allowed his fire to rage out of control. He was later named Fayetteville chief of police, with critics charging that he was awarded this position due to his burning the damaged bridge, which was replaced with a modern steel structure a few months later. (Courtesy N.C. Department of Archives and History.)

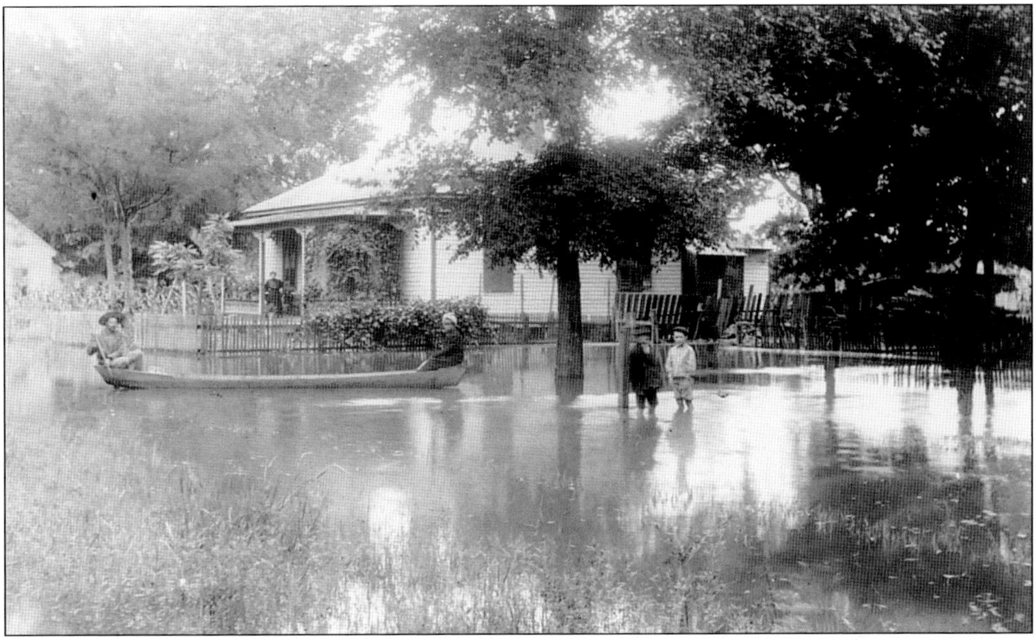

Young children watch as two adults paddle a canoe across the front yard of a Fayetteville home during the flood of 1908. (Courtesy N.C. Department of Archives and History.)

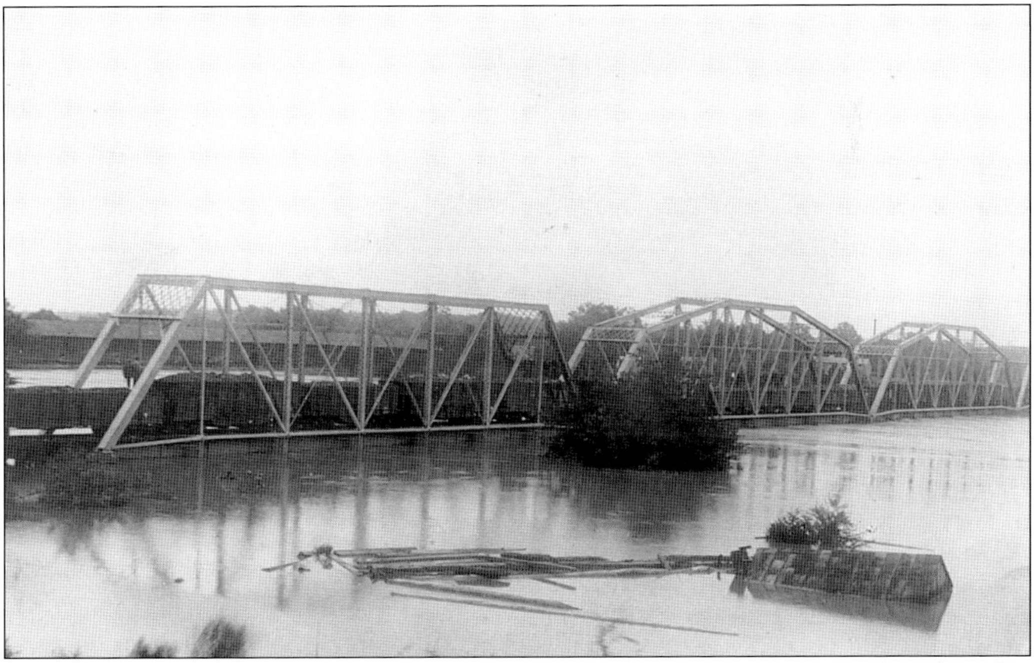

Floodwaters rise to the railroad bridge crossing the Cape Fear in 1908. Note the Clarendon Bridge in the background. (Courtesy N.C. Department of Archives and History.)

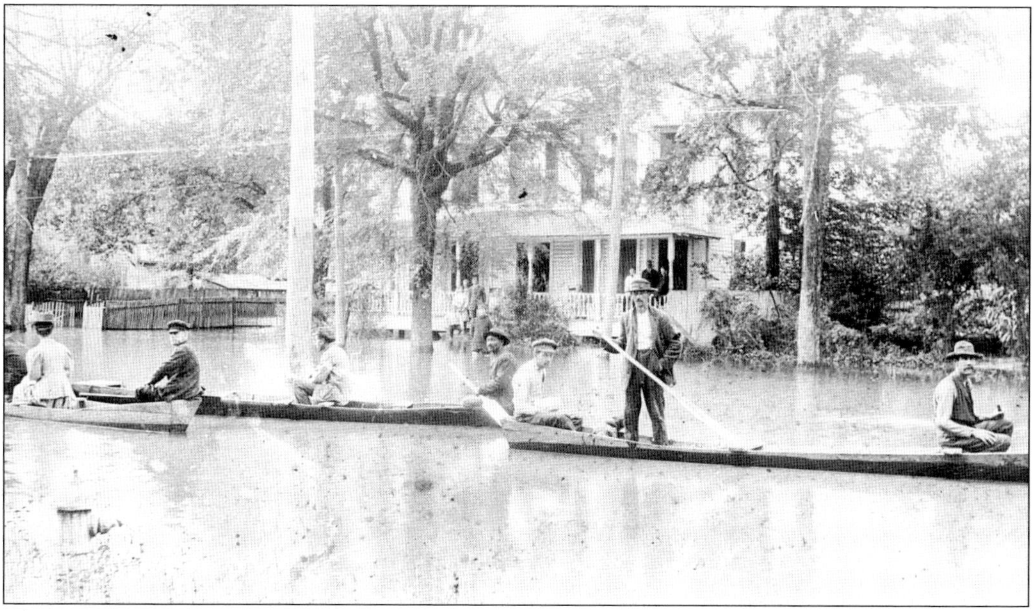

These men depended on boats for transportation while much of Fayetteville was underwater during the flood of 1908. (Courtesy N.C. Department of Archives and History.)

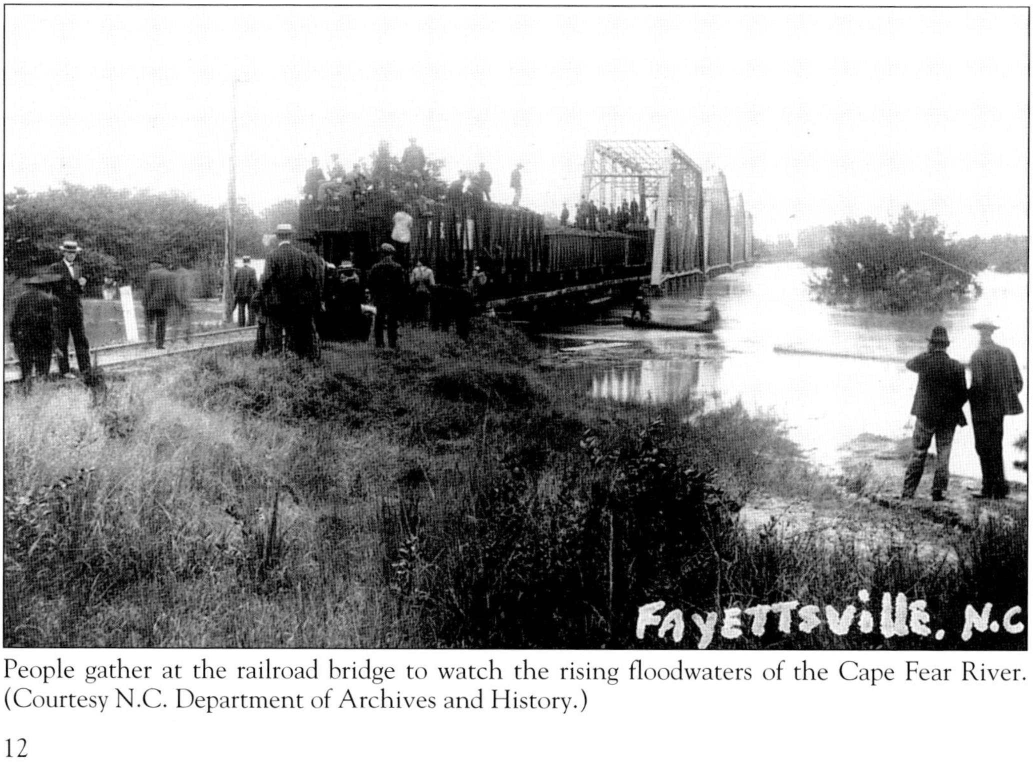

People gather at the railroad bridge to watch the rising floodwaters of the Cape Fear River. (Courtesy N.C. Department of Archives and History.)

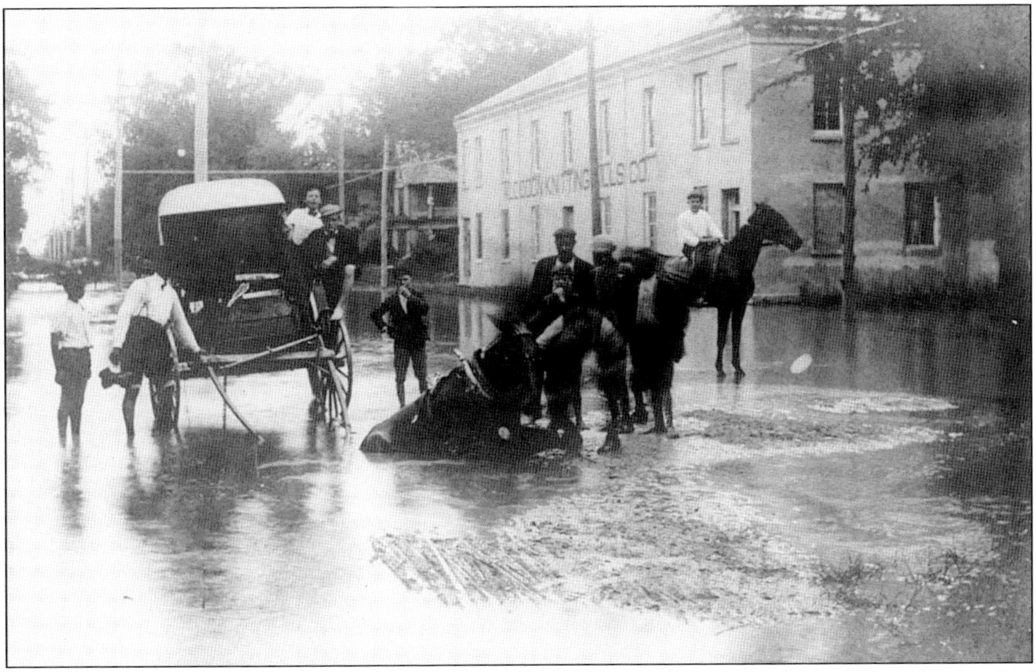

These stranded men are trying to rescue their horse that fell into a deep hole during the flood of 1908. (Courtesy N.C. Department of Archives and History.)

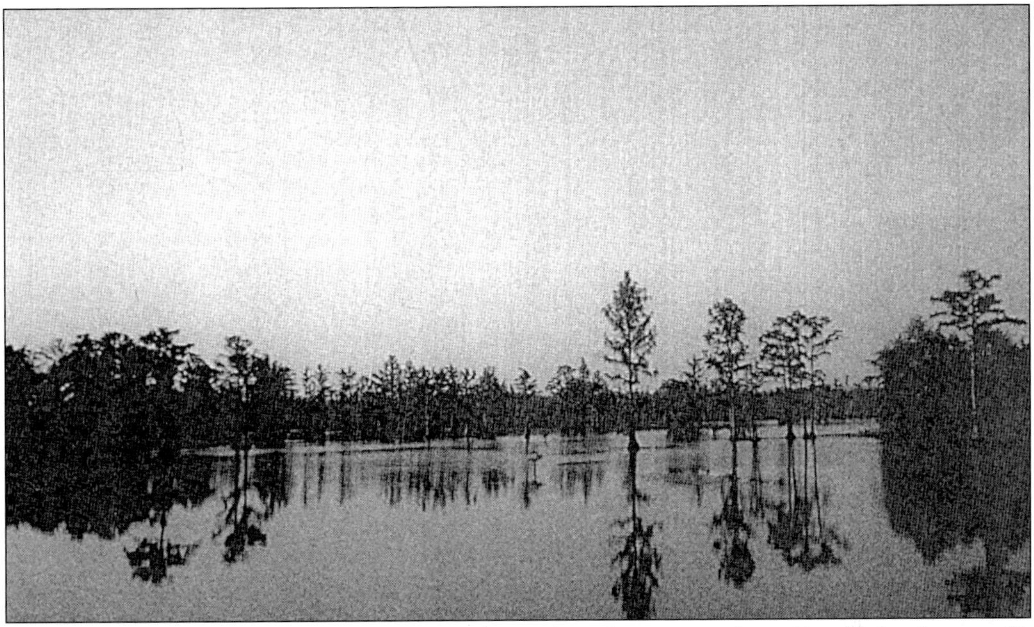

Rhodes Pond, located near the towns of Falcon and Godwin in northern Cumberland, is a well-known fishing spot. It was known earlier as Smith's Mill Pond. A skirmish between Confederate General Joseph Wheeler's cavalry and a Yankee cavalry unit occurred here in March of 1865, just before the Battle of Averasboro was fought a few miles away.

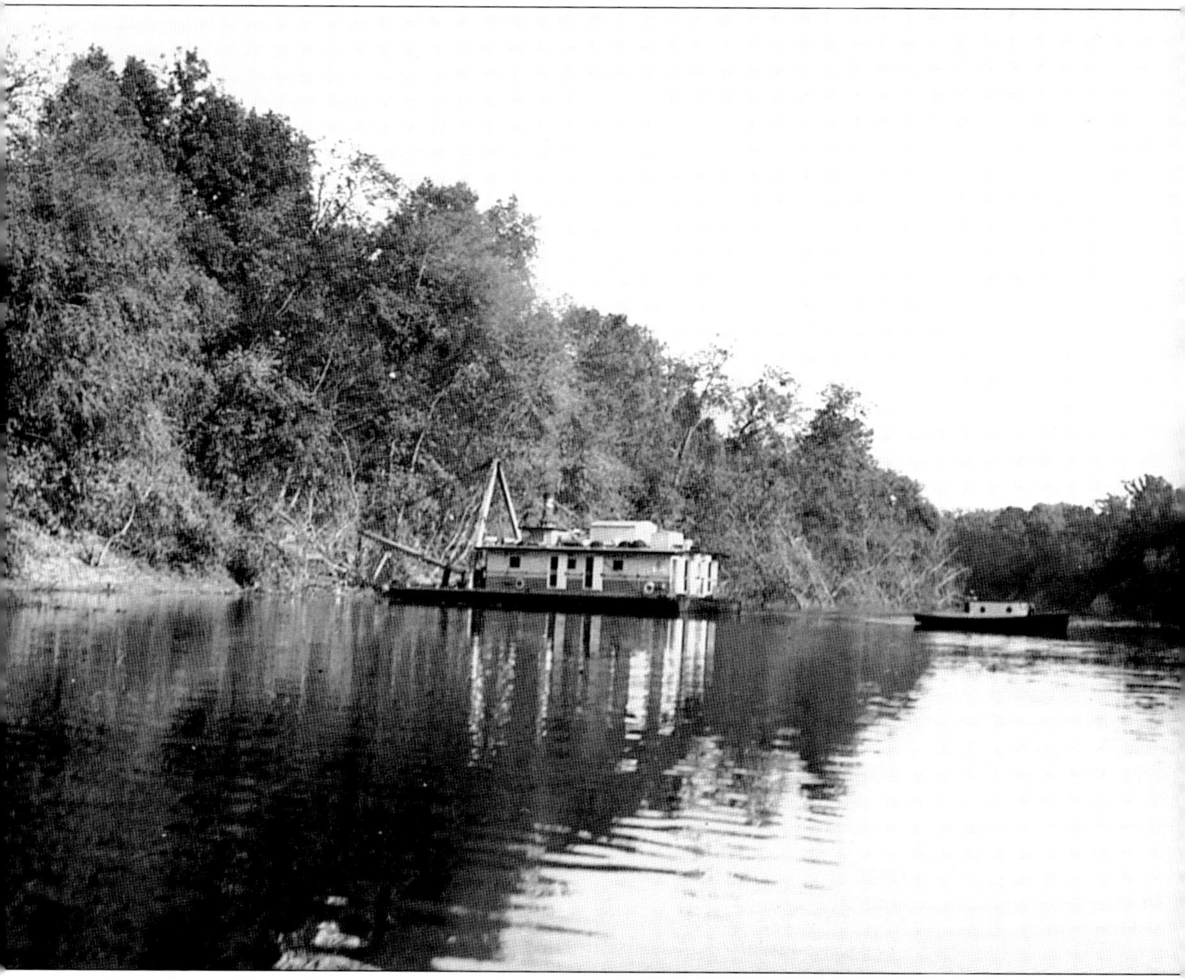

This Cape Fear River scene is from 1939. (Courtesy N.C. Department of Archives and History.)

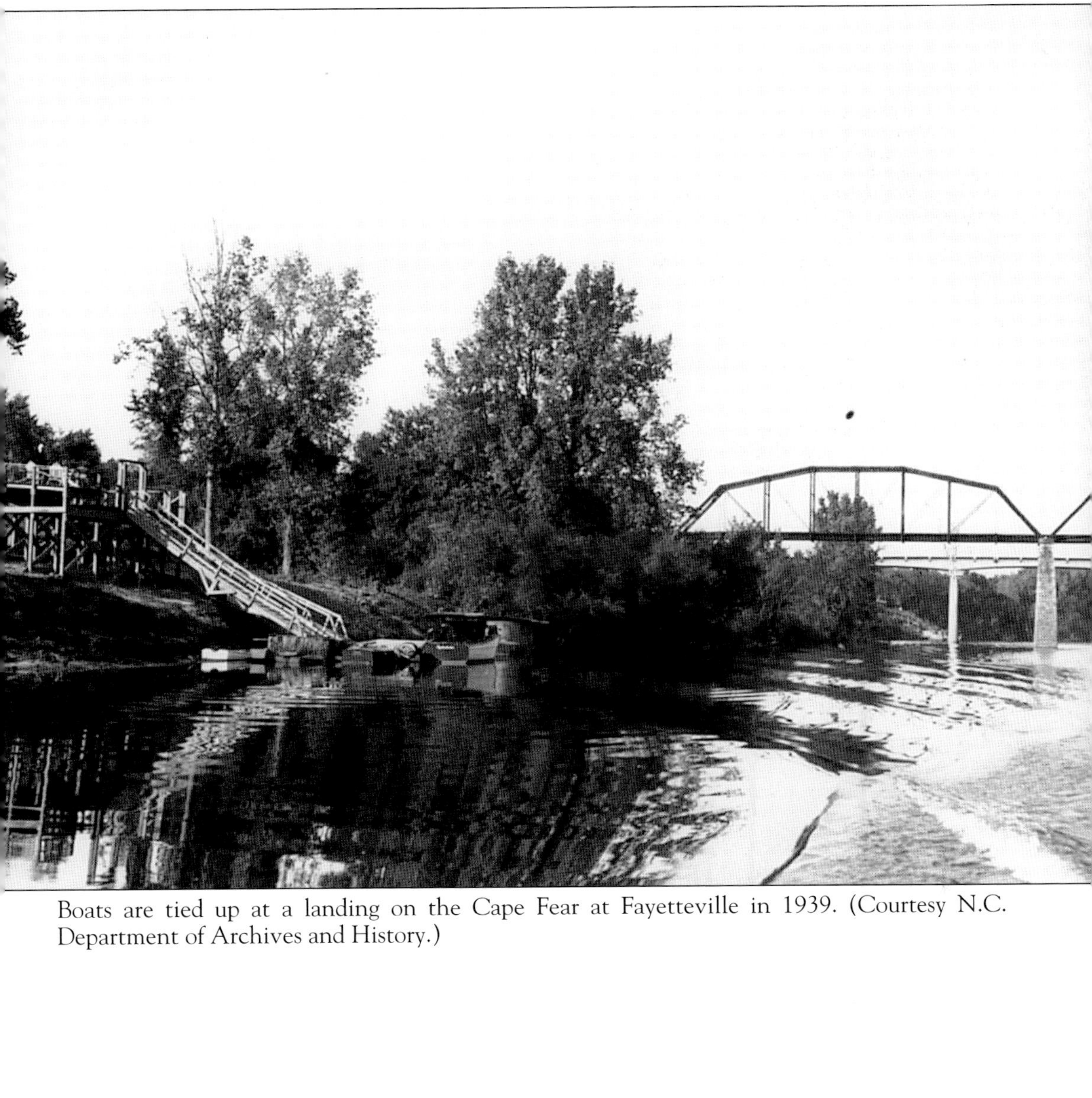

Boats are tied up at a landing on the Cape Fear at Fayetteville in 1939. (Courtesy N.C. Department of Archives and History.)

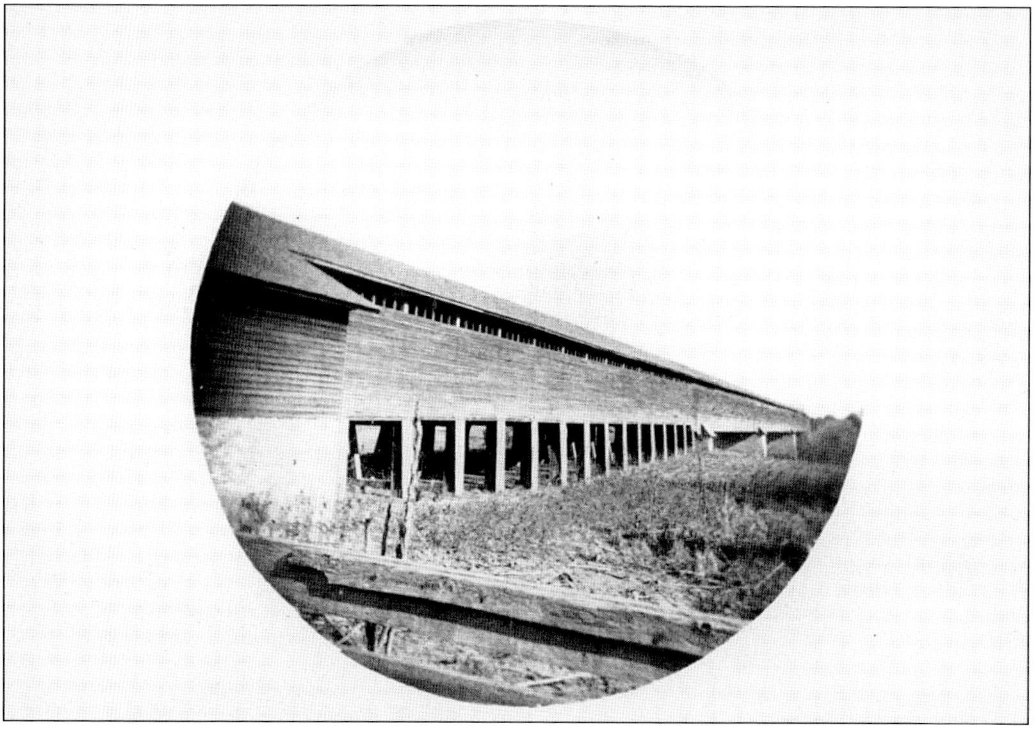

The earliest known photo of the Clarendon Bridge was taken in 1888. This was the second Clarendon Bridge; it replaced the original bridge at the site that was burned by retreating Confederates in March 1865, in an effort to slow the march of the Union Army. (Courtesy N.C. Department of Archives and History.)

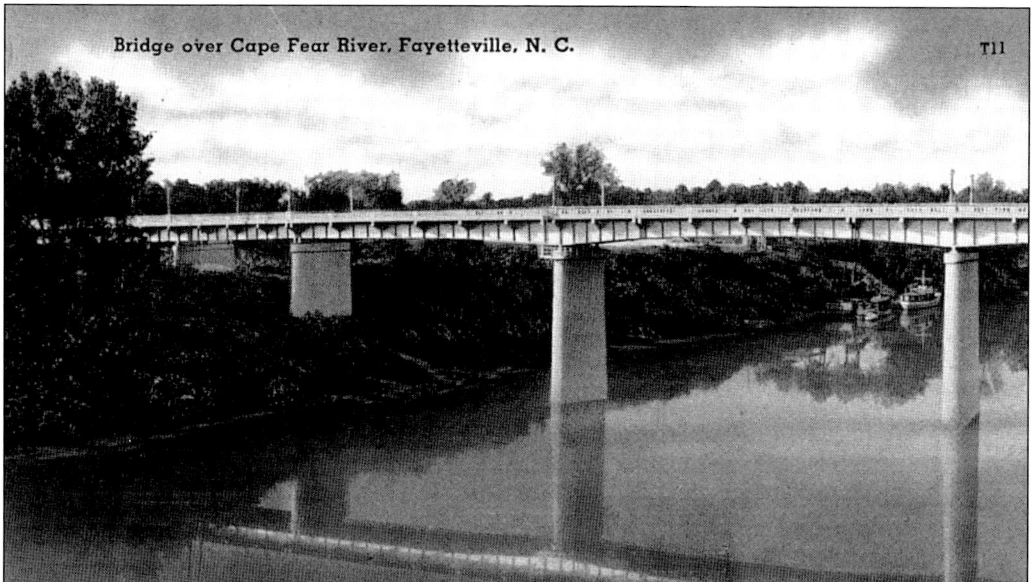

Memorial Bridge in Fayetteville was built in 1937. This is the fourth bridge built at the site. The bridge sits near the port of Fayetteville. Federal government expenditures of nearly $3 million deepened the Cape Fear, making Fayetteville the farthest inland port in North Carolina.

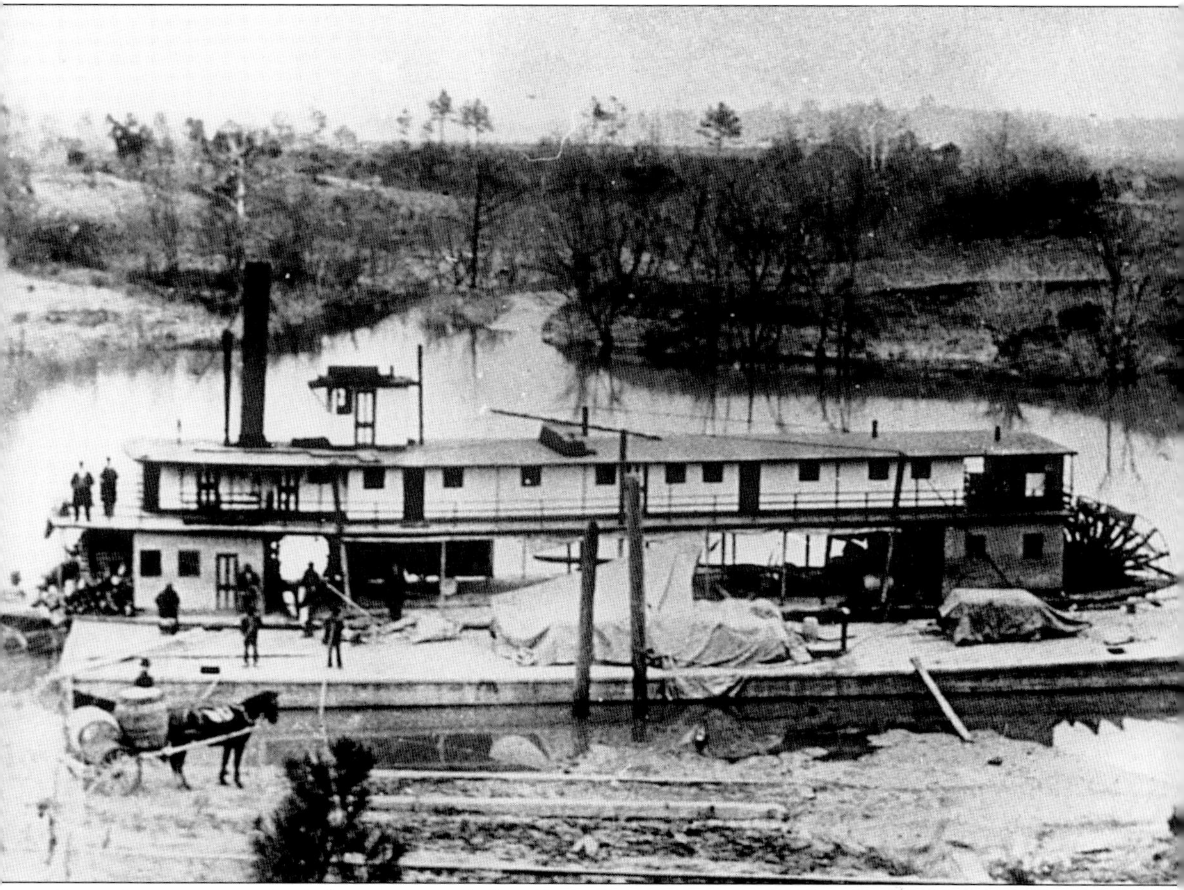

Steamboats once plied the waters of the Cape Fear, running frequently from Wilmington to Fayetteville. Industrious entrepreneurs often cut and stacked wood alongside the river. When steamboats needed fuel, they pulled over to the bank, took the wood, and left a statement for the entrepreneur to bill the owner of the steamboat. Pictured here is the *Thelma,* the last of the stern wheelers to ply the waters of the Cape Fear. (Courtesy N.C. Department of Archives and History.)

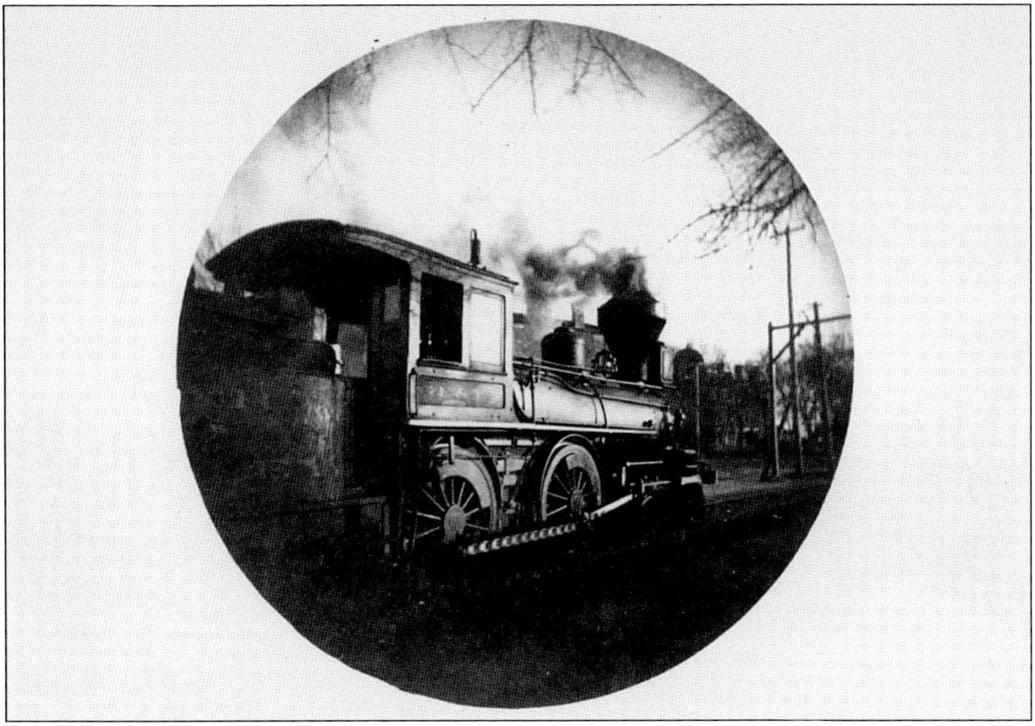

A steam engine locomotive owned by the Cape Fear and Yadkin Valley Railroad races down the tracks in 1888. (Courtesy N.C. Department of Archives and History.)

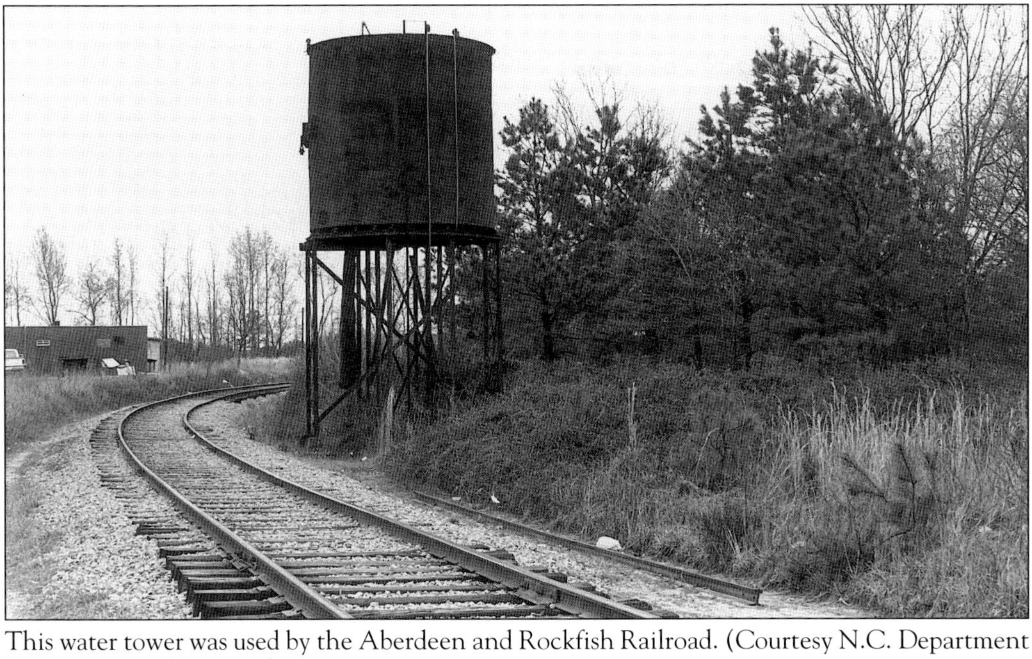

This water tower was used by the Aberdeen and Rockfish Railroad. (Courtesy N.C. Department of Archives and History.)

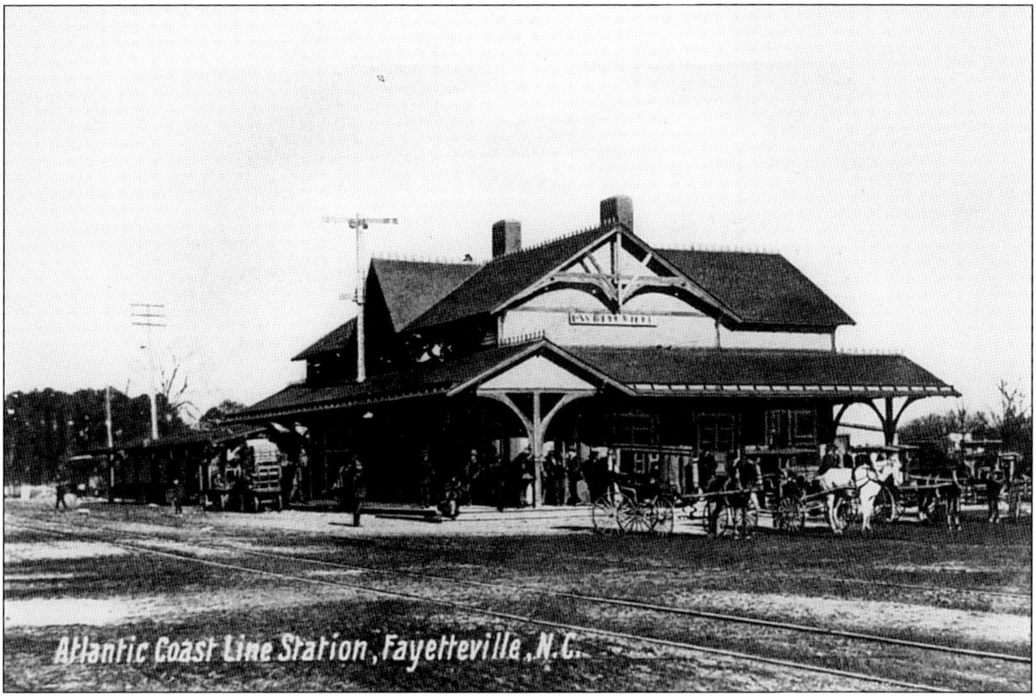

The Atlantic Coast Line Railroad Station, located on Hay Street in downtown Fayetteville, is pictured here in 1908. Note the horse-drawn taxis waiting to carry passengers to their local destinations. (Courtesy N.C. Department of Archives and History.)

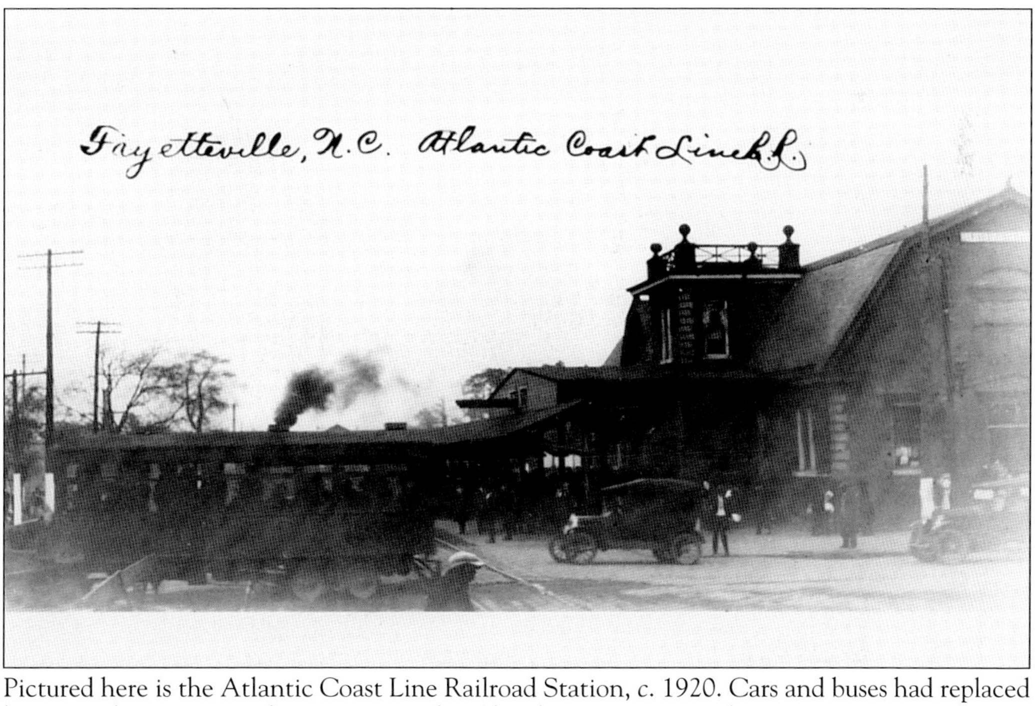

Pictured here is the Atlantic Coast Line Railroad Station, *c.* 1920. Cars and buses had replaced horses and carriages as the primary mode of local transportation. (Courtesy N.C. Department of Archives and History.)

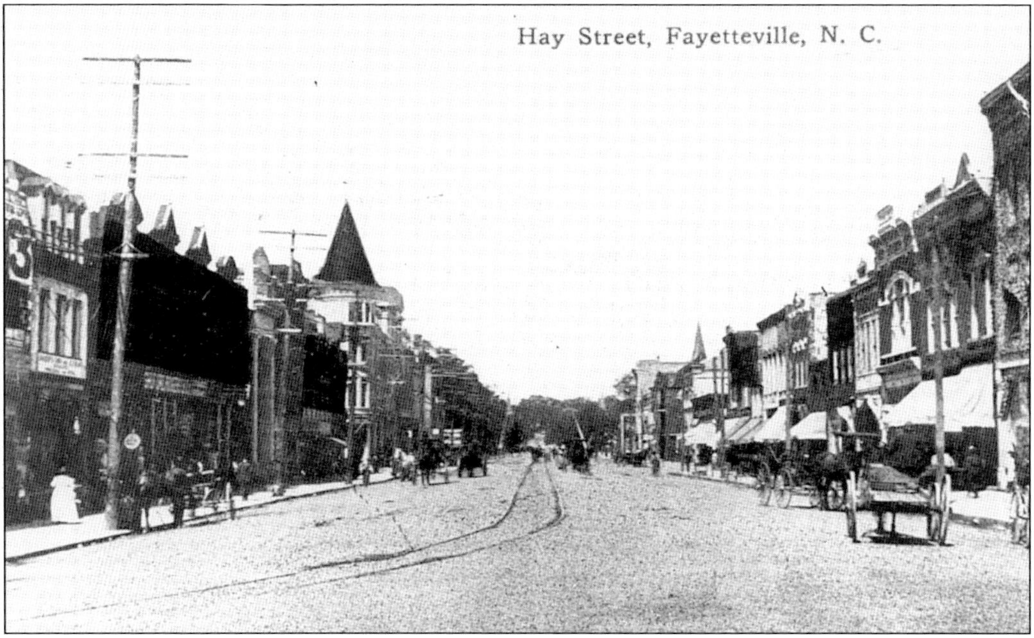

A view of Hay Street in 1913 shows Fayetteville as a blend of the old and the new; trolley car tracks run down the center of the street, flanked on both sides by horses and wagons. (Courtesy N.C. Department of Archives and History.)

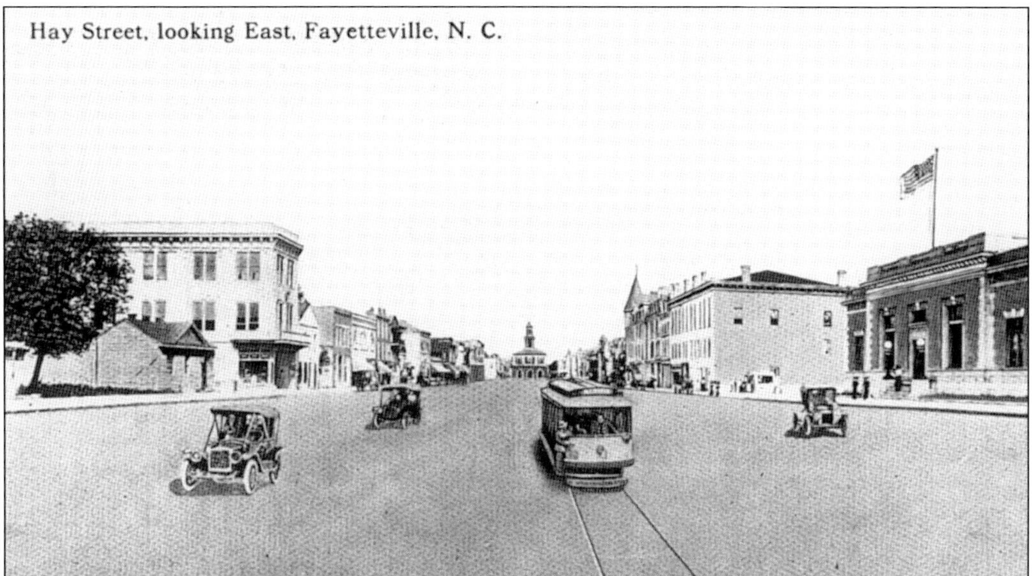

This view of Downtown Fayetteville was taken looking east down Hay Street, *c.* 1920. The old post office, now the Arts Center, is on the right underneath the flag. (Courtesy N.C. Department of Archives and History.)

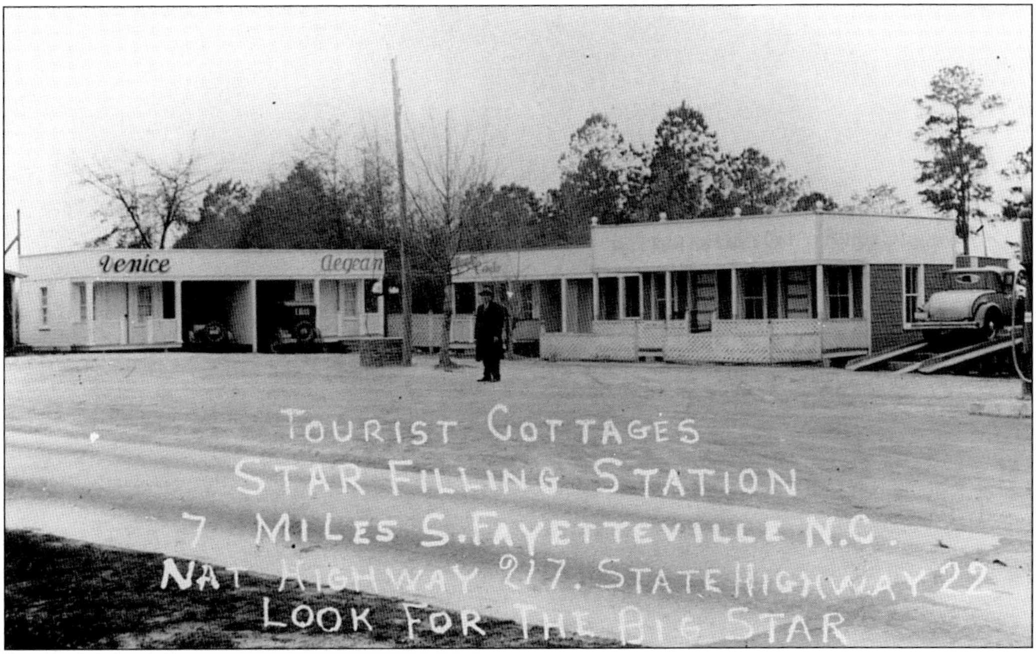

The Star Filling Station and Tourist Cottages were located 7 miles south of Fayetteville, *c.* 1930. Notice the names given the cottages: Venice, Aegean, and Monte Carlo. (Courtesy N.C. Department of Archives and History.)

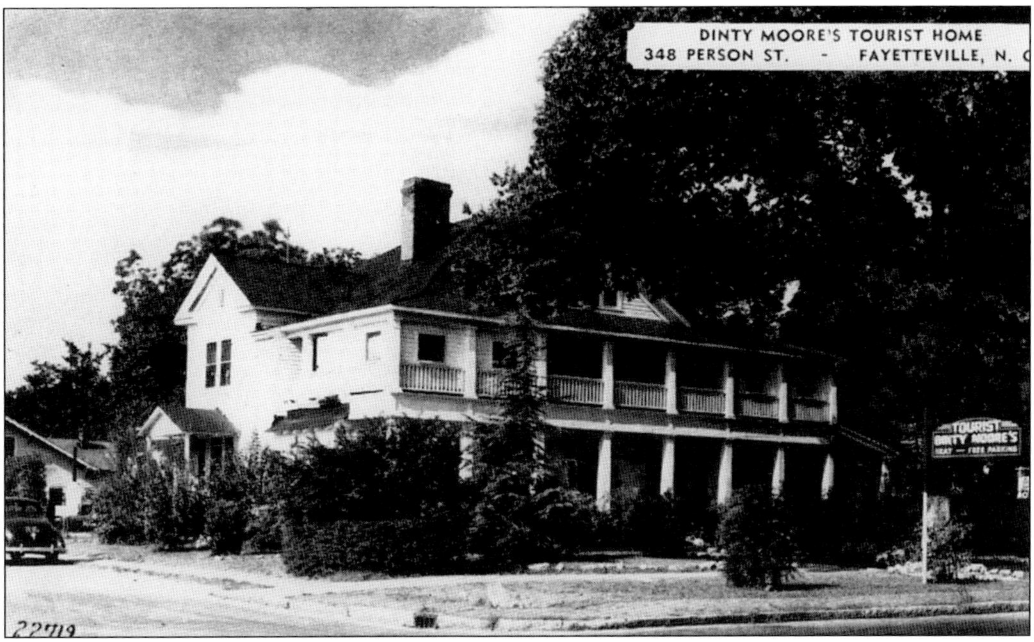

Dinty Moore's Tourist Home was located on Person Street in Fayetteville in 1940. Tourist homes such as these offered an alternative to higher-priced downtown hotels, servicing travelers until motels and the interstate highway system became a reality in the 1950s. (Courtesy N.C. Department of Archives and History.)

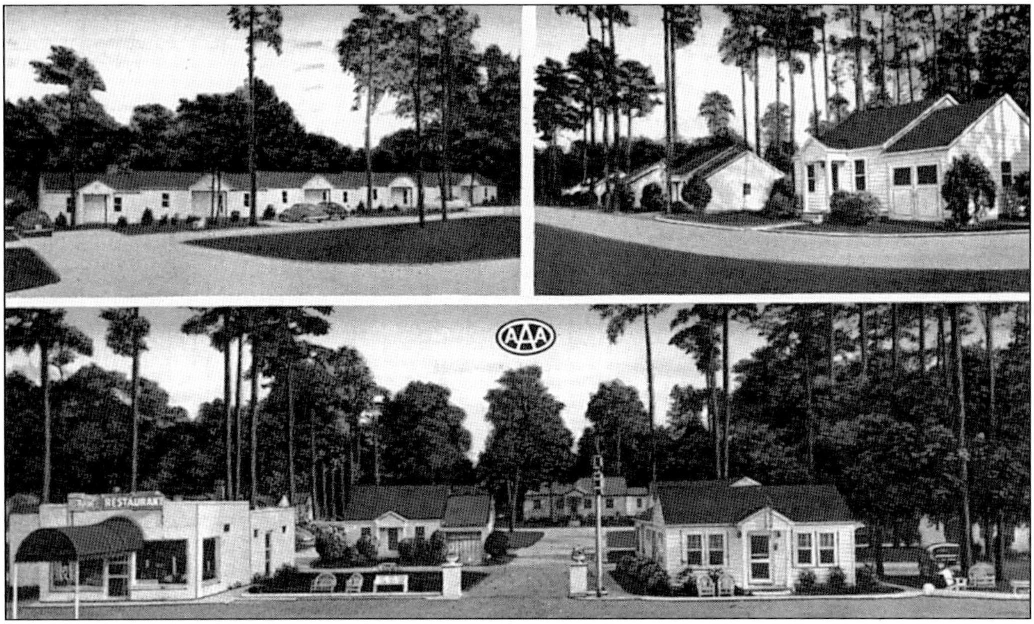

This postcard is postmarked 1951 of Thompson's Cottage Court, located one mile south of Fayetteville on U.S. 15A, now U.S. 401. Owners Mr. and Mrs. Joe Thompson advertised 26 rooms, all with such modern conveniences as tile baths and steam heat. A restaurant was located on the premises.

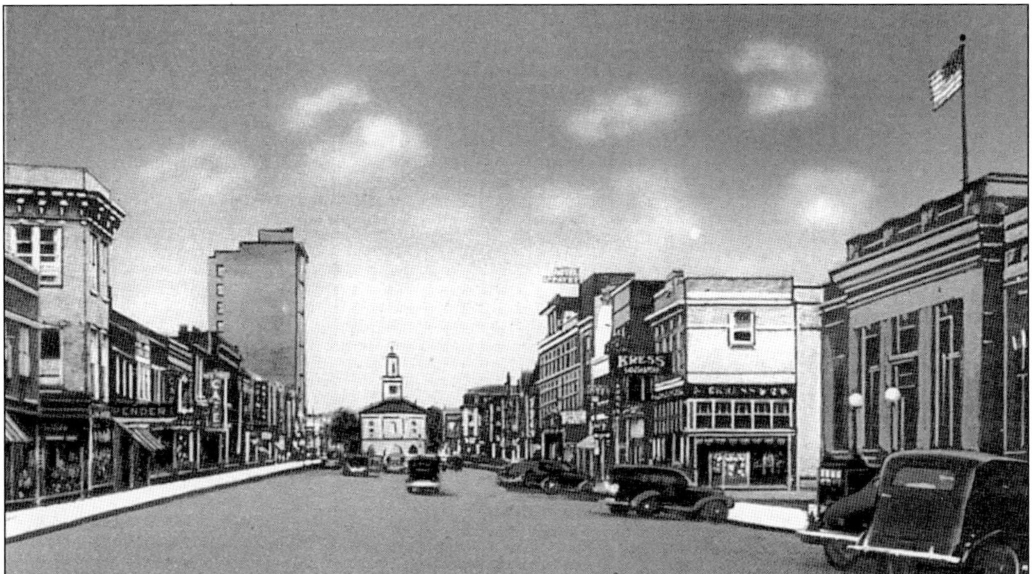

This postcard scene shows the business district of Fayetteville on Hay Street, looking toward the Market House.

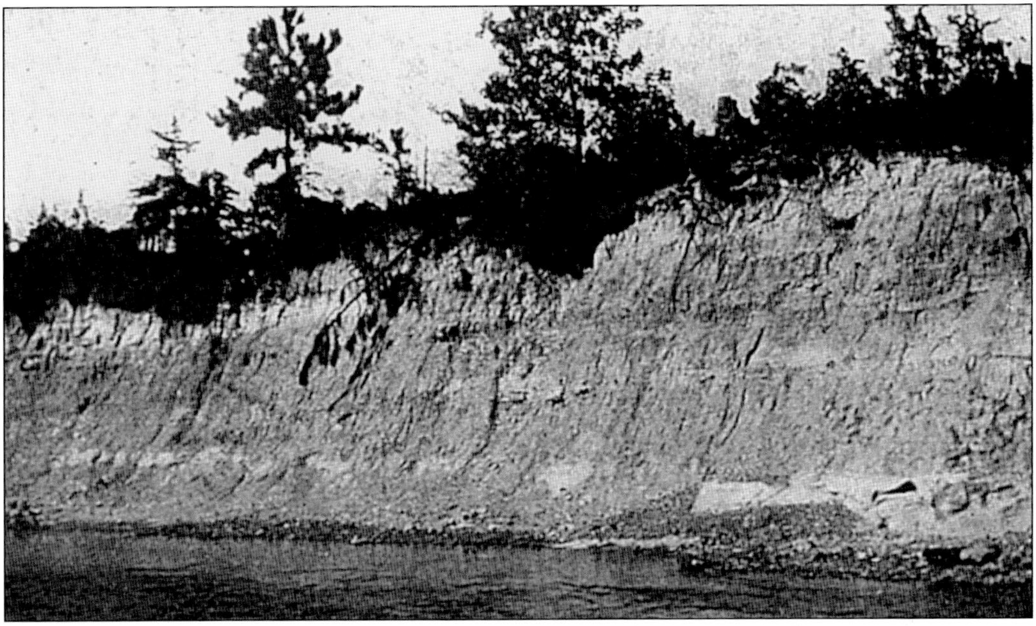

A view of the Patuxent geographic formation along the Lower Little River is seen near Manchester in 1907.

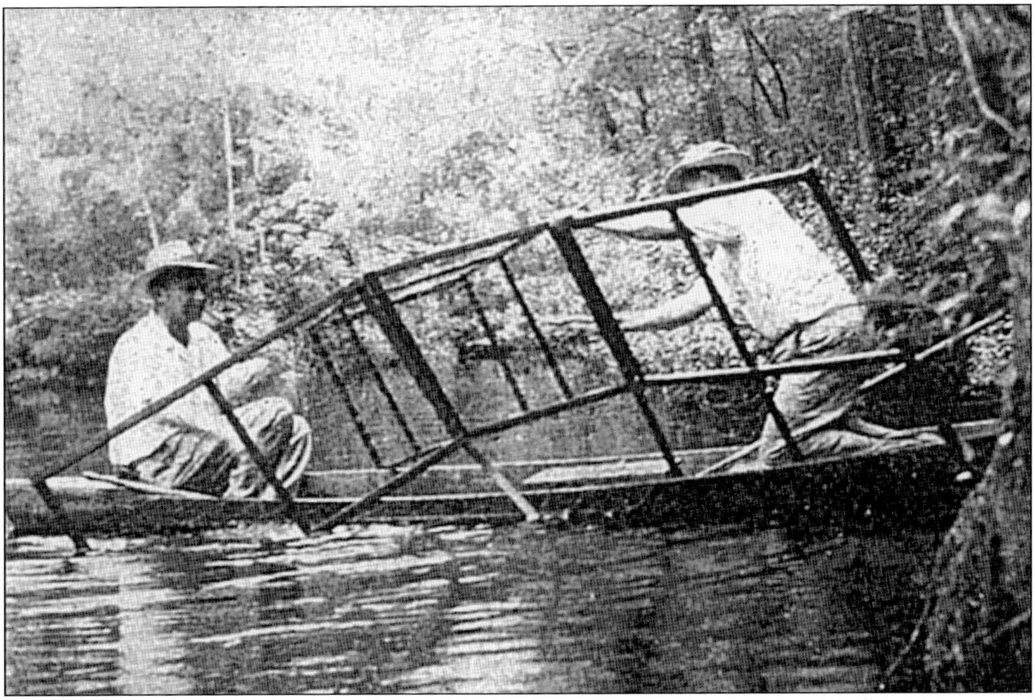

E.W. Caine and Oscar Chadwick remove an illegal device used to trap fish from the South River near Falcon in 1947.

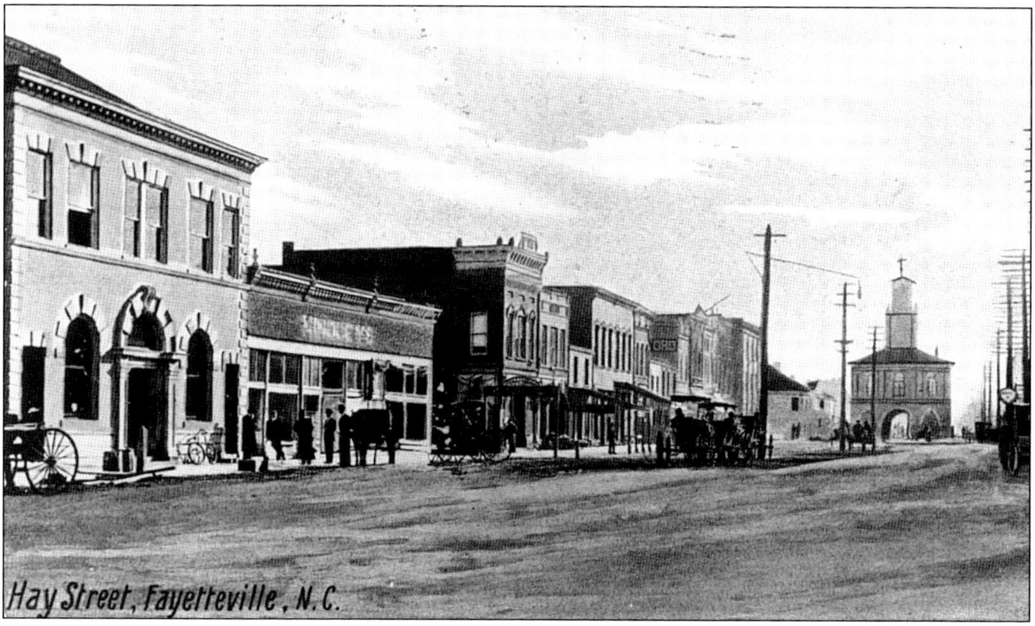

This view of downtown Fayetteville was taken around 1900. (Courtesy N.C. Department of Archives and History.)

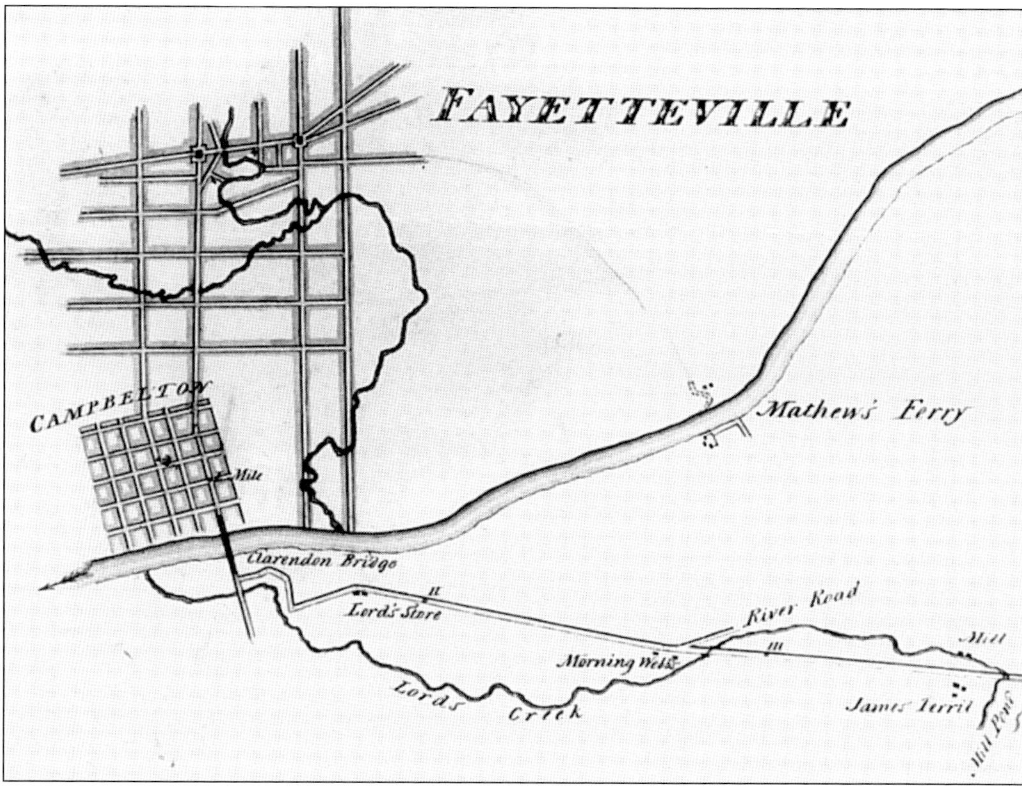

A map shows Fayetteville, along with old Campbellton on the Cape Fear. Mathews Ferry is located upstream. (Courtesy N.C. Department of Archives and History.)

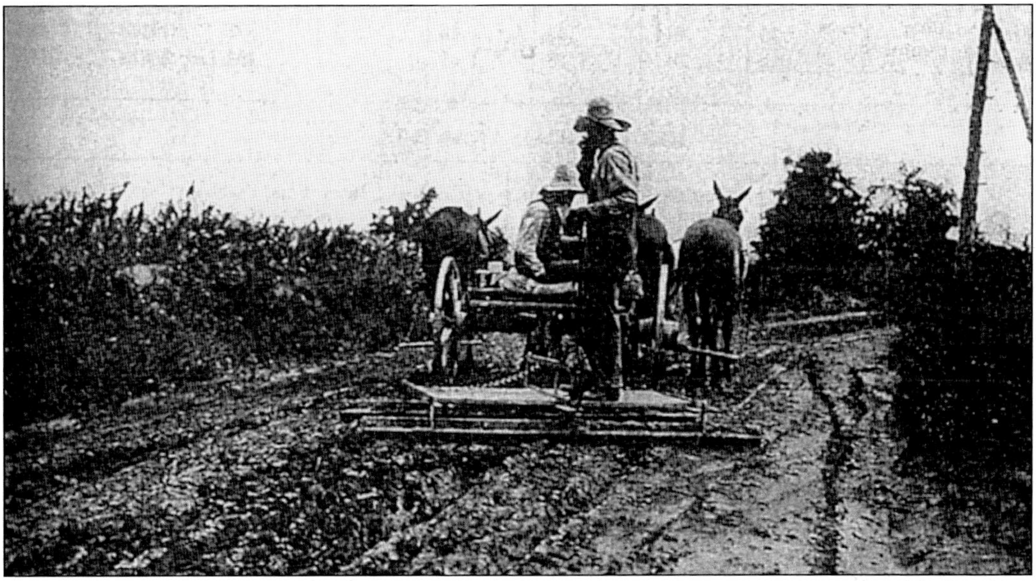

Before the state took over maintenance of roads, local communities were responsible for their upkeep. These men are using mules to grade a muddy road near Hope Mills in 1900.

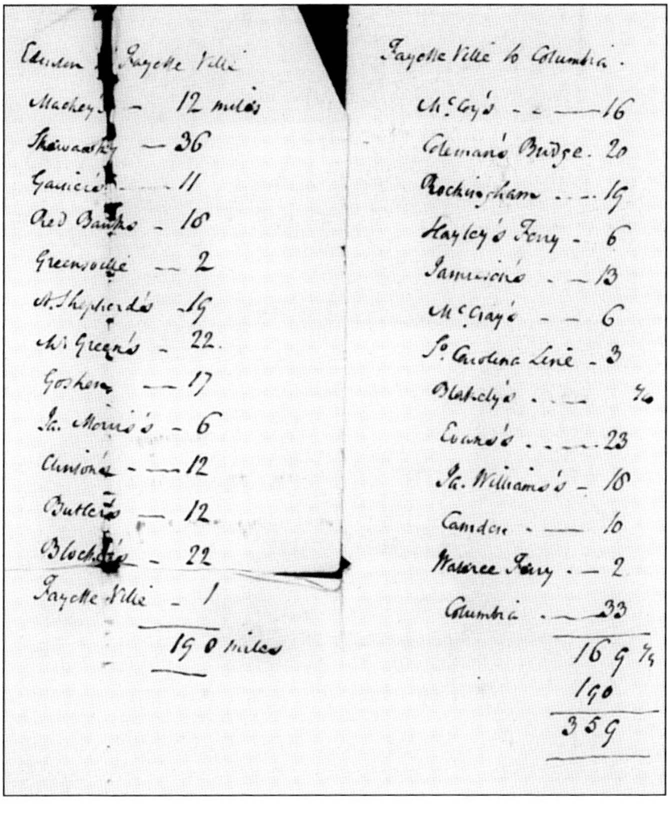

Edenton to Fayette Ville	
Mackey's	12 miles
Skewarkey	36
Gainer's	11
Red Banks	18
Greensville	2
N. Shepherd's	19
Mr. Green's	22.
Goshen	17
Jn. Morris's	6
Clinton's	12
Butler's	12.
Blocker's	22
Fayette Ville	1
	190 miles

Fayette Ville to Columbia.	
McCoy's	16
Coleman's Bridge	20
Rockingham	19
Hayley's Ferry	6
Jamieson's	13
McGray's	6
So. Carolina Line	3
Blakely's	½
Evans's	23
Jn. Williams's	18
Camden	10
Wateree Ferry	2
Columbia	33
	169 ½
	190
	359

Mileage chart of James Iredell from Fayetteville to Columbia, South Carolina. A North Carolina revolutionary leader, Iredell was appointed by President George Washington as an associate justice to the first U.S. Supreme Court in 1789. (Courtesy N.C. Department of Archives and History.)

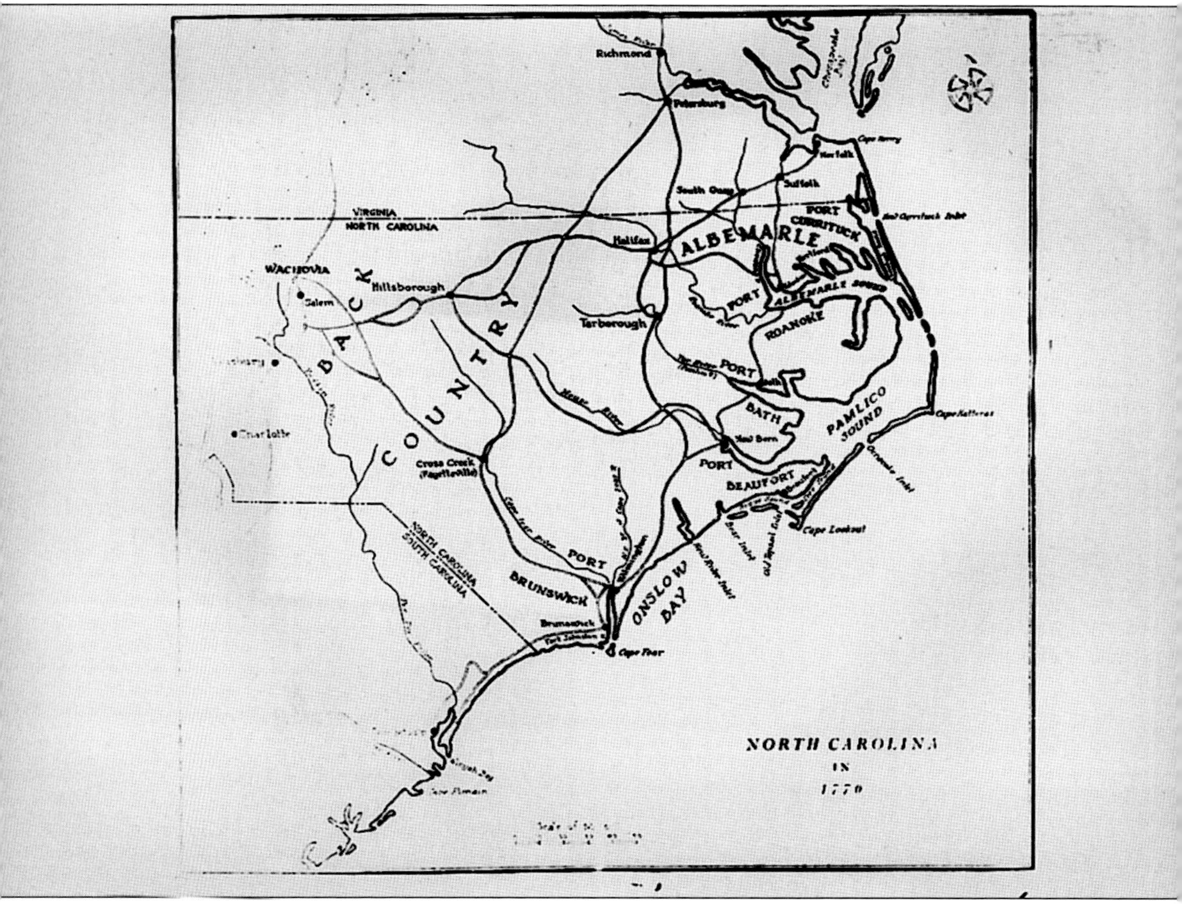

A 1770 map of North Carolina shows Cross Creek, which merged with Campbellton to become Fayetteville. Also seen are roads from that town leading to Wilmington, Salem, and Petersburg, Virginia. (Courtesy N.C. Department of Archives and History.)

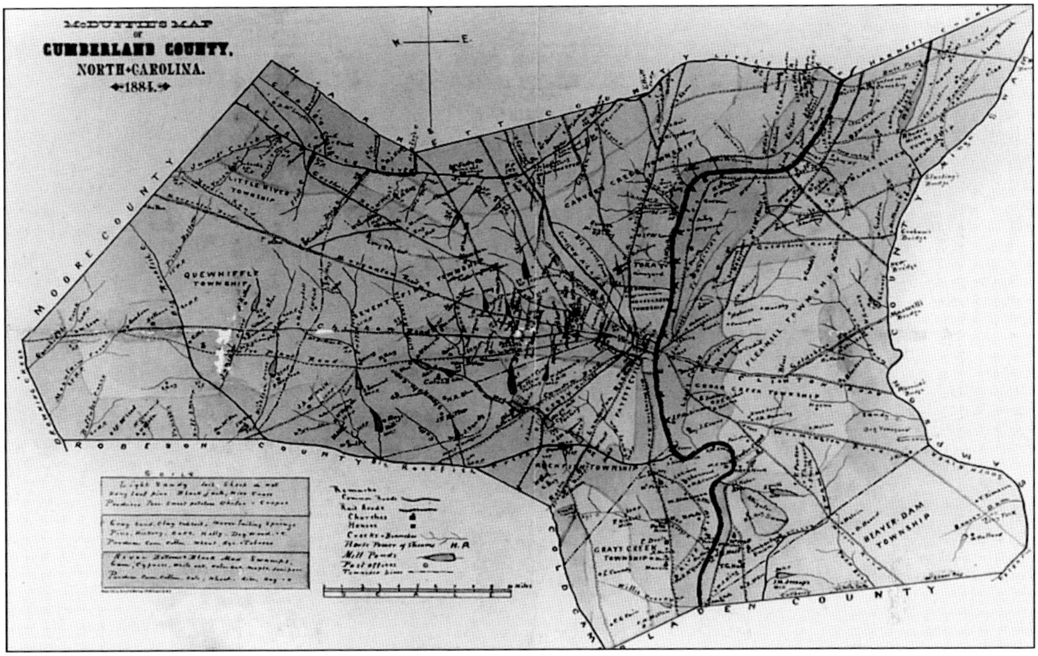

The McDuffie Map of Cumberland County was made in 1884, prior to the creation of Hoke County from Cumberland's western lands.

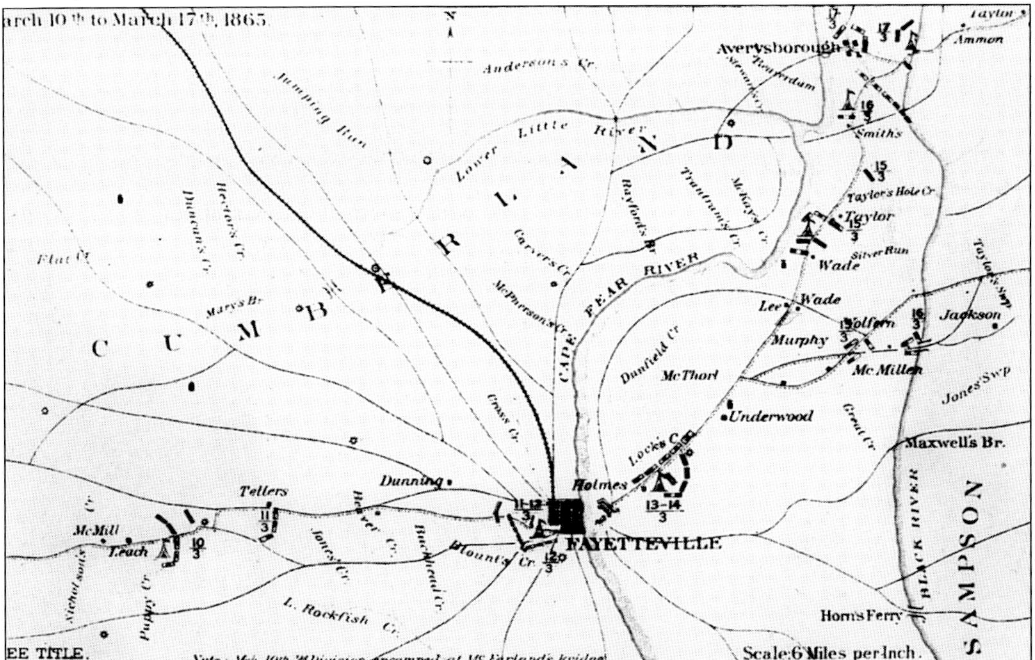

An 1865 map of Cumberland County was made during the occupation by the Union Army. Shown are troop positions during the Battle of Averasboro, which was fought from March 15 to March 17. The railroad leading to the northwest ran to the Egypt Coal Mine, where much of the machinery from the Fayetteville Arsenal was sent for safekeeping. (Courtesy N.C. Department of Archives and History.)

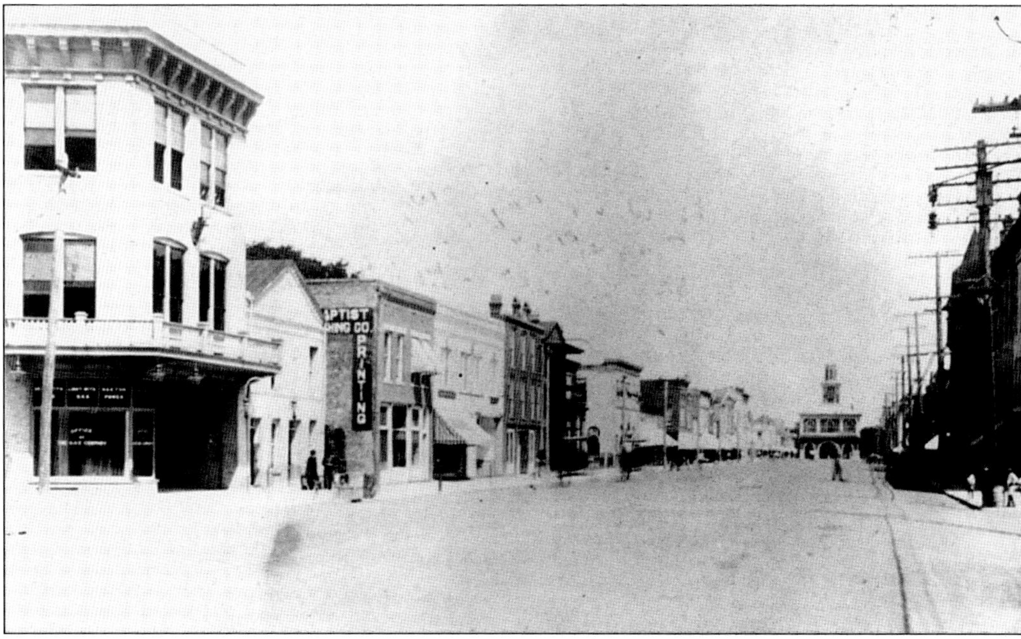

Hay Street is pictured in May of 1909. The Baptist Publishing Company is located on the left. (Courtesy N.C. Department of Archives and History.)

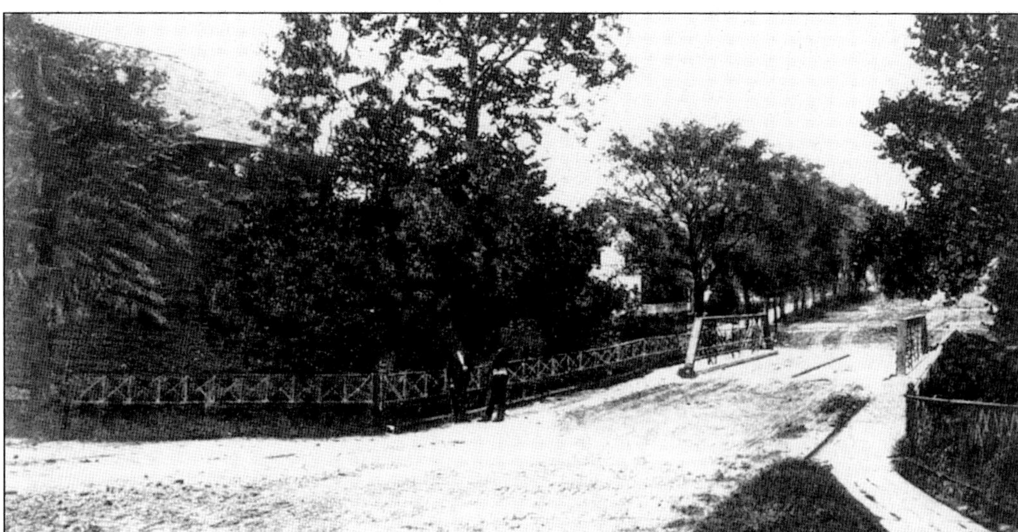
Eccles Bridge over Cross Creek on Green Street is pictured *c.* 1900. (Courtesy N.C. Department of Archives and History.)

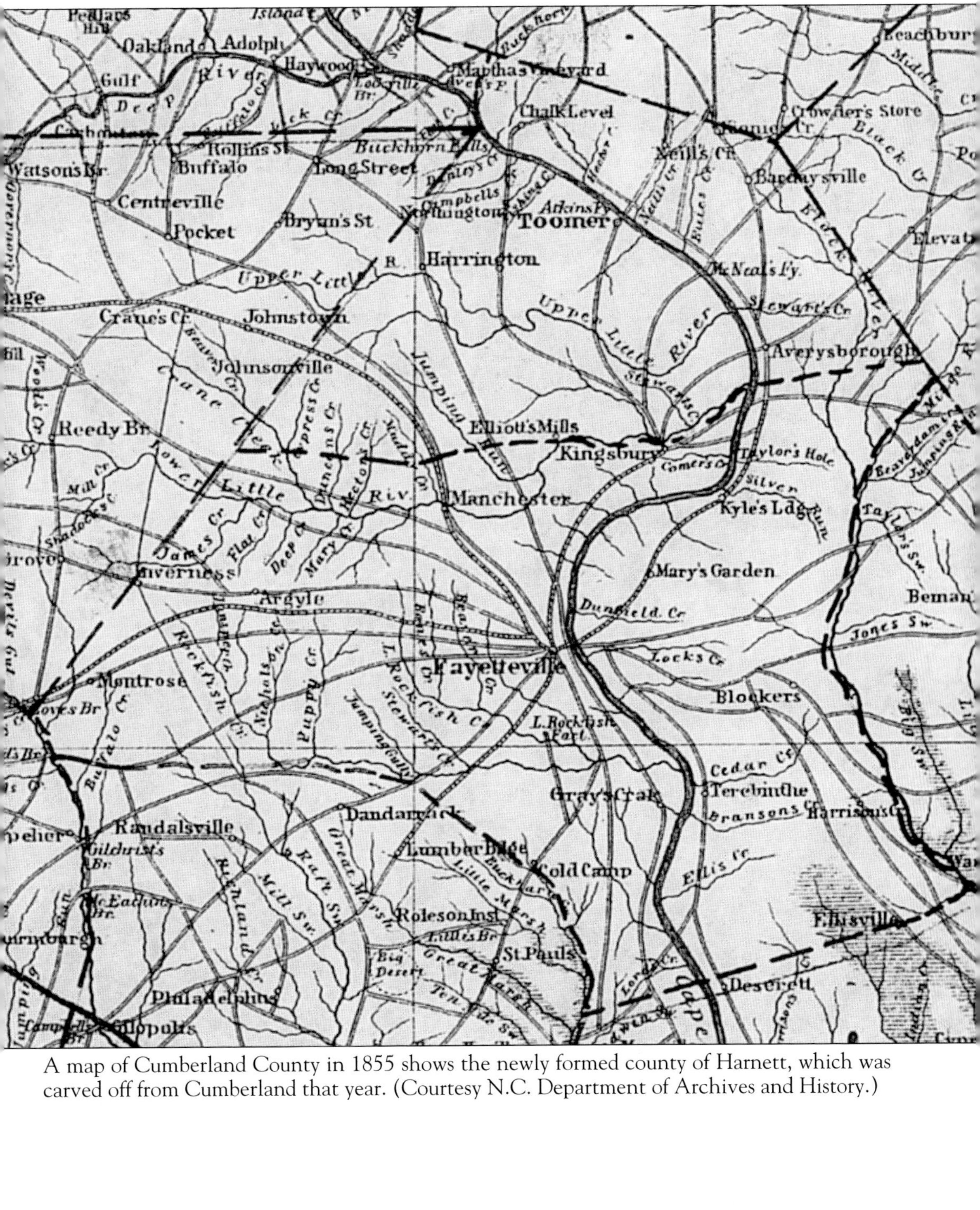

A map of Cumberland County in 1855 shows the newly formed county of Harnett, which was carved off from Cumberland that year. (Courtesy N.C. Department of Archives and History.)

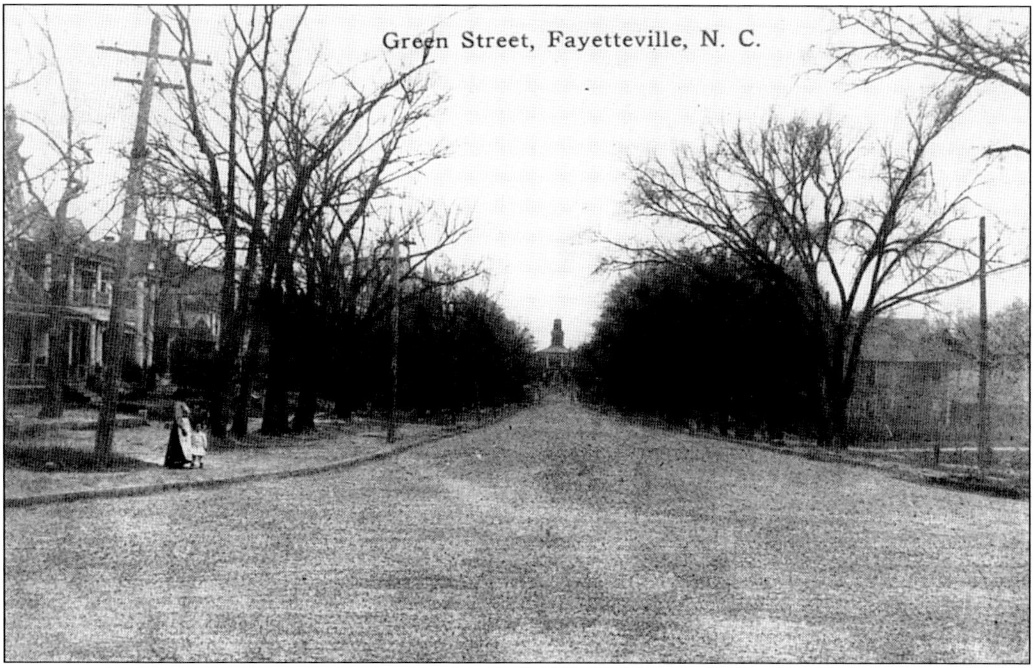

Green Street in Fayetteville is pictured looking toward the Market House from the old courthouse on St. James Square, *c.* 1890. (Courtesy N.C. Department of Archives and History.)

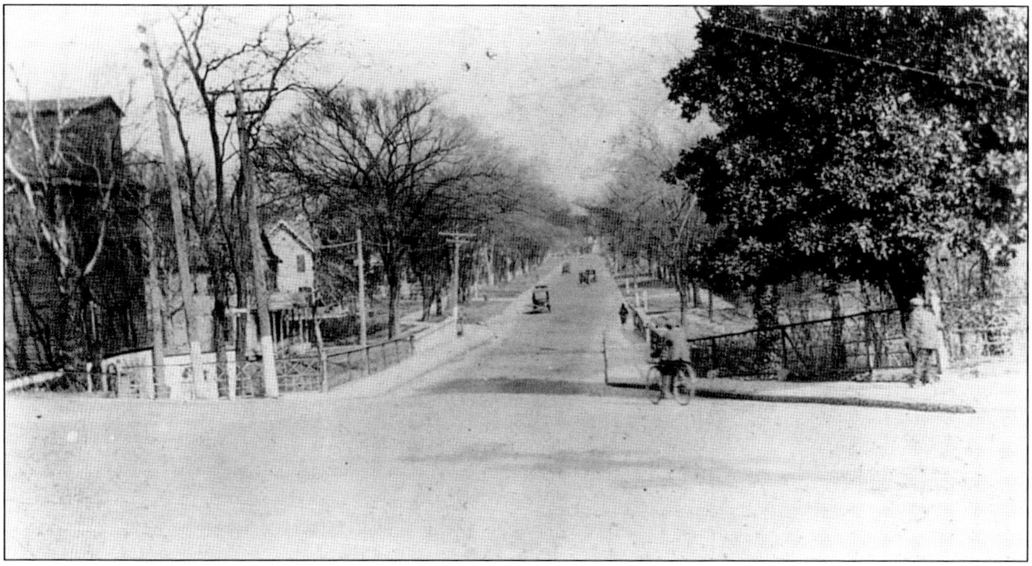

Green Street is seen looking north from the Market House toward the old courthouse on St. James Square. McNeill's Mill is on the left. (Courtesy N.C. Department of Archives and History.)

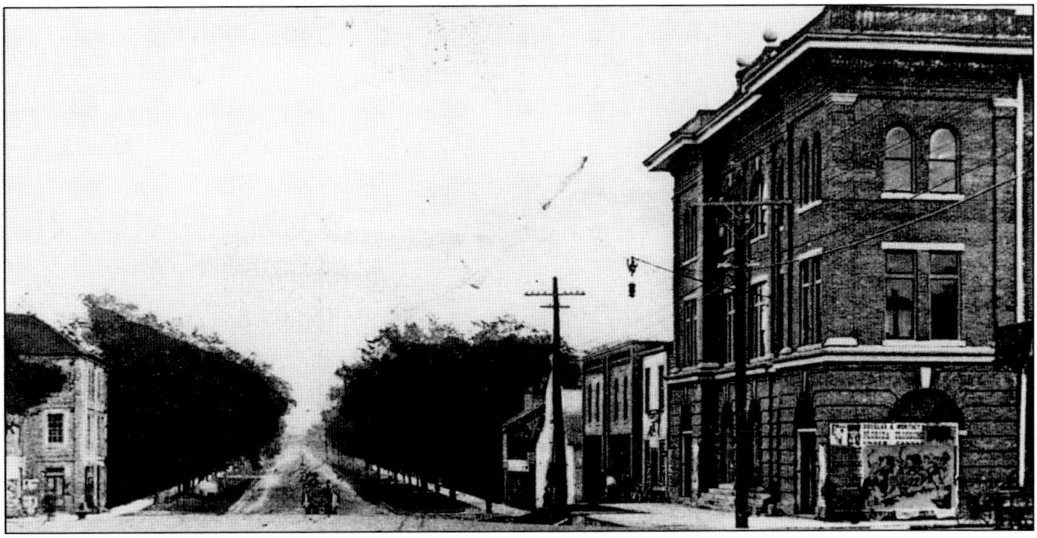

This image is of Person Street in Fayetteville, looking east from the Market House toward the Cape Fear River, *c.* 1900. (Courtesy N.C. Department of Archives and History.)

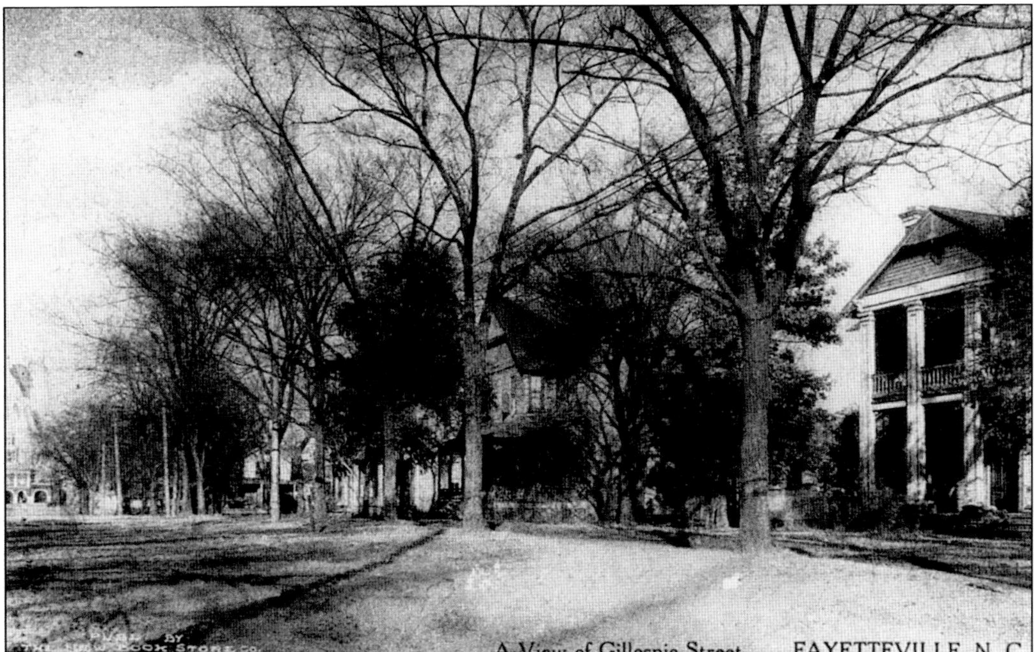

Pictured here is a view of the fine homes that once lined Gillespie Street in Fayetteville, *c.* 1900. (Courtesy N.C. Department of Archives and History.)

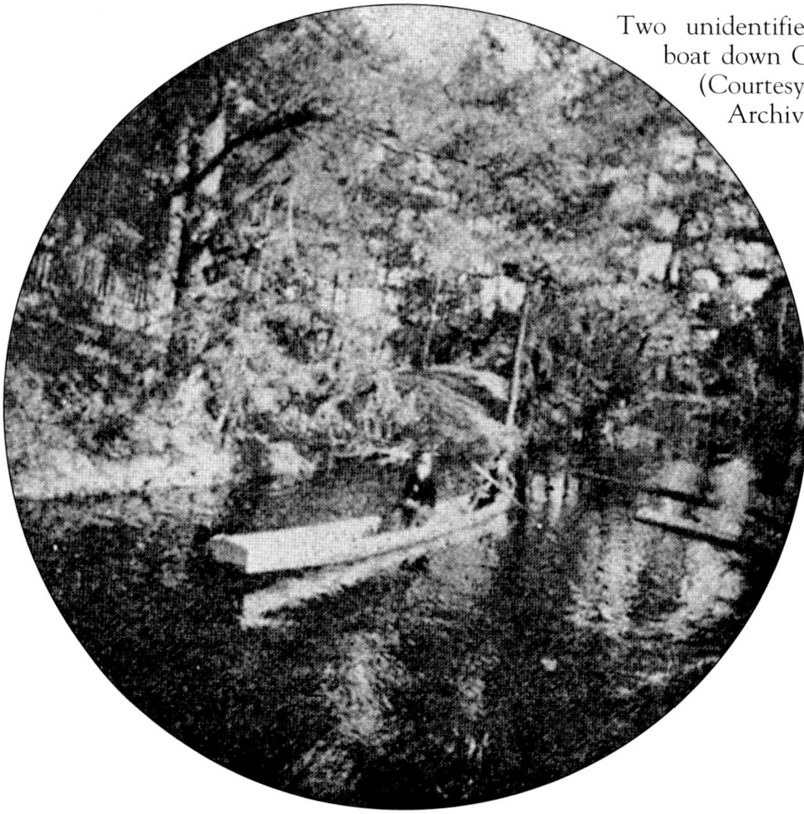

Two unidentified people paddle a boat down Cross Creek in 1888. (Courtesy N.C. Department of Archives and History.)

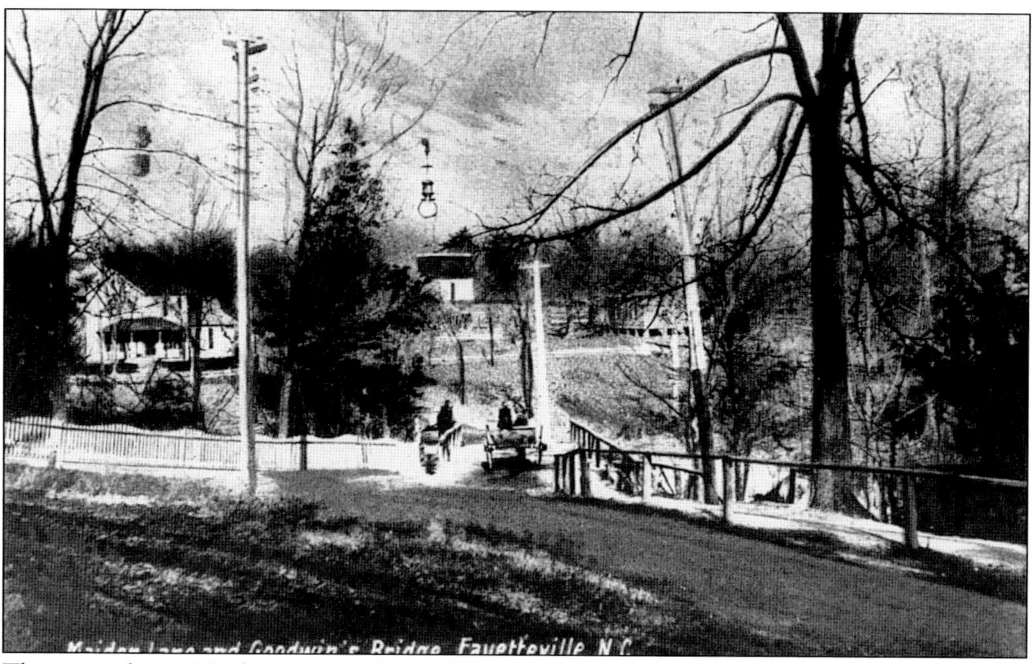

This view shows Maiden Lane and Goodwin's Bridge across Cross Creek, *c.* 1900. (Courtesy N.C. Department of Archives and History.)

Two

Business and Industry

A variety of businesses and industries have operated in Cumberland County since its creation in 1754. Farming was the occupation of most early settlers, but businesses were soon established to meet the needs of a growing population. Gristmills were necessities in the mid-18th century, and Cumberland had several to grind grain for its residents. The MacRae Map of 1825 showed eight gristmills in the town limits of Fayetteville, not counting the many that were operating in the Cumberland countryside.

Other early businesses included blacksmith shops and livery stables to care for transportation needs. Publishing had an early start in Cumberland. One of the earliest printing firms in the state was the Bowen and Howard Company, which was printing government documents as early as the 1780s. Another publishing venture, the *Fayetteville Observer*, began publication in 1816 as the *Carolina Observer*. With the exception of an interruption in publishing due to the destruction of its office and presses by Yankee troops during the Civil War, the *Fayetteville Observer* has continued publication to the present day.

A number of businesses and industrial firms opened in Fayetteville after World War II. This growth climaxed with the opening of the Kelly Springfield tire plant in the late 1960s. This company is the largest private employer in Cumberland County.

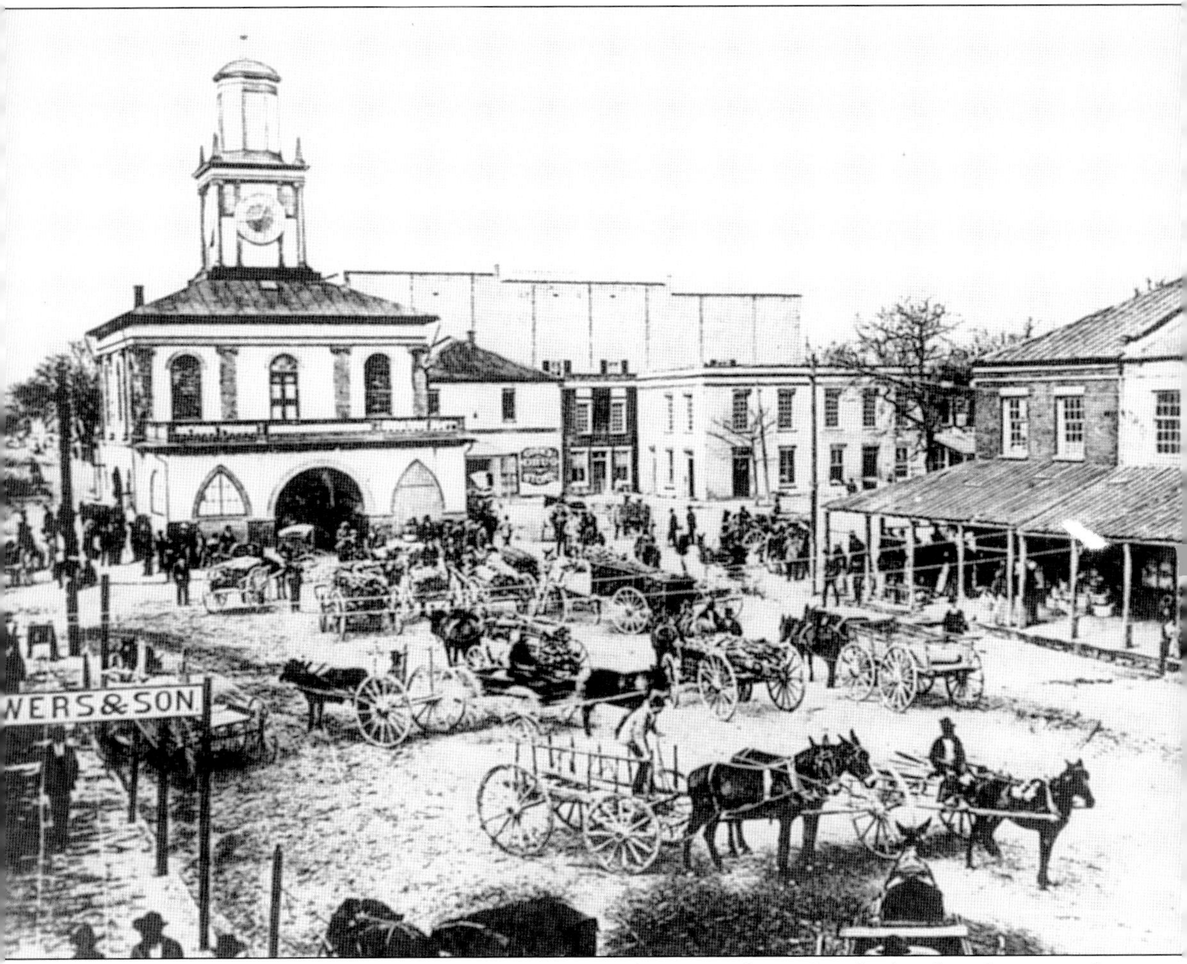

Fayetteville's City Market is pictured *c.* 1890. Farmers from Cumberland and surrounding counties brought wagonloads of produce and other farm products to the county seat to trade. (Courtesy N.C. Department of Archives and History.)

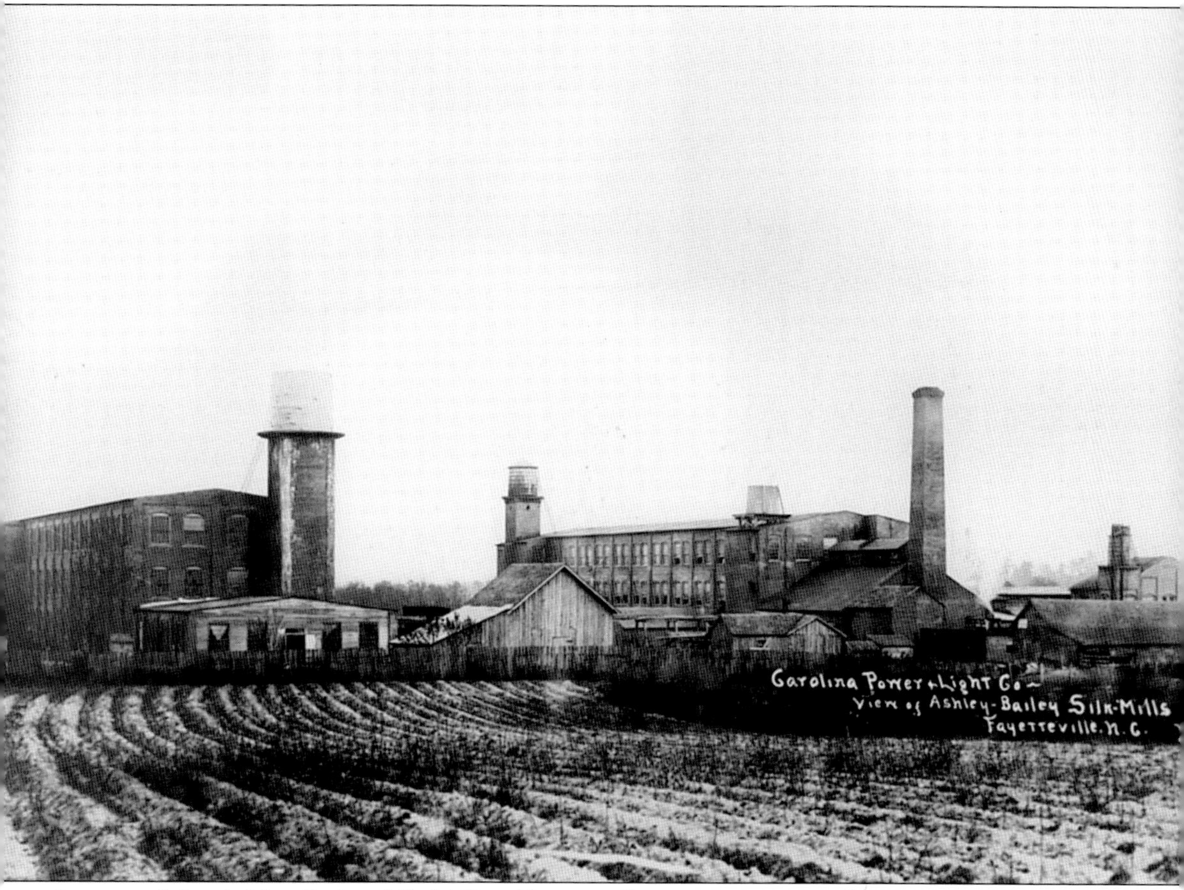

A view of the Ashley-Bailey Silk Mill in Fayetteville is seen in a Carolina Power and Light Company photograph from 1910. Many farmers experimented with silk production in the early 1900s without success. (Courtesy N.C. Department of Archives and History.)

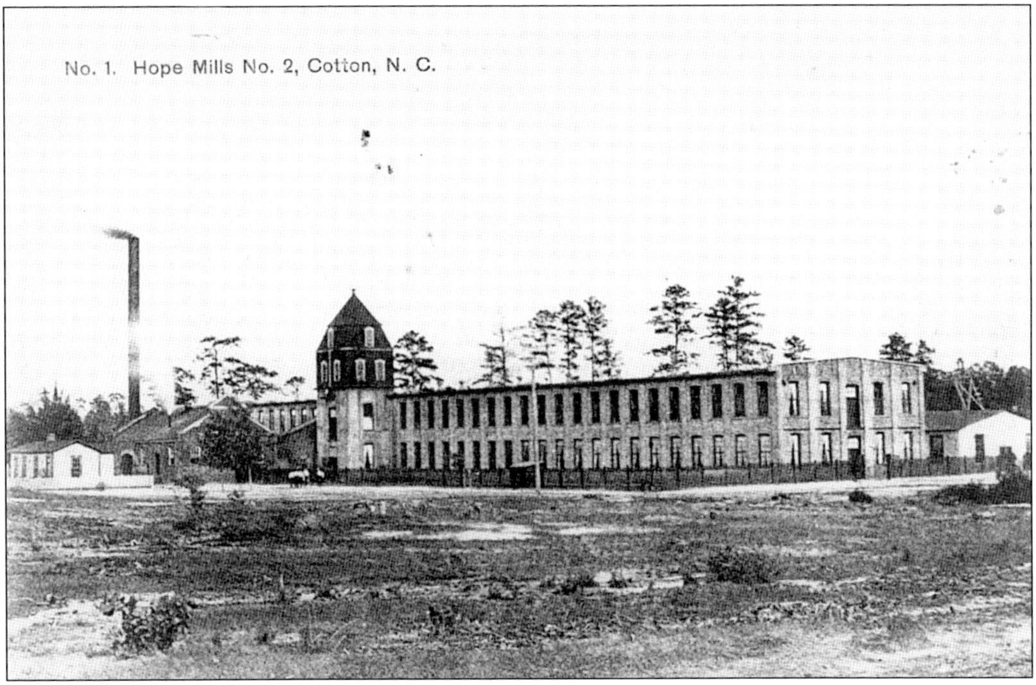

Hope Mills Cotton Mill is pictured in 1910. (Courtesy N.C. Department of Archives and History.)

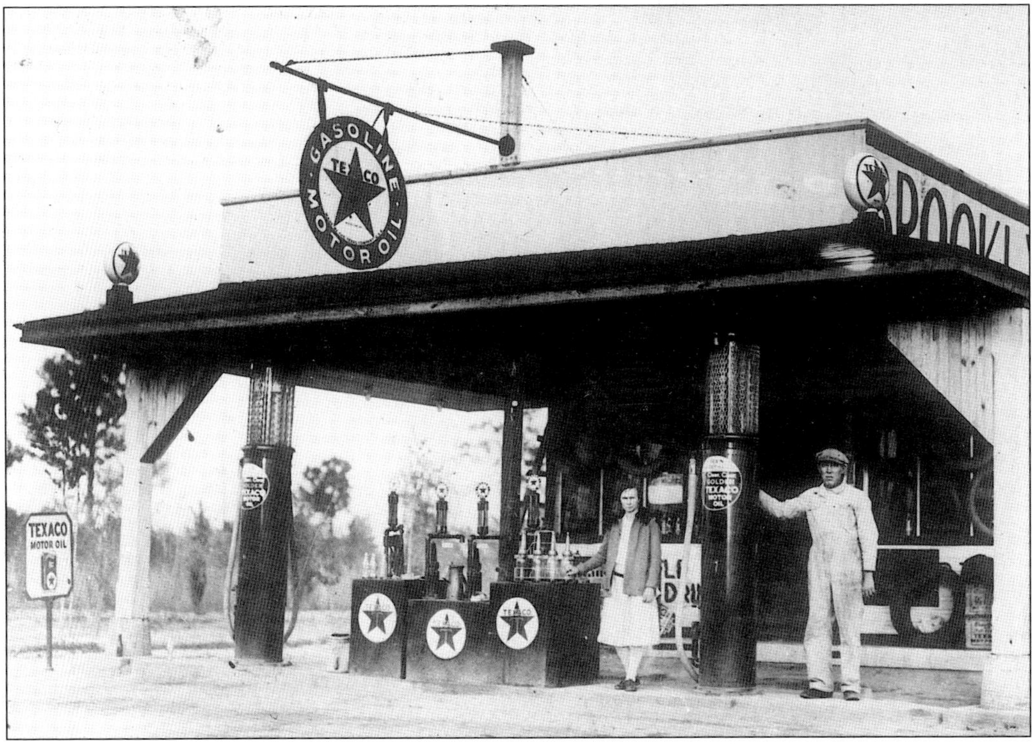

The Brooklyn Service Station in Gray's Creek offered Texaco products for sale to motorists in 1930. (Courtesy N.C. Department of Archives and History.)

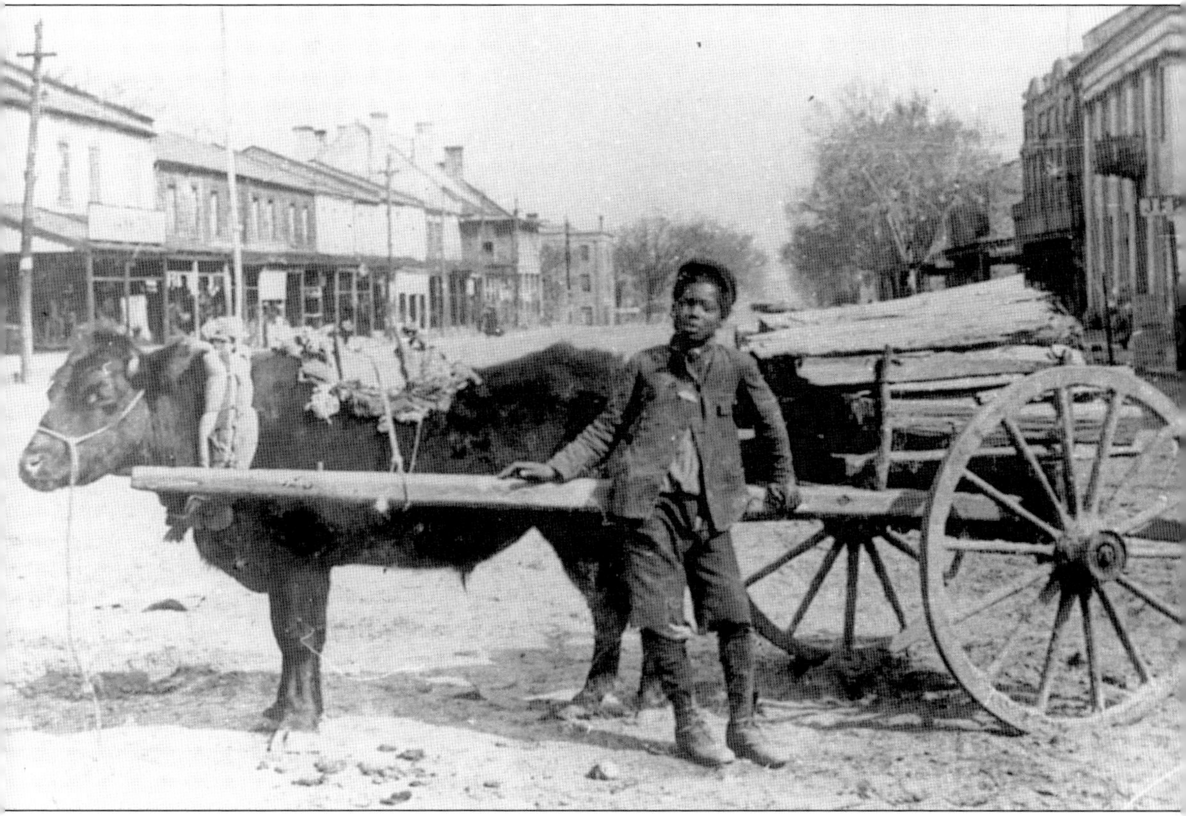

This young man was selling wood in downtown Fayetteville from a bull-driven wood cart, *c.* 1898. (Courtesy N.C. Department of Archives and History.)

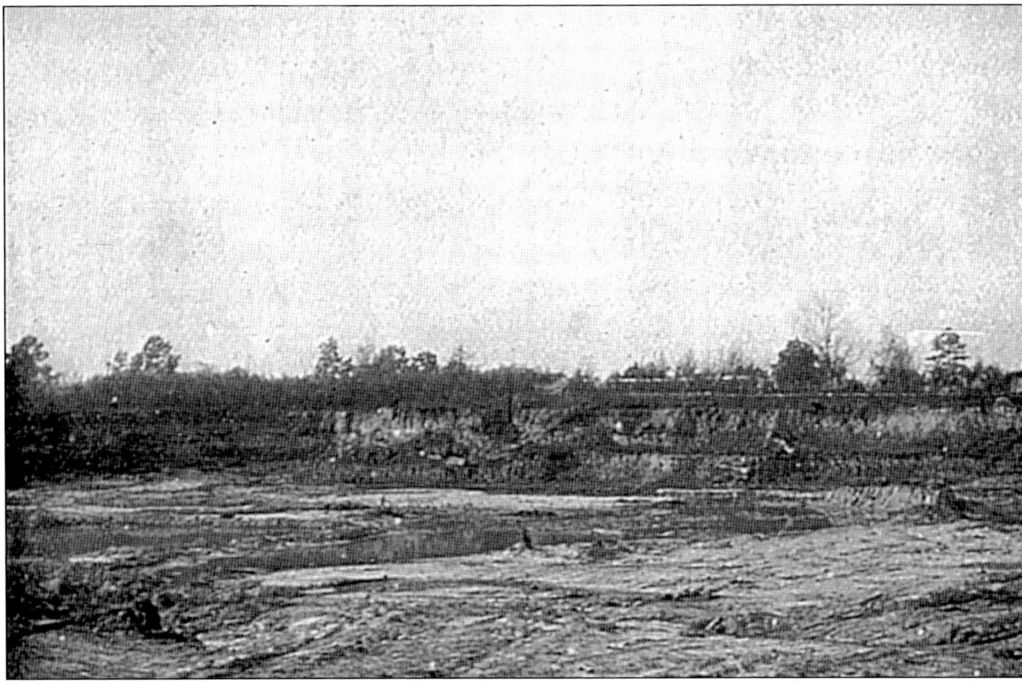

The Poe Brothers brick clay bank south of Fayetteville is pictured in 1906. This pit produced a fine grained, bluish-white clay that was used in brick making. Smooth clay found in some parts of the bank was used to produce stoneware.

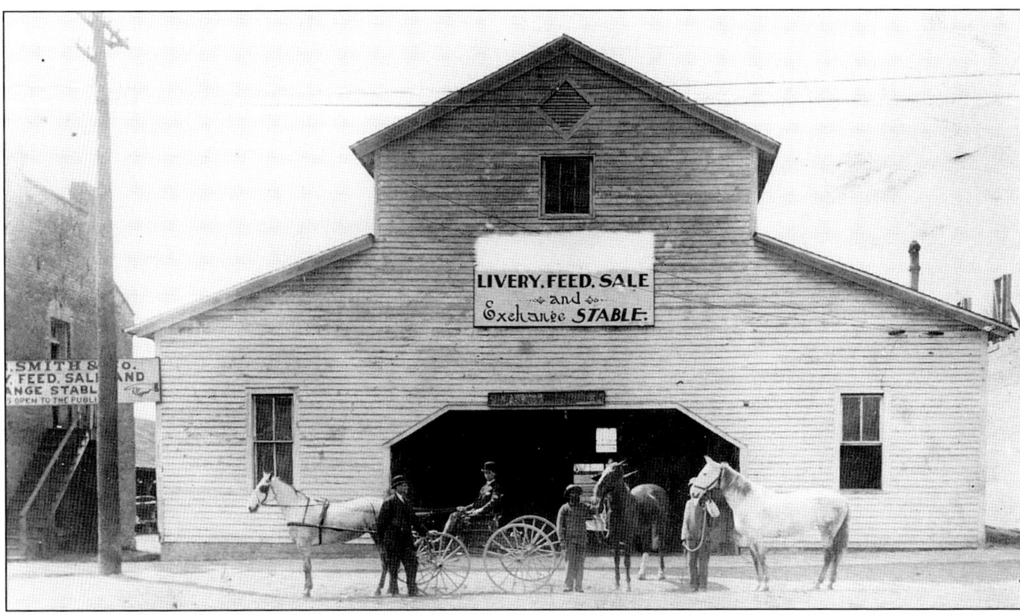

Livery stables were an essential business until automobiles became prevalent on the roads in the 1900s. Horses belonging to people visiting town were boarded at stables, and people could also buy and trade horses there. Pictured here is Smith's Livery, Feed, Sale, and Exchange Stable, c. 1890. (Courtesy N.C. Department of Archives and History.)

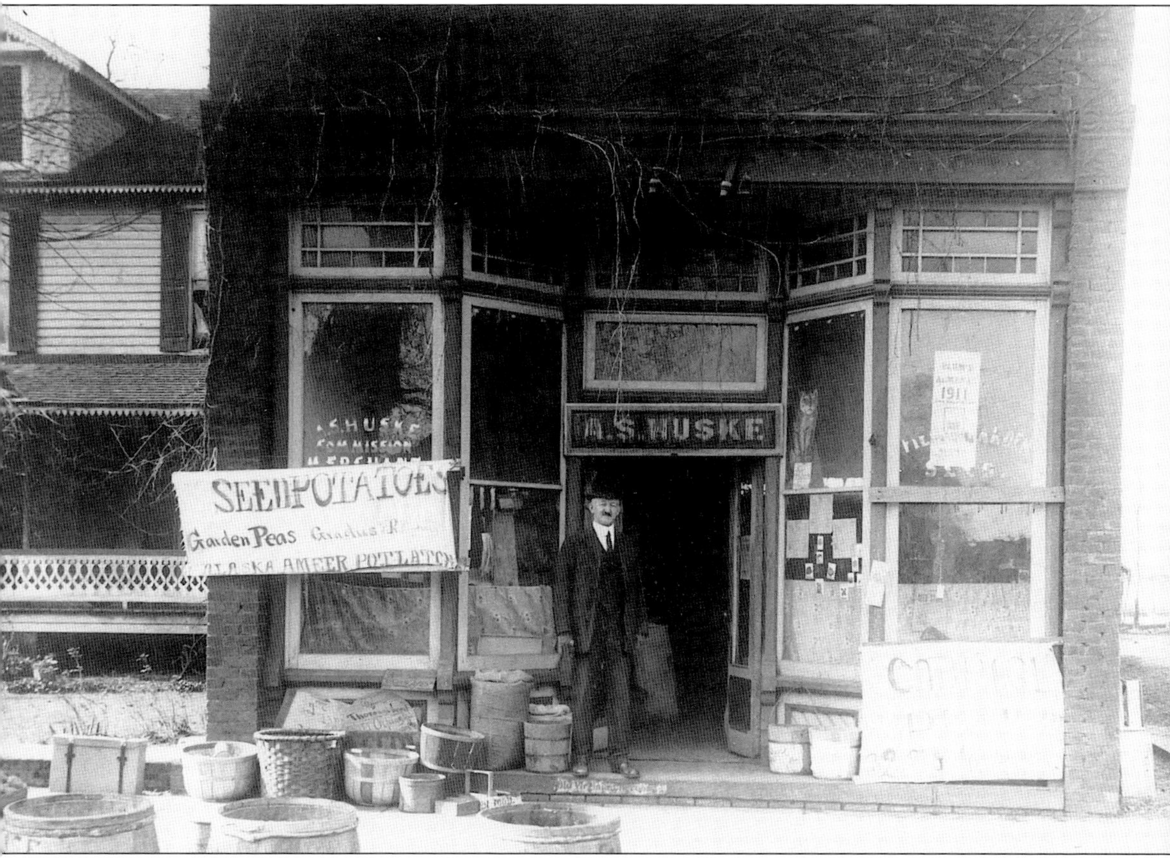

A.S. Huske stands outside his hardware store in downtown Fayetteville in 1910. (Courtesy N.C. Department of Archives and History.)

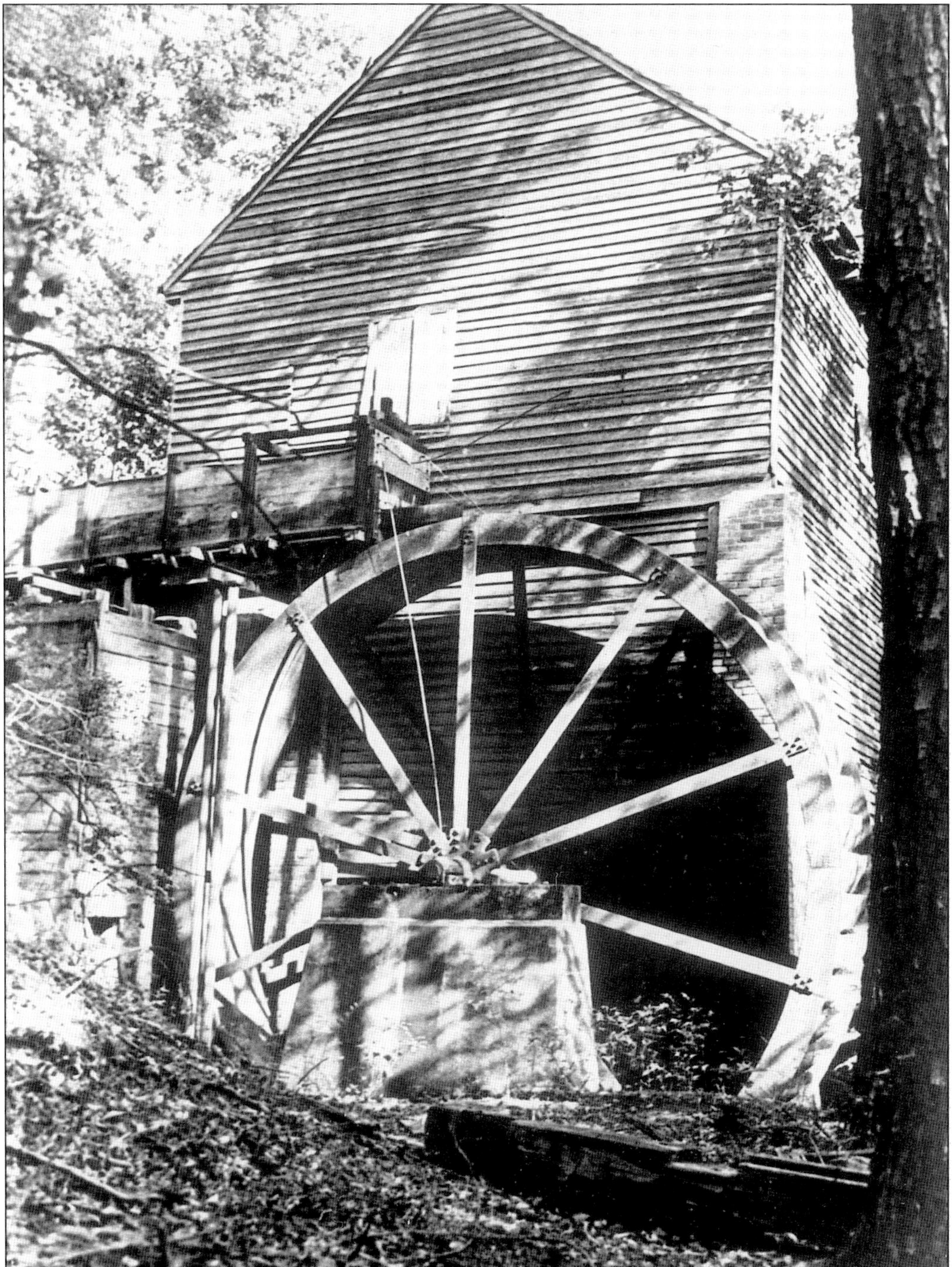

Gulley Mill was located between Fayetteville and Eastover. Operated by Norman Lucas and his son Lloyd, this mill used the overshot wheel for power production. The mill ground corn for meal and wheat for flour. While some paid to have their grain ground, the most common method of payment was for the miller to keep a portion of the grain in lieu of money. (Courtesy N.C. Department of Archives and History.)

Edward Jones Hale, editor of the *Fayetteville Observer*, is pictured here. Due to its strong Southern sentiment, the newspaper was destroyed by Yankee troops on orders from General William T. Sherman in 1865. Hale left Fayetteville after the destruction of his paper and opened a successful publishing house. (Courtesy *Biographical History of North Carolina* by Samuel A. Ashe.)

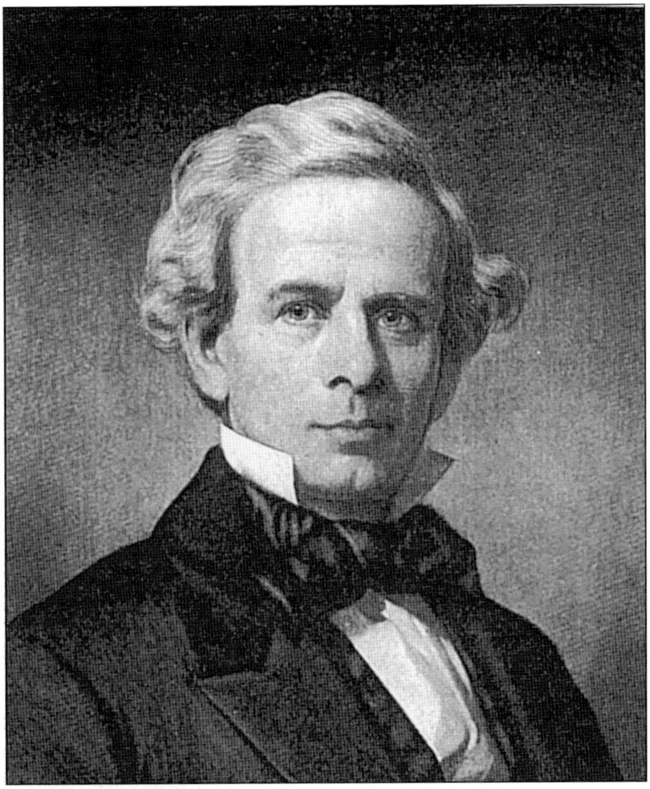

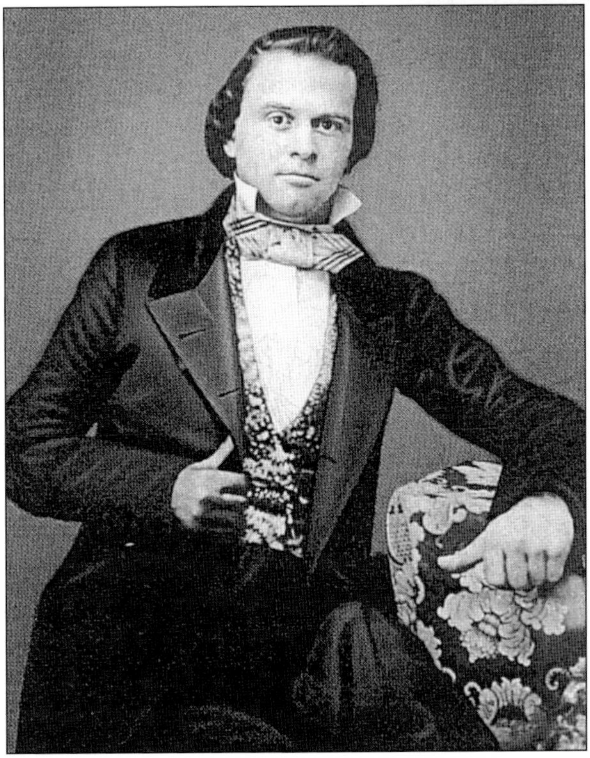

Peter Hale was the son of Edward Jones Hale, his business partner in printing and newspaper publishing. (Courtesy *Biographical History of North Carolina* by Samuel A. Ashe.)

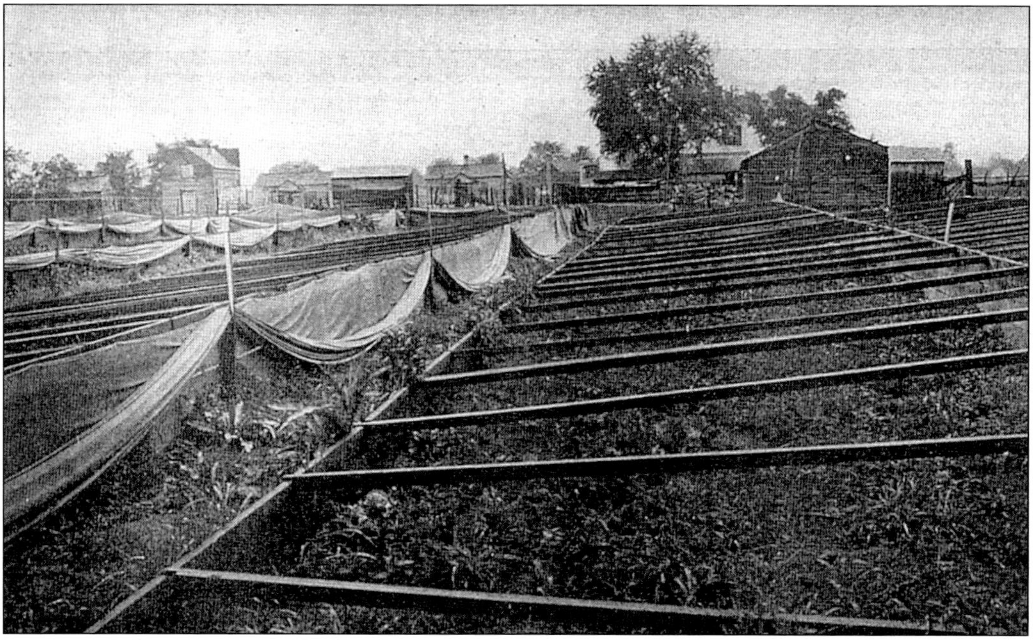

Lettuce production in Cumberland County is pictured in 1910. This Cumberland farmer was experimenting with new methods of raising lettuce for market.

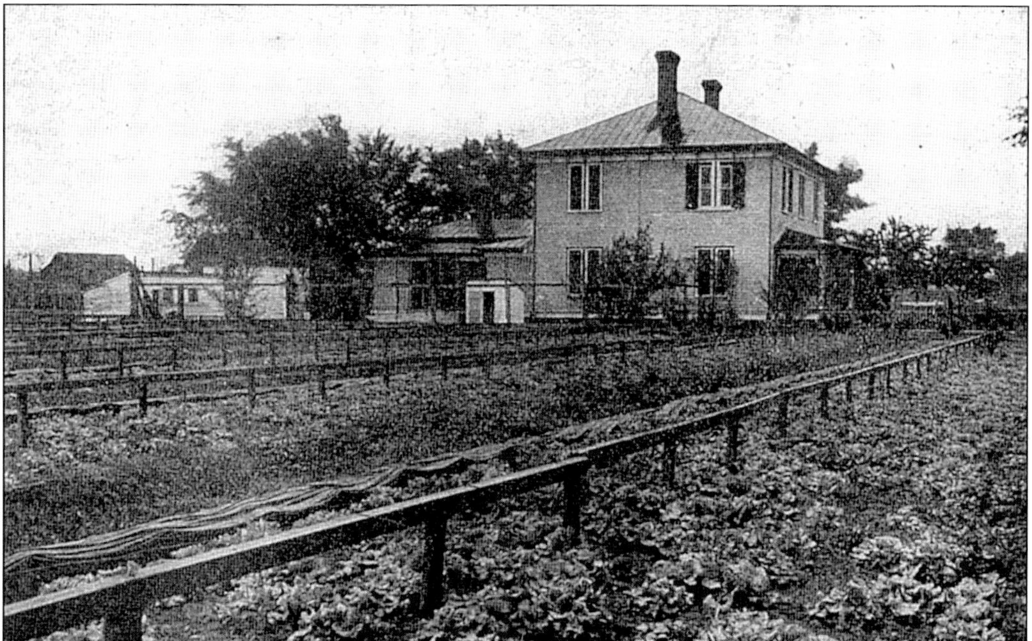

Pictured here are lettuce frames on a small farm in suburban Fayetteville in 1910.

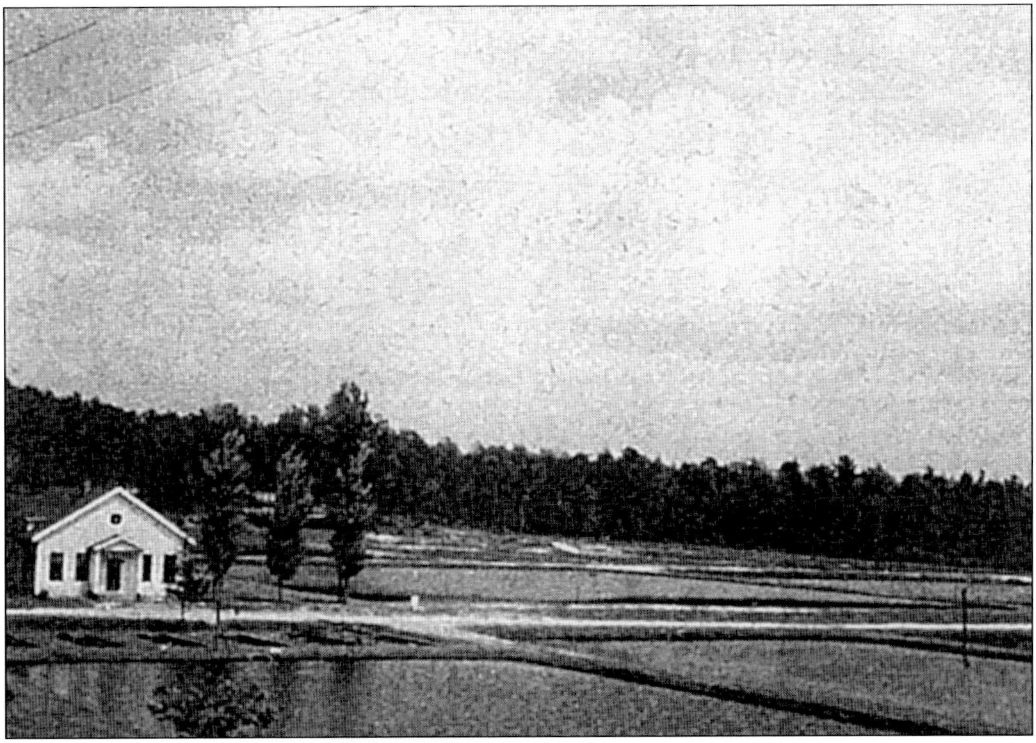

Pictured in 1947, this Cumberland County fish hatchery was created due to a $500,000 appropriation by the General Assembly. This site, near Fayetteville, was one of five such hatcheries in the state.

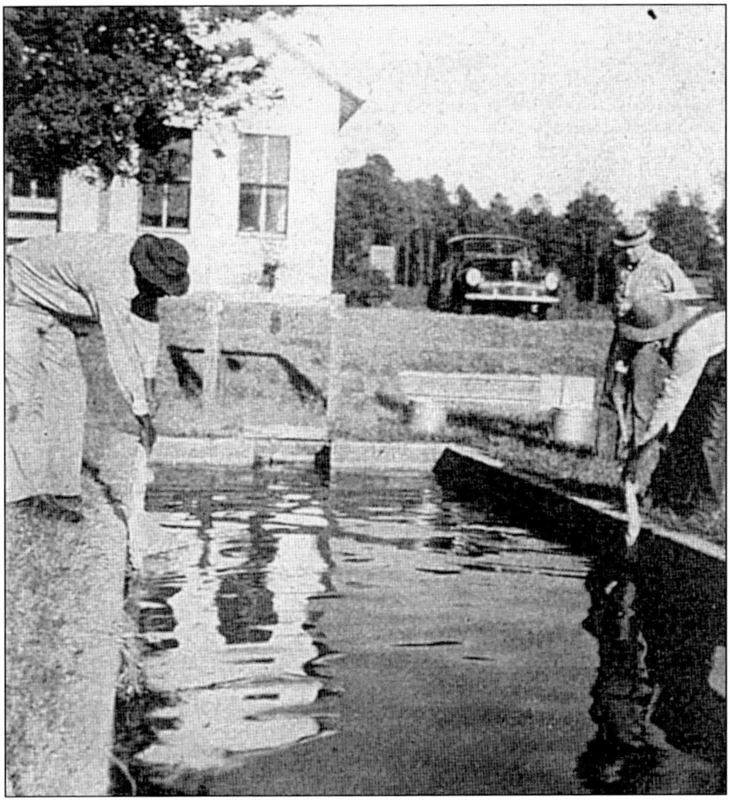

Workers seine bluegill fingerlings at the Cumberland County Hatchery. These young fish were used to stock farm ponds countywide.

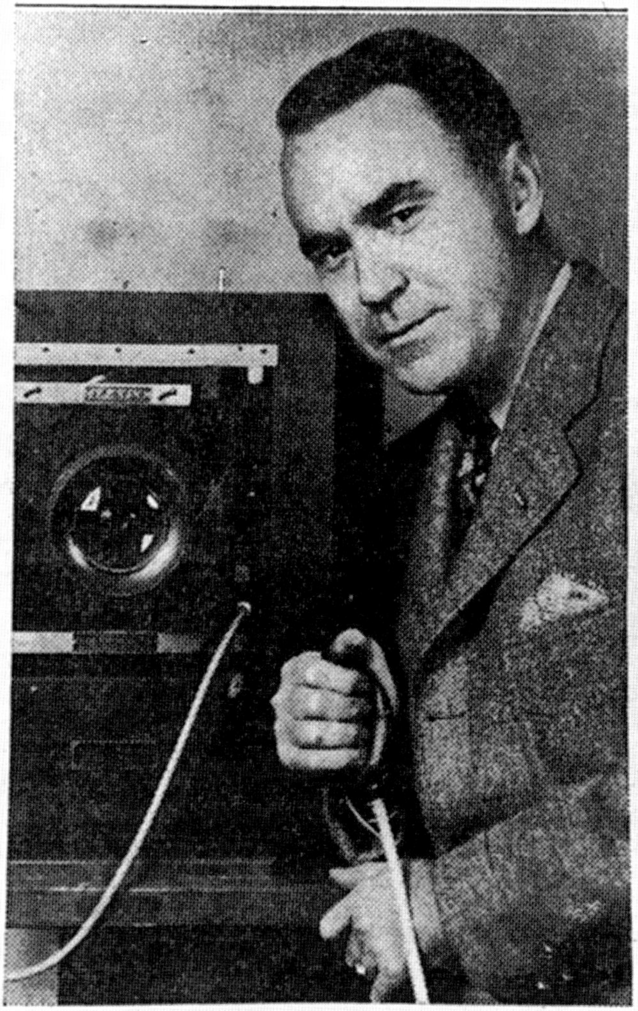

NOEL PATON
"The Man Who Made The Pictures"
(A Self-Portrait)

The Paton Studi

1897 - - - 1939

Two hundred and twenty Business Professional and Social Leaders o Fayetteville, Cumberland Count and vicinity were photographed b us especially for this Sesqui-Cen tennial Edition of The Fayettevill Observer.

Two Hundred and Twenty Cumberland County Scotchm Can't Be Wrong:-

"While You're About It, Get A Good Picture."

Somebody, Somewhere Wants Your Picture THIS Christmas.

A self-portrait and advertisement for Noel Paton, owner of the Paton Studio, was made in 1939. Paton made several pictures of historical interest in Cumberland County. (Courtesy N.C. Department of Archives and History.)

A 1788 booklet printed in Fayetteville by Bowen & Howard dealing with tariffs and trade regulations was published in French. (Courtesy N.C. Department of Archives and History.)

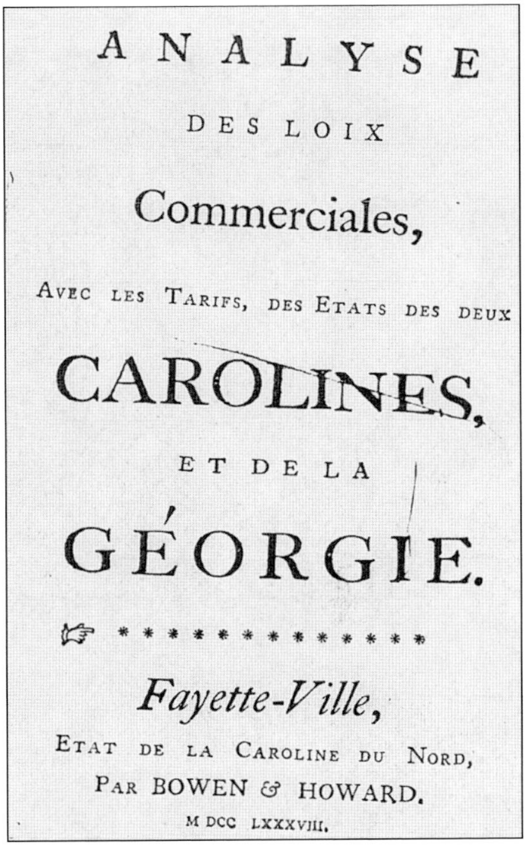
ANALYSE

DES LOIX

Commerciales,

AVEC LES TARIFS, DES ETATS DES DEUX

CAROLINES,

ET DE LA

GÉORGIE.

☞ * * * * * * * * * * * * * *

Fayette-Ville,

ETAT DE LA CAROLINE DU NORD,

PAR BOWEN & HOWARD.

M DCC LXXXVIII.

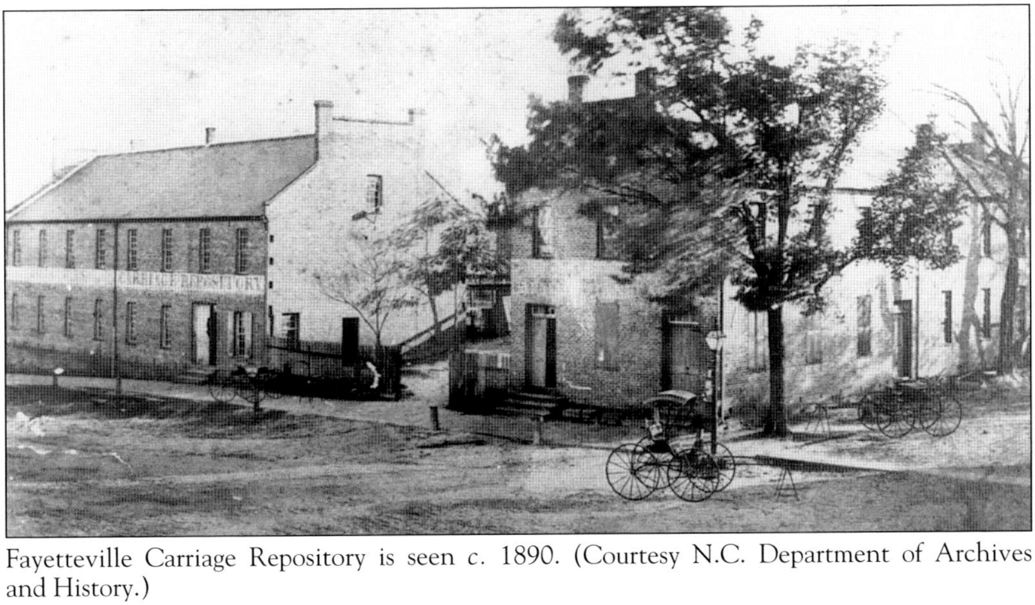

Fayetteville Carriage Repository is seen *c.* 1890. (Courtesy N.C. Department of Archives and History.)

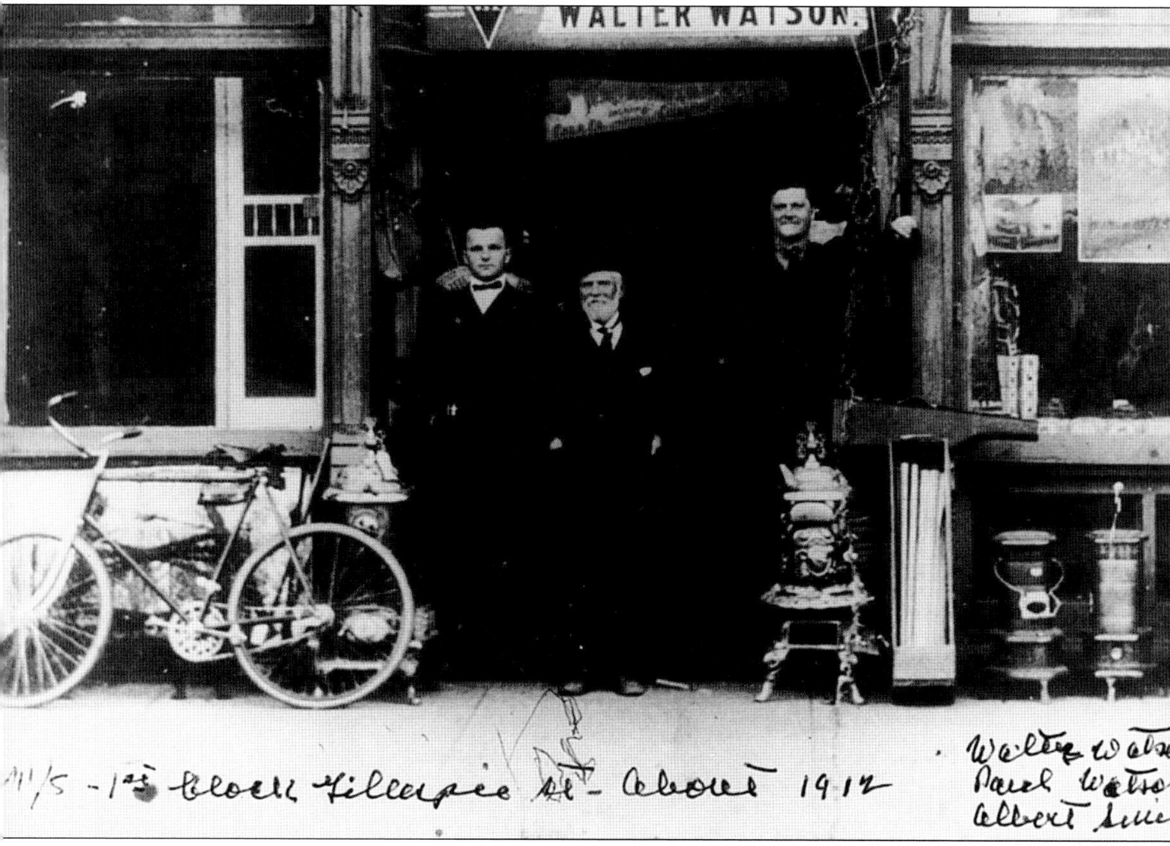

Walter Watson, Paul Watson, and Albert Smith pose for this picture outside of Watson's Hardware store on Gillespie Street, *c*. 1912.

Three

Military History

Cumberland has one of the richest military heritages in the state. One of its earliest recorded military events occurred in 1712 when a small army of colonists and friendly Native Americans from South Carolina passed through the county en route to help defend New Bern from the attacking Tuscaroras. Led by "Tuscarora Jack" Barnwell, this force marched up Green's Path and crossed the Cape Fear near the mouth of Lower Little River, near present-day Linden.

Cumberland saw considerable action during the American Revolution. Cross Creek was a mustering ground for Loyalists, before they began a march toward their own defeat by Patriot forces at the Battle of Moore's Creek in February 1776. Five years later, the main British army in the South, commanded by Lord Charles Cornwallis, camped there during its march to Wilmington following the Battle of Guilford Courthouse. Shortly afterward, the feared Loyalist commander, David Fanning, led a raid on the town and took several prisoners.

The Fayetteville Independent Light Infantry, formed in 1793, is the oldest continuously operating militia Unit in the South.

Cumberland County was invaded by Yankees in 1865 during the historical segment known as Sherman's March. Commanded by General William T. Sherman, this invading force occupied Fayetteville in March of 1865, and caused much destruction. On March 15, 1865, a wing of this army was attacked by entrenched Confederates in northern Cumberland; this was the beginning of the Battle of Averasboro.

Cumberland received a huge boost both economically and militarily in 1918 when a site between Fayetteville and Manchester was selected for a new army post, Camp Bragg. Pope Field was added the following year. Named for Confederate General Braxton Bragg, Camp Bragg was renamed Fort Bragg in 1922; it is the home of the famed 82nd Airborne, whose soldiers are flown worldwide from Pope Air Force Base.

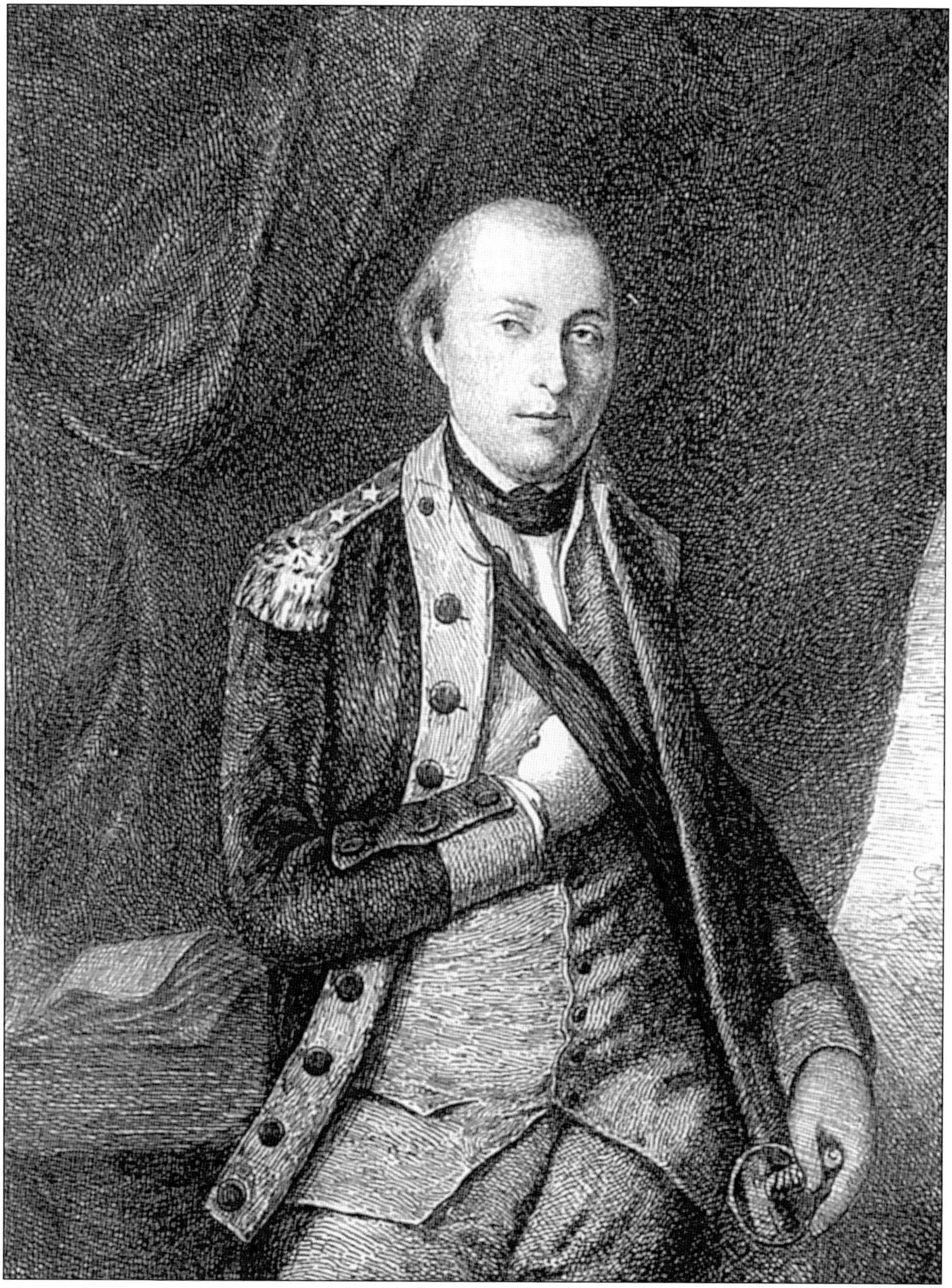

Pictured is the Marquis de Lafayette in 1780. Lafayette was a Frenchman who assisted General George Washington and the American forces against the British during the Revolutionary War. Fayetteville was named in his honor when the villages of Cross Creek and Campbellton merged in 1783. (Courtesy *The Marquis de Lafayette In The American Revolution*, by Charlemagne Tower Jr.)

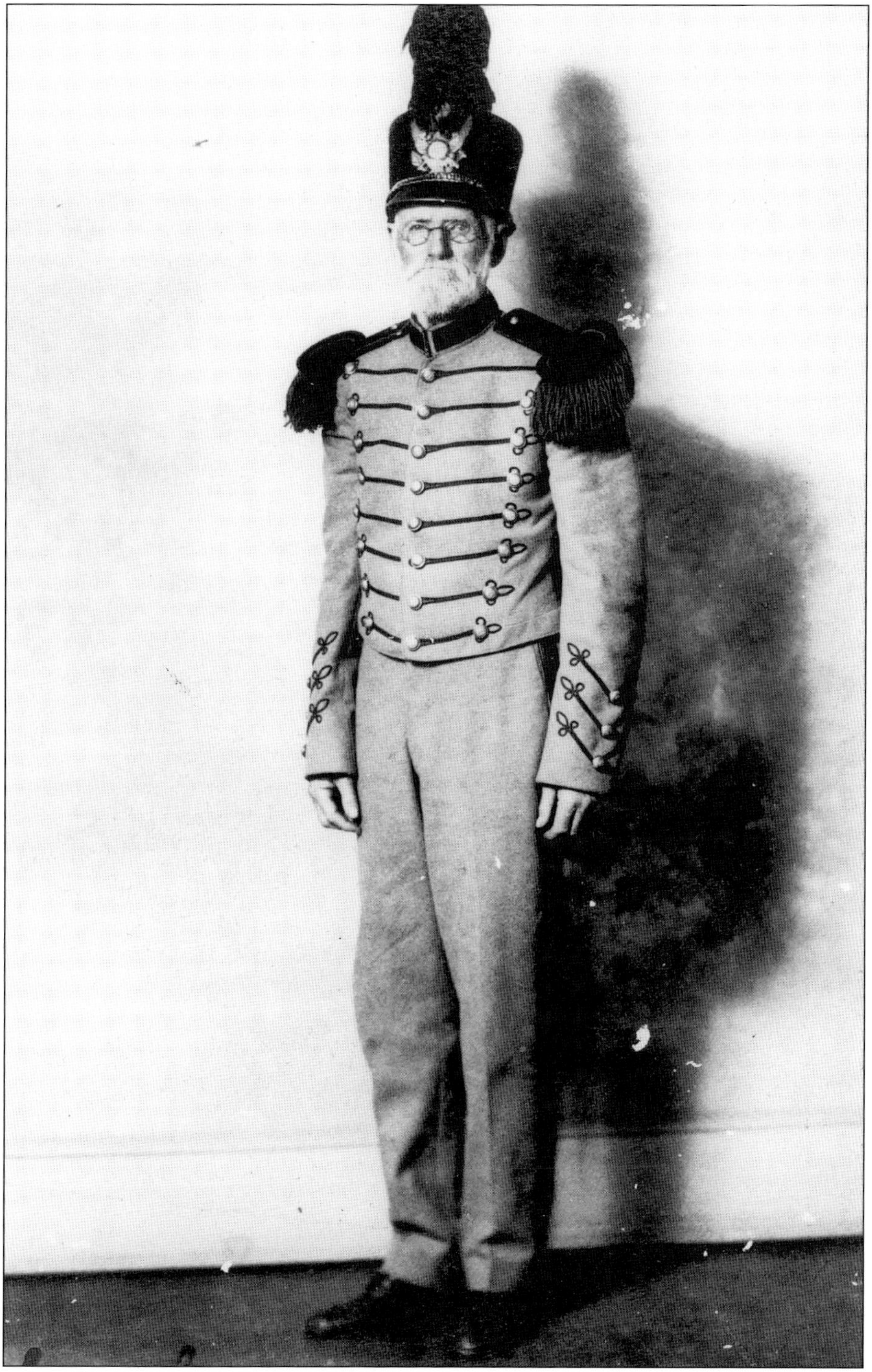

John T. Williams, a member of the Fayetteville Independent Light Infantry, models his uniform in 1926. The Fayetteville Independent Light Infantry, organized in 1793, is the oldest continuously operating militia unit in the South. (Courtesy N.C. Department of Archives and History.)

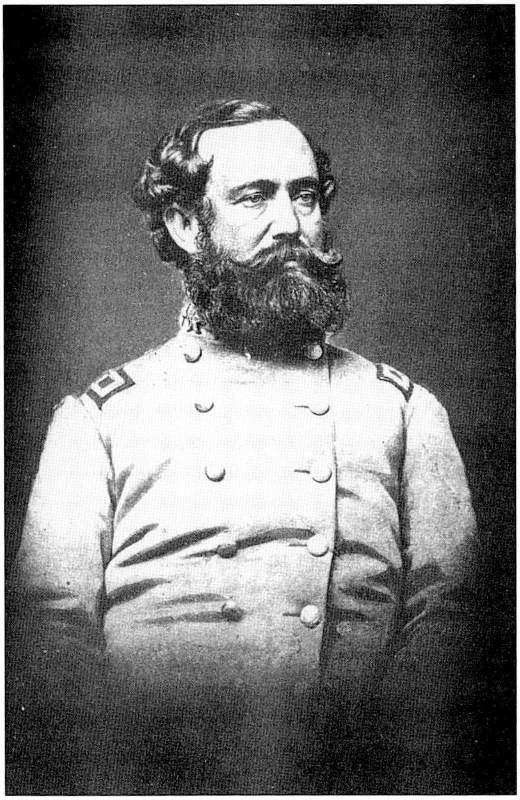

Confederate General Wade Hampton led a successful cavalry skirmish with five men against a much larger Yankee force on Hay Street on the morning of March 11, 1865. His small force killed 13 Union soldiers and captured 12. (Courtesy *Lee's Lieutenants* by Douglas Southall Freeman.)

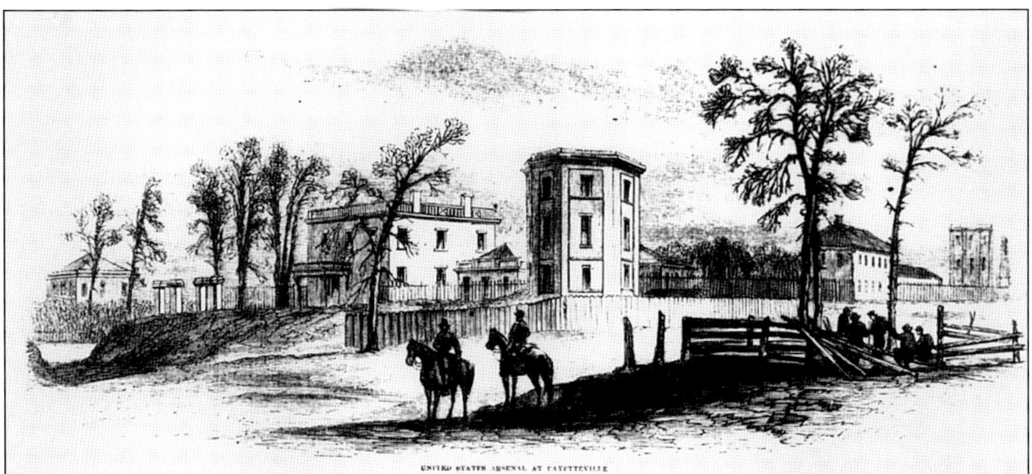

The Fayetteville Arsenal was built in 1834 and destroyed by Union forces commanded by General William T. Sherman on March 14, 1865. The arsenal produced rifles and ammunition. (Courtesy N.C. Department of Archives and History.)

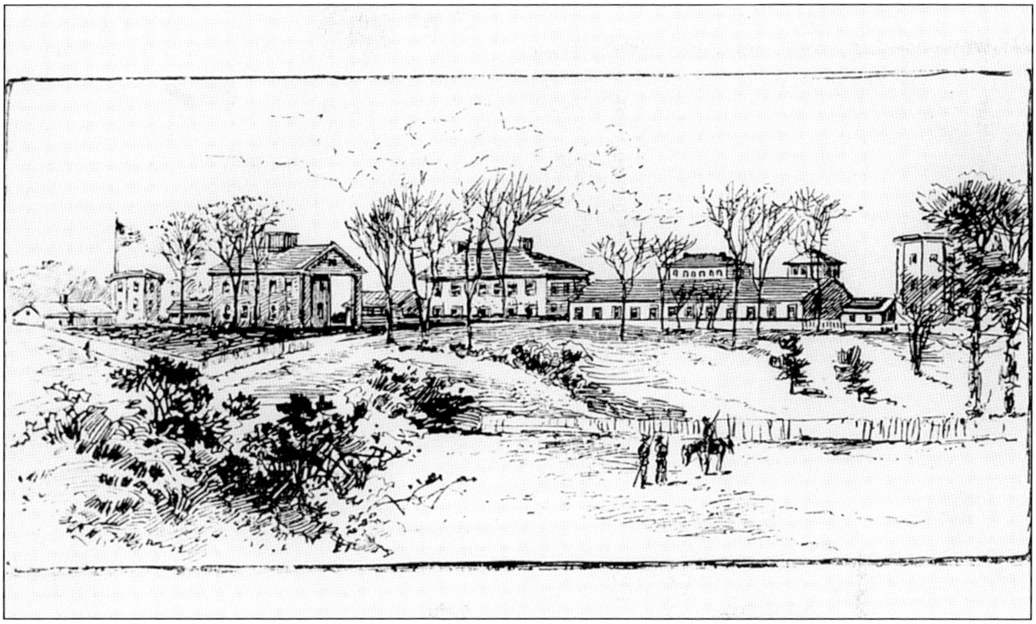

Seen here is another view of the Fayetteville Arsenal before its destruction in 1865. The fortress-like structure stood on Haymount Hill. (Courtesy N.C. Department of Archives and History.)

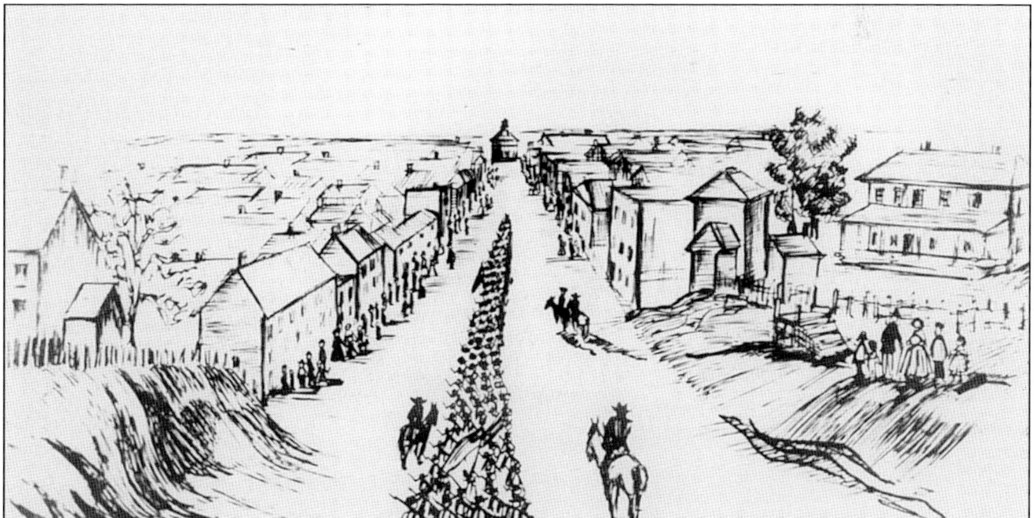

The Twentieth Corps of the Union Army invaded Fayetteville on March 11, 1865. To insult the residents, its band played "Dixie," the Confederate national anthem, as it marched into town. (Courtesy N.C. Department of Archives and History.)

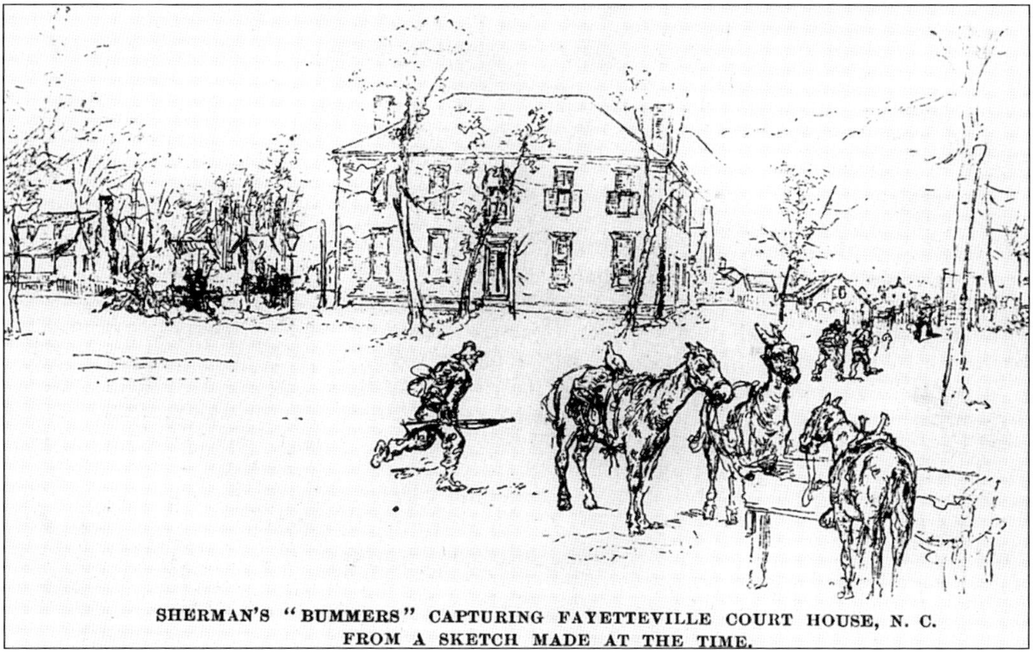

Yankee "bummers" wasted little time in stealing food and valuables from residents after entering Fayetteville. These bummers are looting at the old courthouse that stood on St. James Square. (Courtesy N.C. Department of Archives and History.)

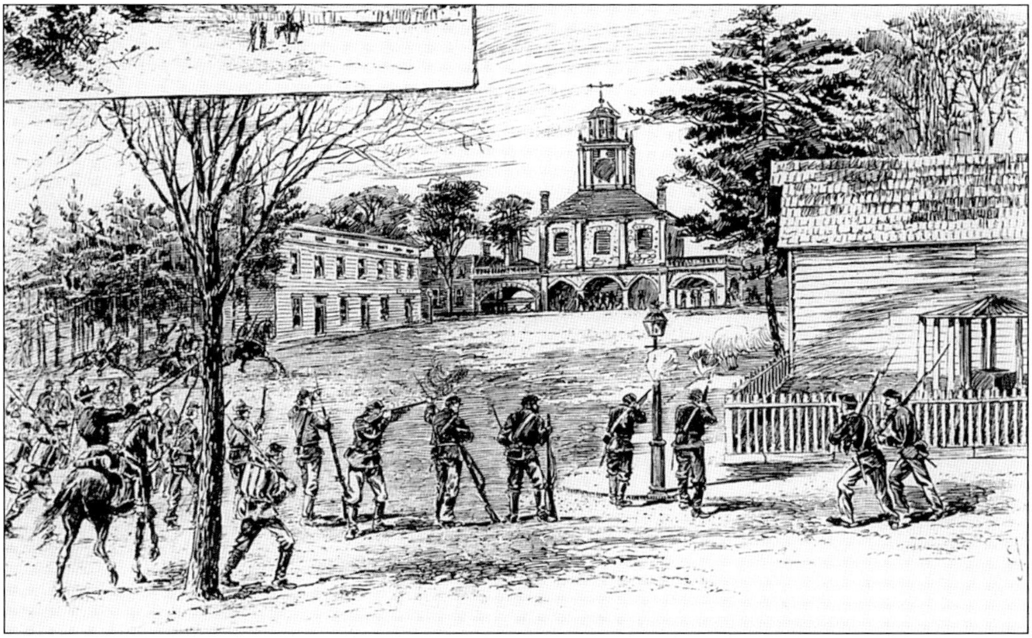

Yankee soldiers drove the remaining Confederates out of Fayetteville at the Market House. The Confederates retreated across the Clarendon Bridge, which was then set on fire in an attempt to slow the Yankee crossing of the flooded Cape Fear River. (Courtesy N.C. Department of Archives and History.)

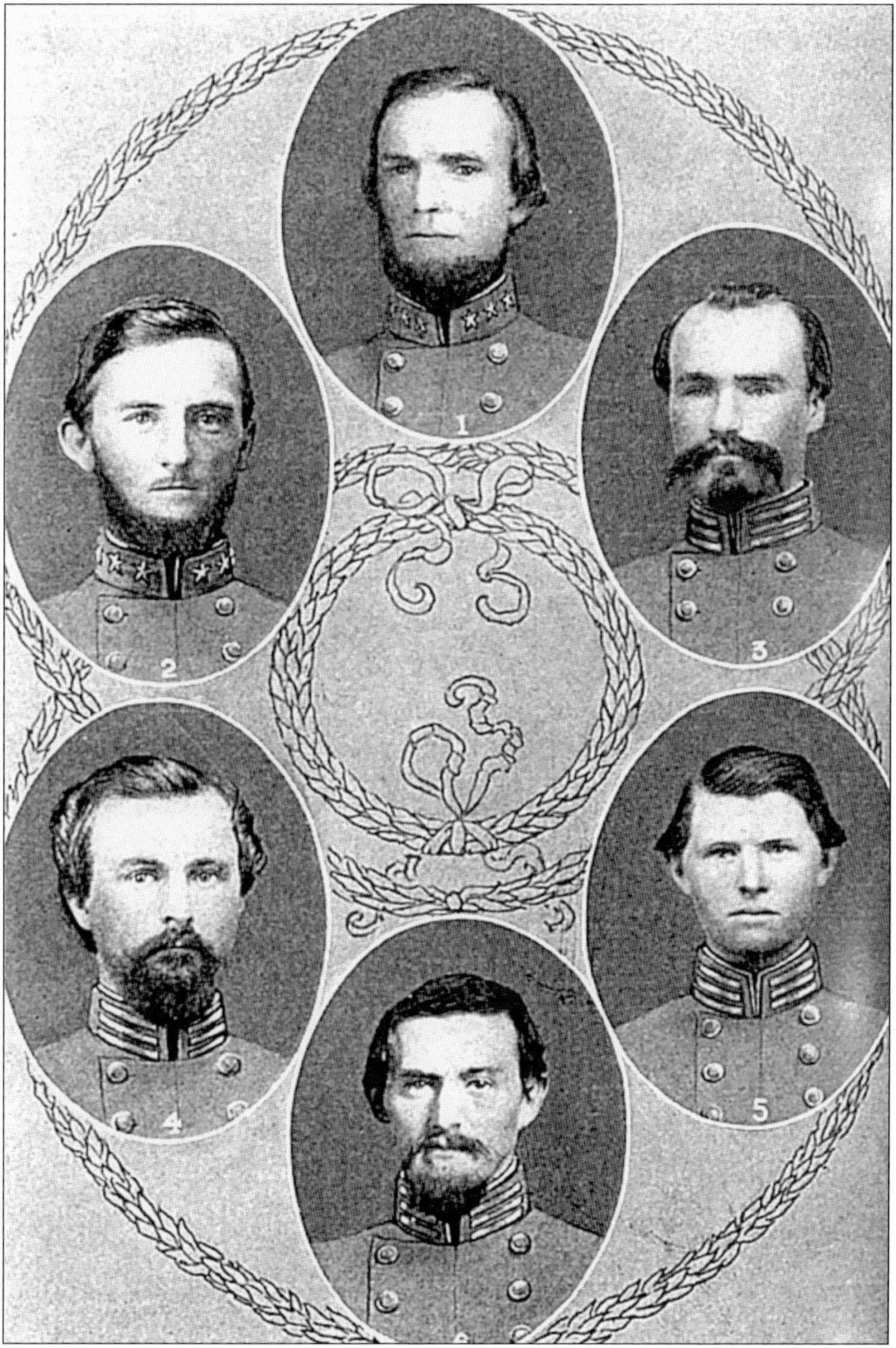

Seen here are the commanding officers of the 51st Regiment of the Confederate Army. This unit was comprised of men from Cumberland County.

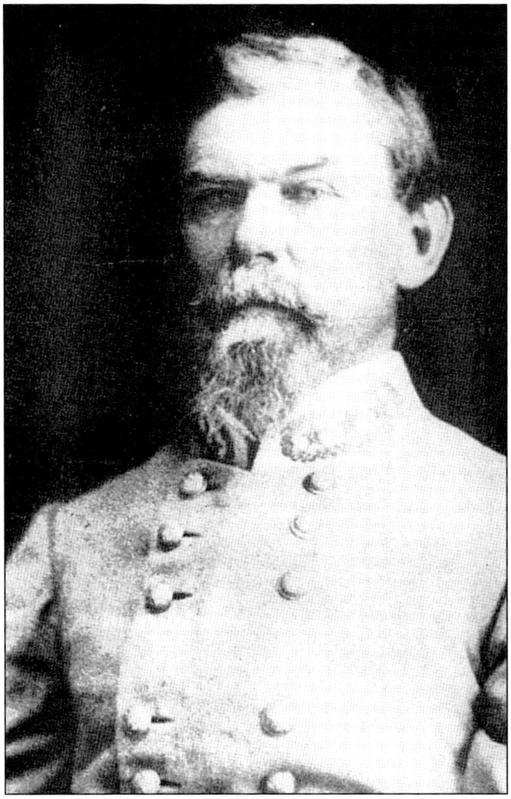

General William Joseph Hardee was the commanding Confederate General in Fayetteville; upon orders from General Joseph Johnston, he planned the Battle of Averasboro and commanded Confederate forces there on March 15–17, 1865.

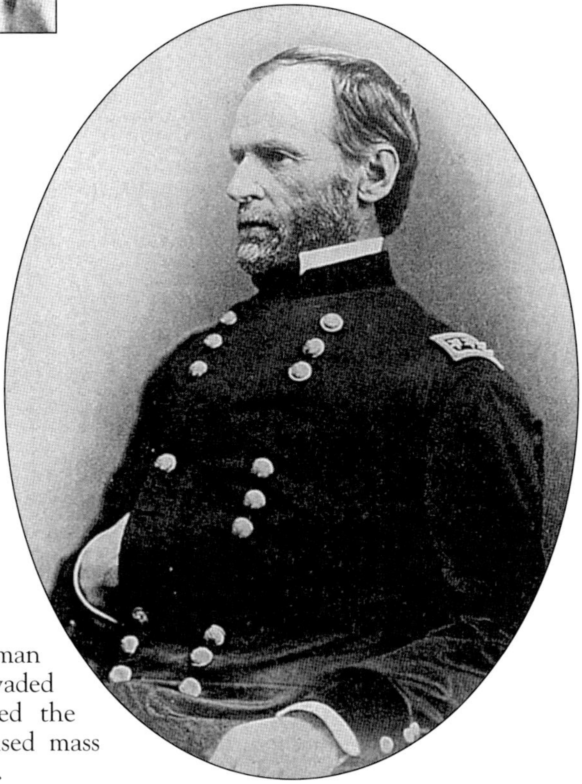

General William Tecumseh Sherman commanded the Union Army that invaded Fayetteville in March of 1865. He led the infamous Sherman's March, which caused mass destruction in Georgia and the Carolinas.

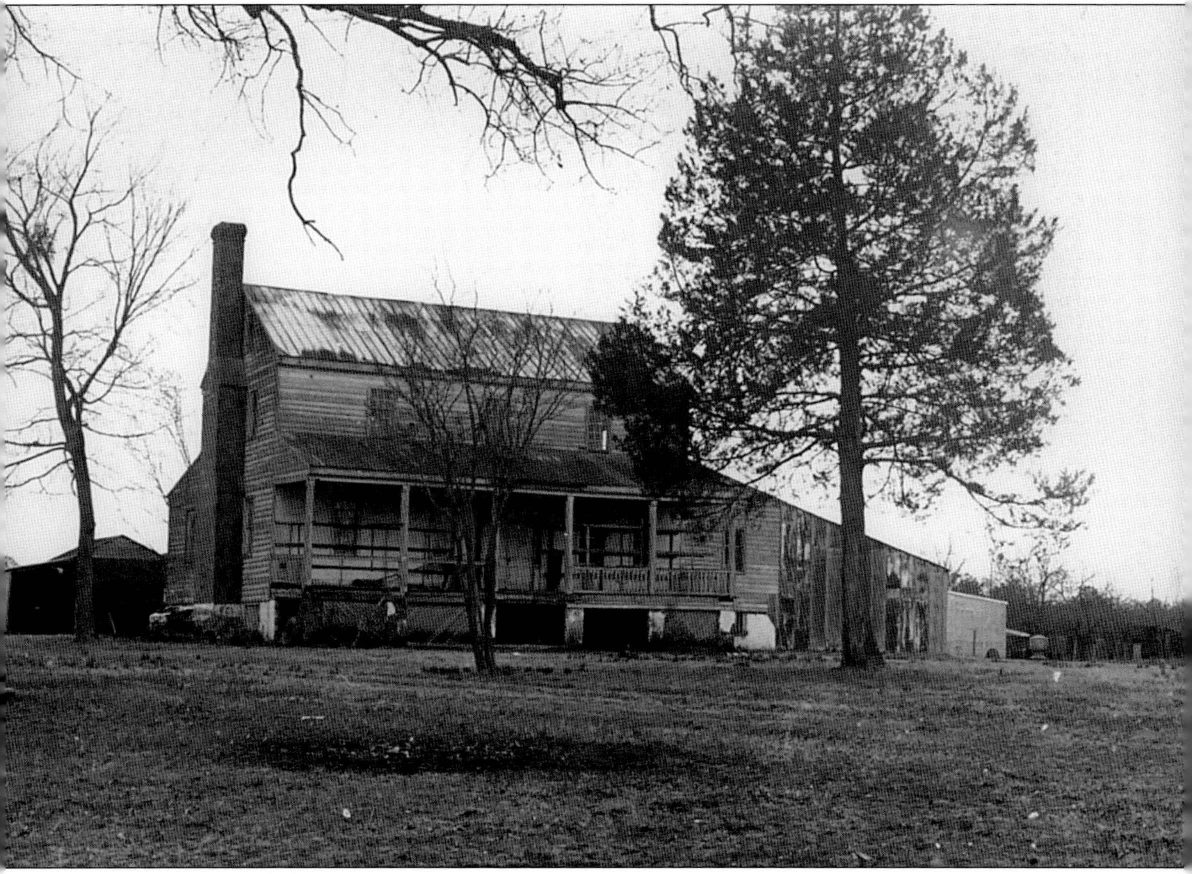

Oak Grove was the plantation home of John Smith, and was used as a hospital during the Battle of Averasboro. Several remnants of the battle are still visible, including the attic where an artillery shell pierced the roof near its pitch and shattered a rafter, and dried bloodstains on the hardwood floors of the downstairs living room where operations and amputations were performed on top of a piano. (Courtesy N.C. Department of Archives and History.)

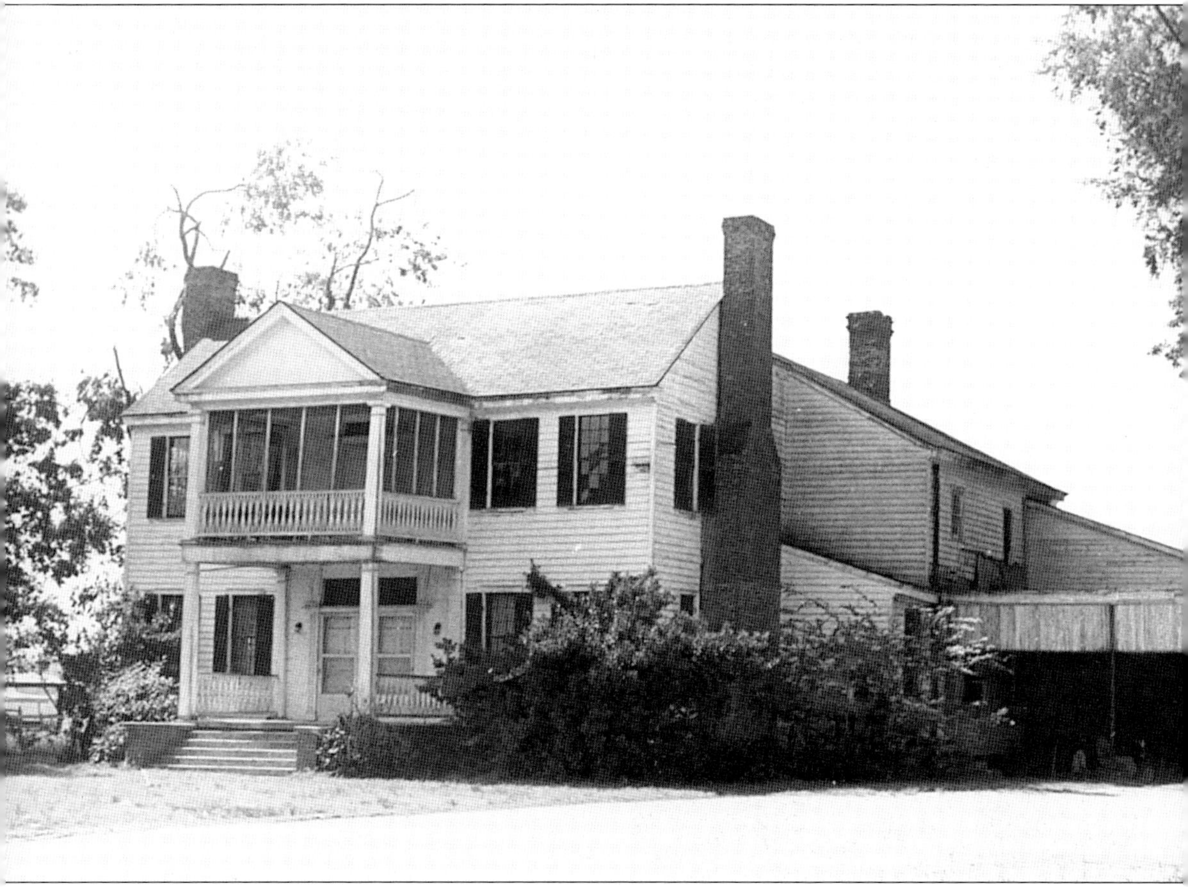

The William Smith home near Godwin was used as a Yankee hospital during the Battle of Averasboro. William Smith's brother, John, owned Oak Grove, and another brother, Farquard Smith, owned Lebanon Plantation a short distance away in neighboring Harnett County. (Courtesy N.C. Department of Archives and History.)

Fayetteville's Confederate Monument was erected in 1902 in the center of St. James Square, located on the site of the old courthouse that was torn down the previous decade. The monument was later moved a short distance to the corner of Ramsey and Grove Streets to improve traffic flow.

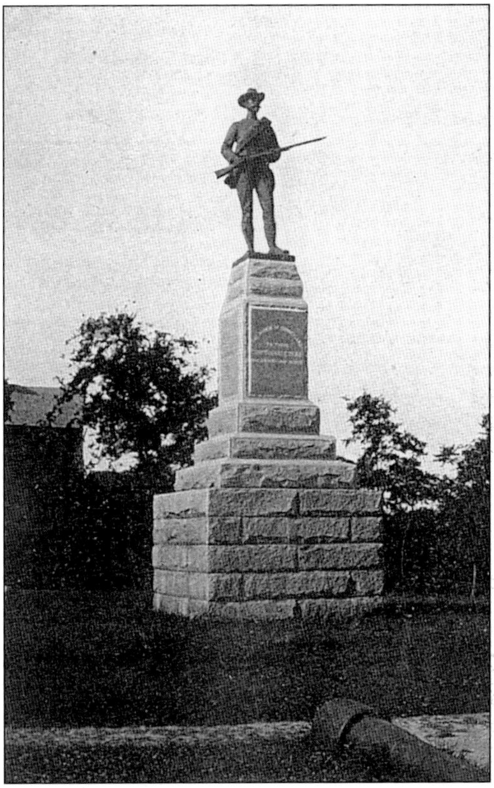

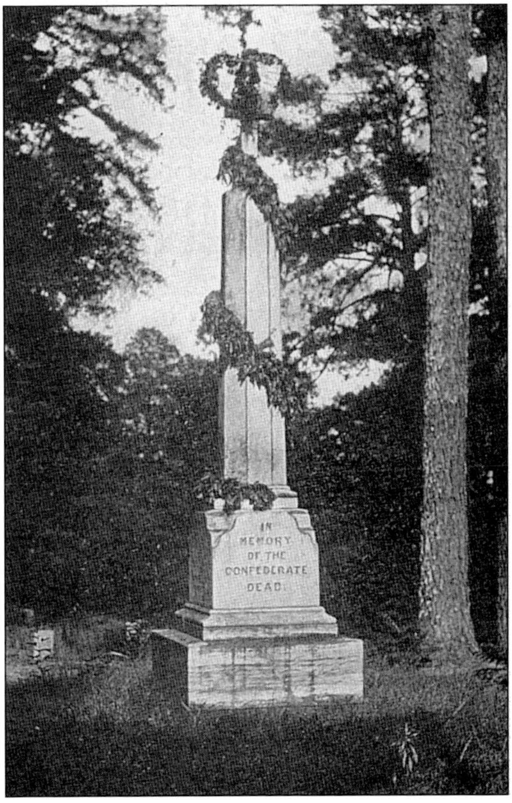

The Confederate Monument in Cross Creek Cemetery, dedicated in 1868, was one of the first memorials honoring the Confederate dead in the South. Ladies belonging to an organization that later became the United Daughters of the Confederacy made and raffled a quilt to raise funds for the marker.

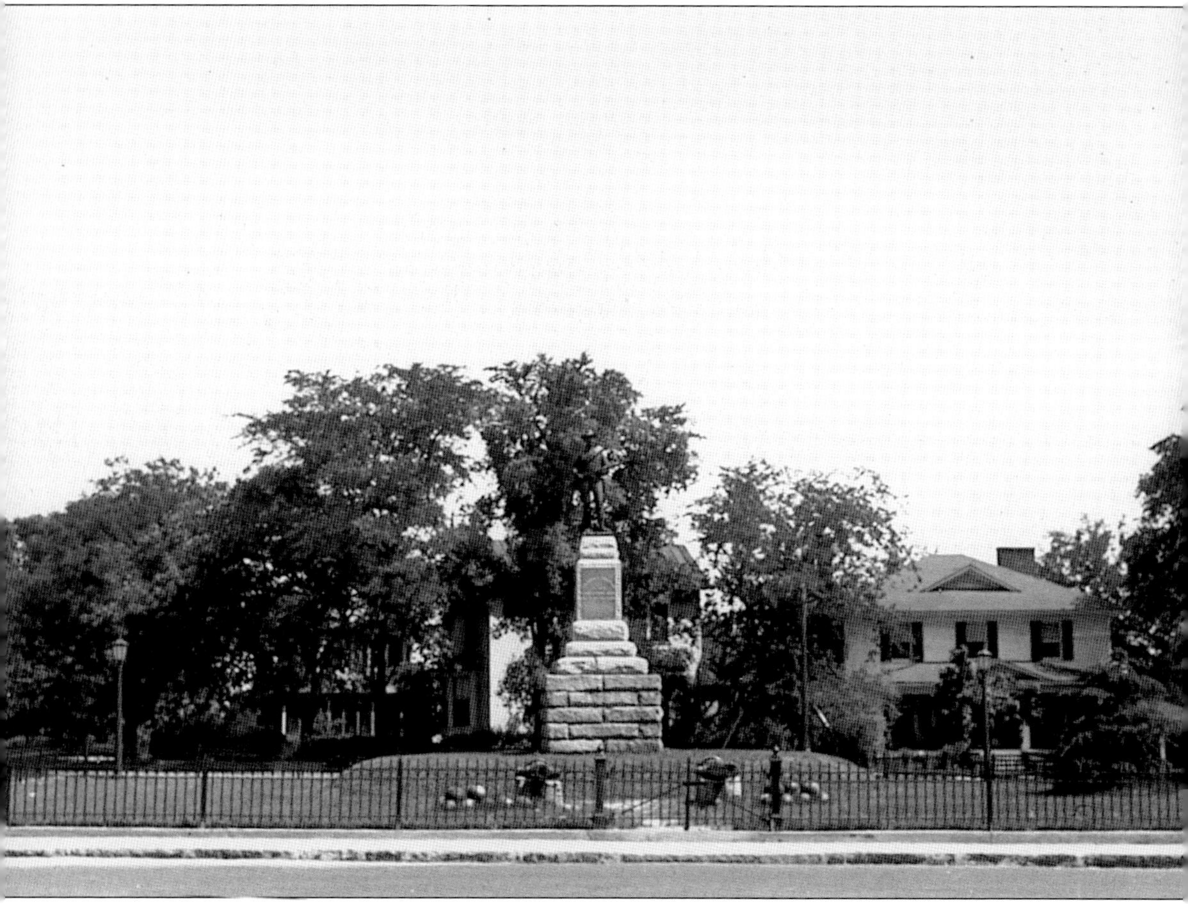

Pictured is another view of the Confederate Monument on St. James Square. (Courtesy N.C. Department of Archives and History.)

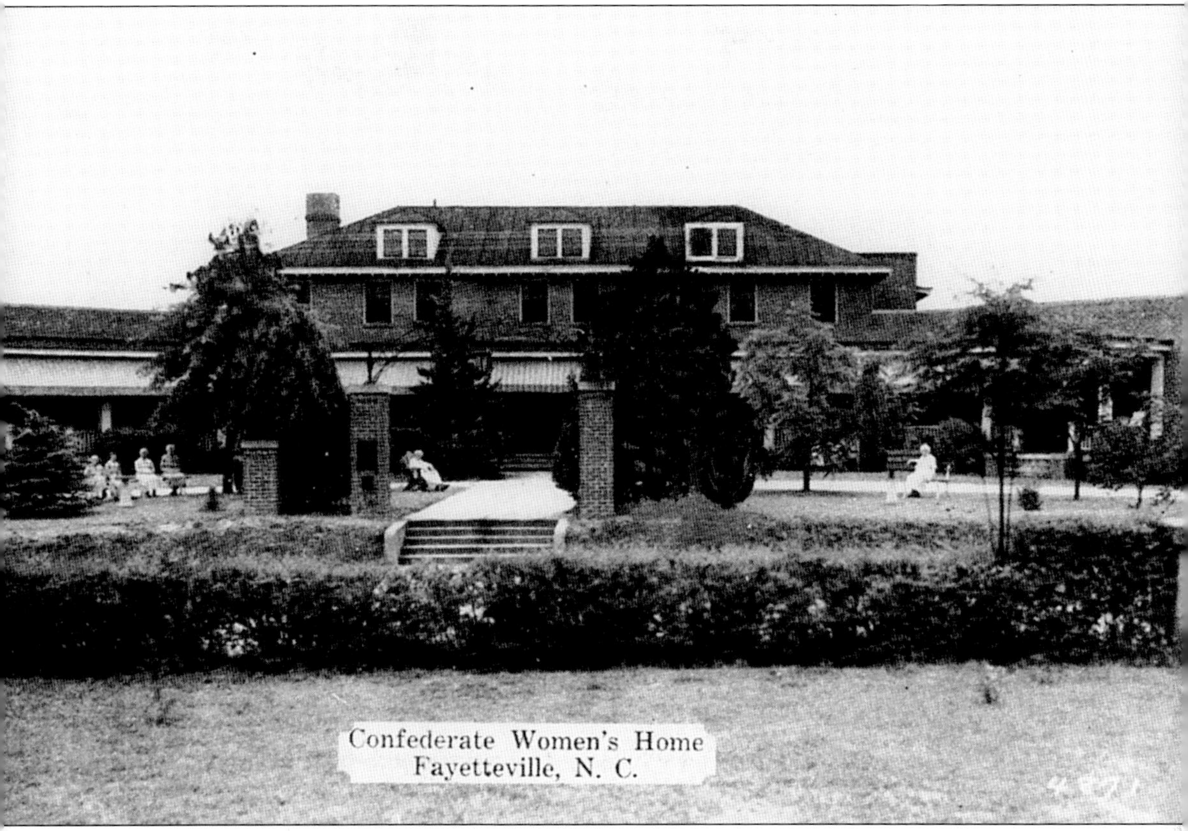

The Confederate Women's Home, shown here in 1920, was built in 1915 for the wives and daughters of Confederate veterans, and stood on Fort Bragg Road near Terry Sanford High School. It was torn down in the early 1980s. (Courtesy N.C. Department of Archives and History.)

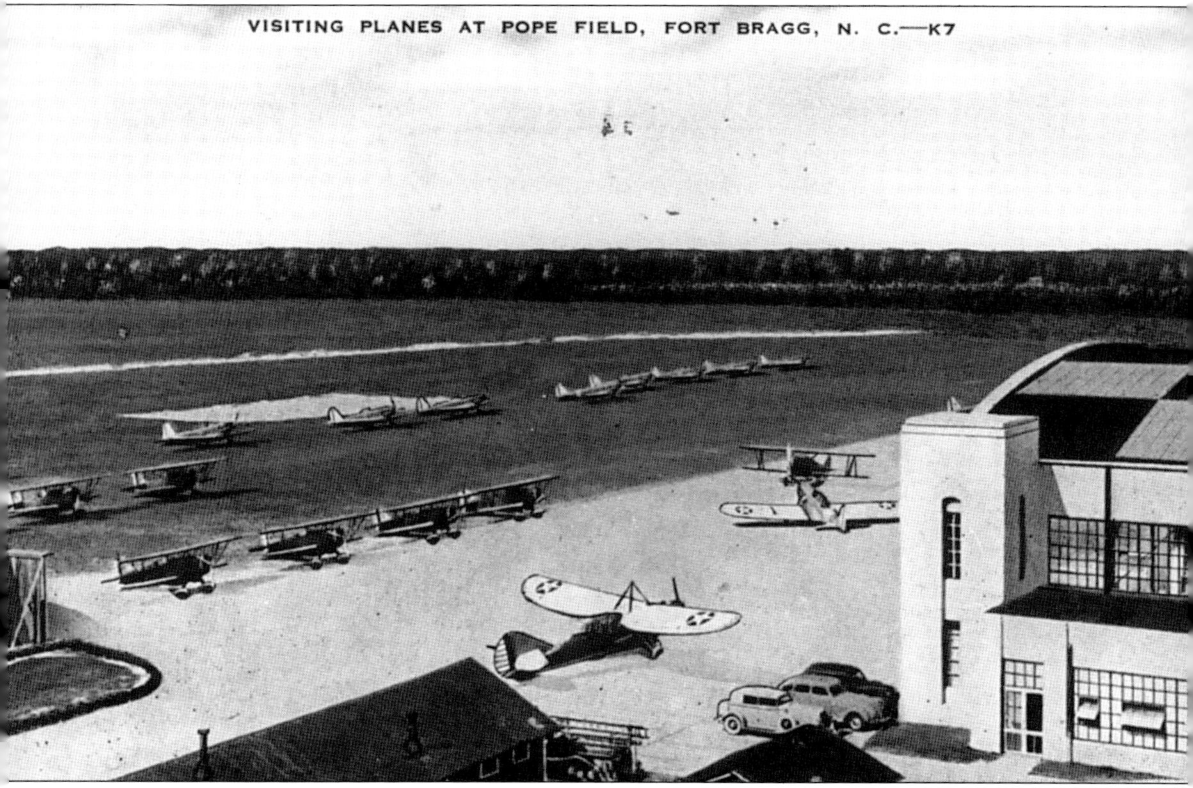

Airplanes at Pope Field, now known as Pope Air Force Base, are seen in 1943. Pope Field was created in 1919 as the flying field of Camp Bragg, and was named in honor of Lt. Harley Pope, an army pilot who was killed when his plane crashed into the Cape Fear River near Fayetteville. Today, Pope Air Force Base is used as the base for transporting Fort Bragg soldiers and their supplies on missions worldwide. (Courtesy N.C. Department of Archives and History.)

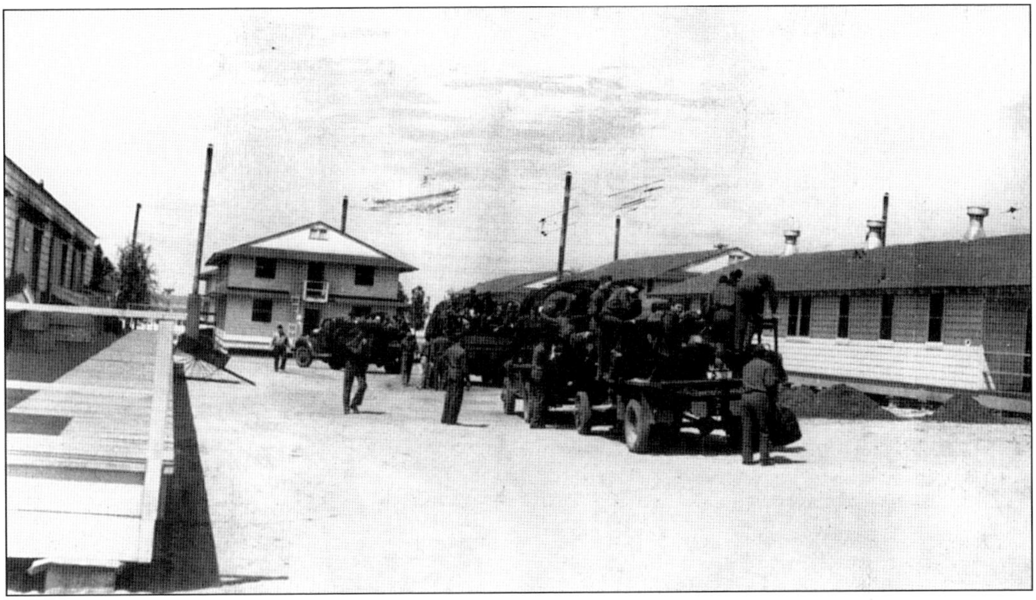

Soldiers preparing to go off to World War II arrive at the Fort Bragg reception center in 1941. (Courtesy N.C. Department of Archives and History.)

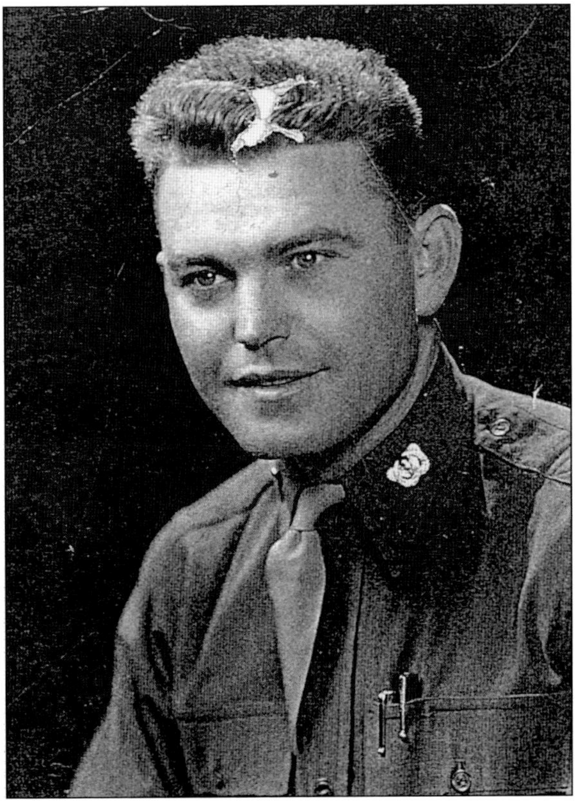

U.S. Army warrant officer Astor C. Lucas was stationed at Fort Bragg. He fought in the European Theater during World War II.

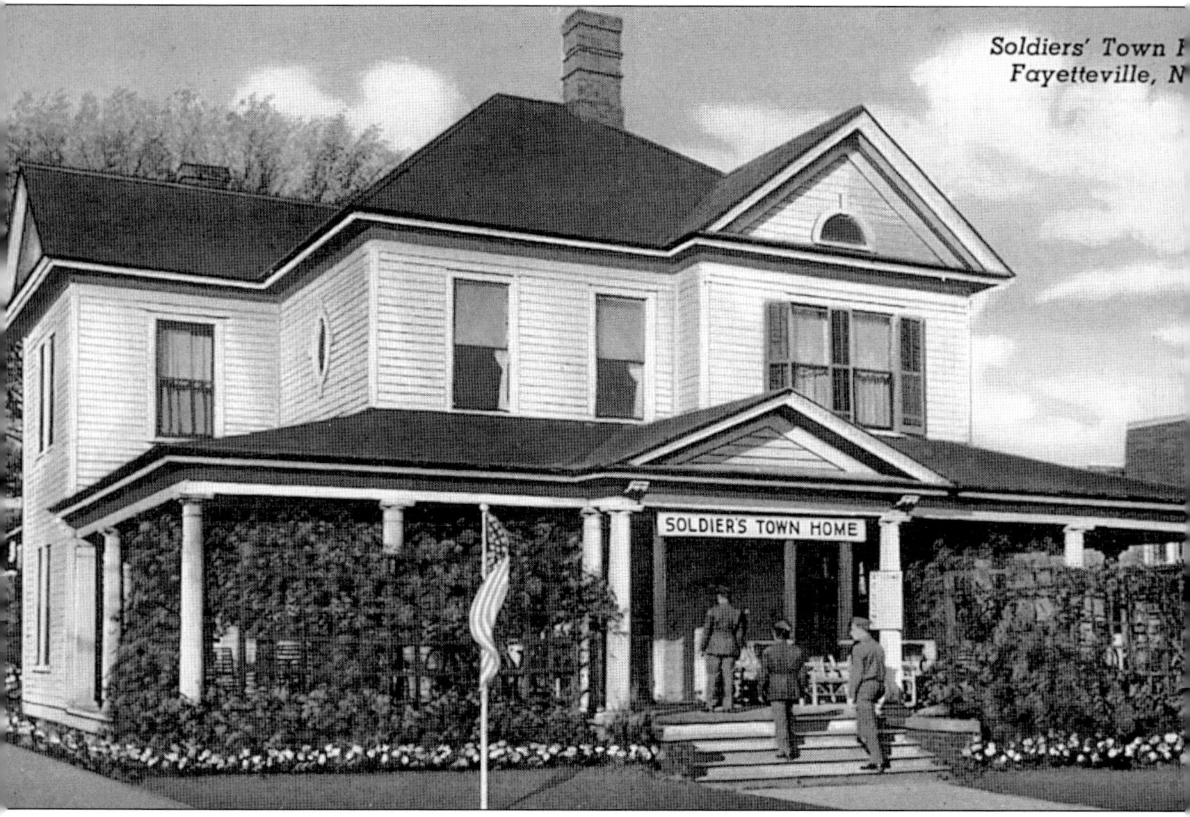

The Soldiers' Town Home in Fayetteville provided recreation for soldiers stationed at Fort Bragg. It was the original recreation home for soldiers and their wives in the United States.

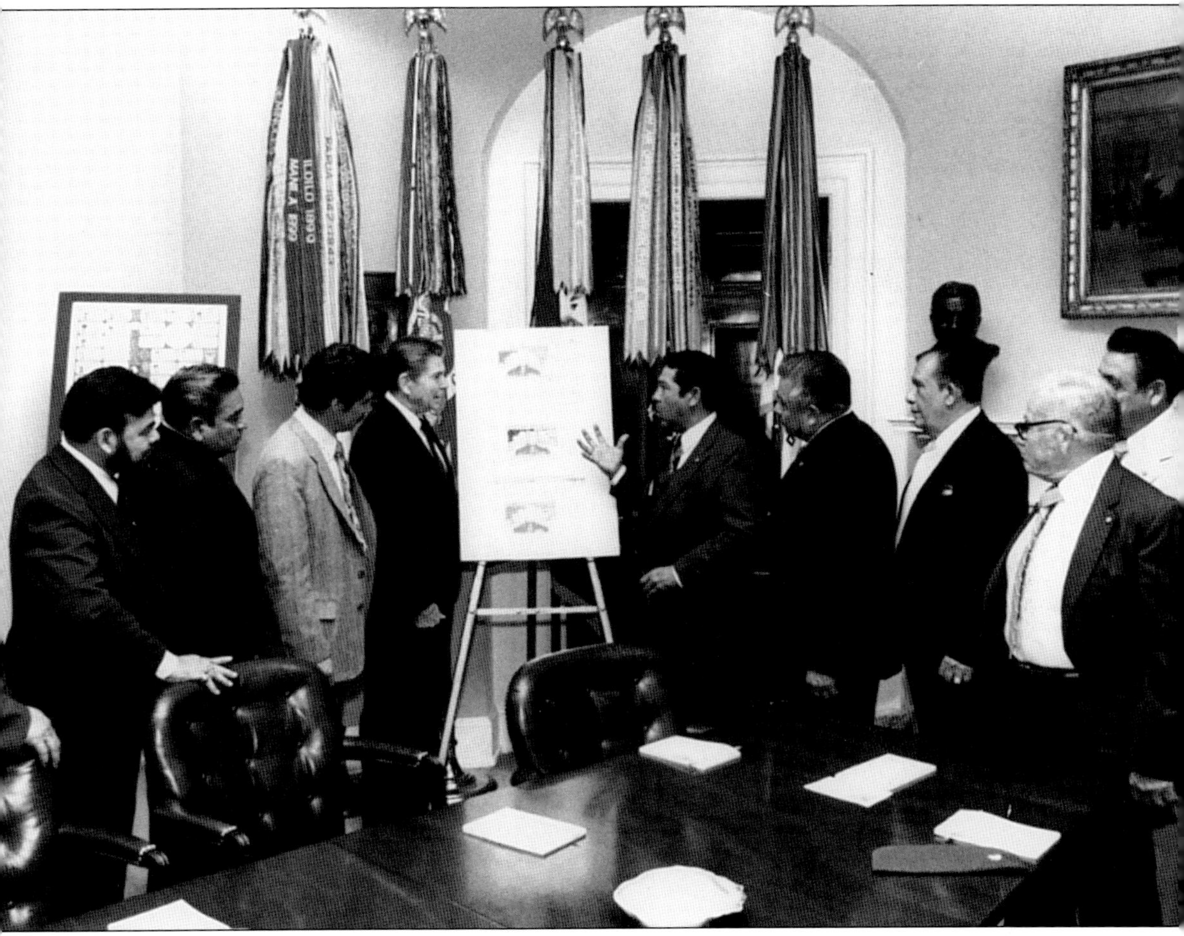

Corporal Rudy Hernandez of the 187th Airborne Regiment Combat Team at Fort Bragg is pictured with President Ronald Reagan in 1984. (Courtesy N.C. Department of Archives and History.)

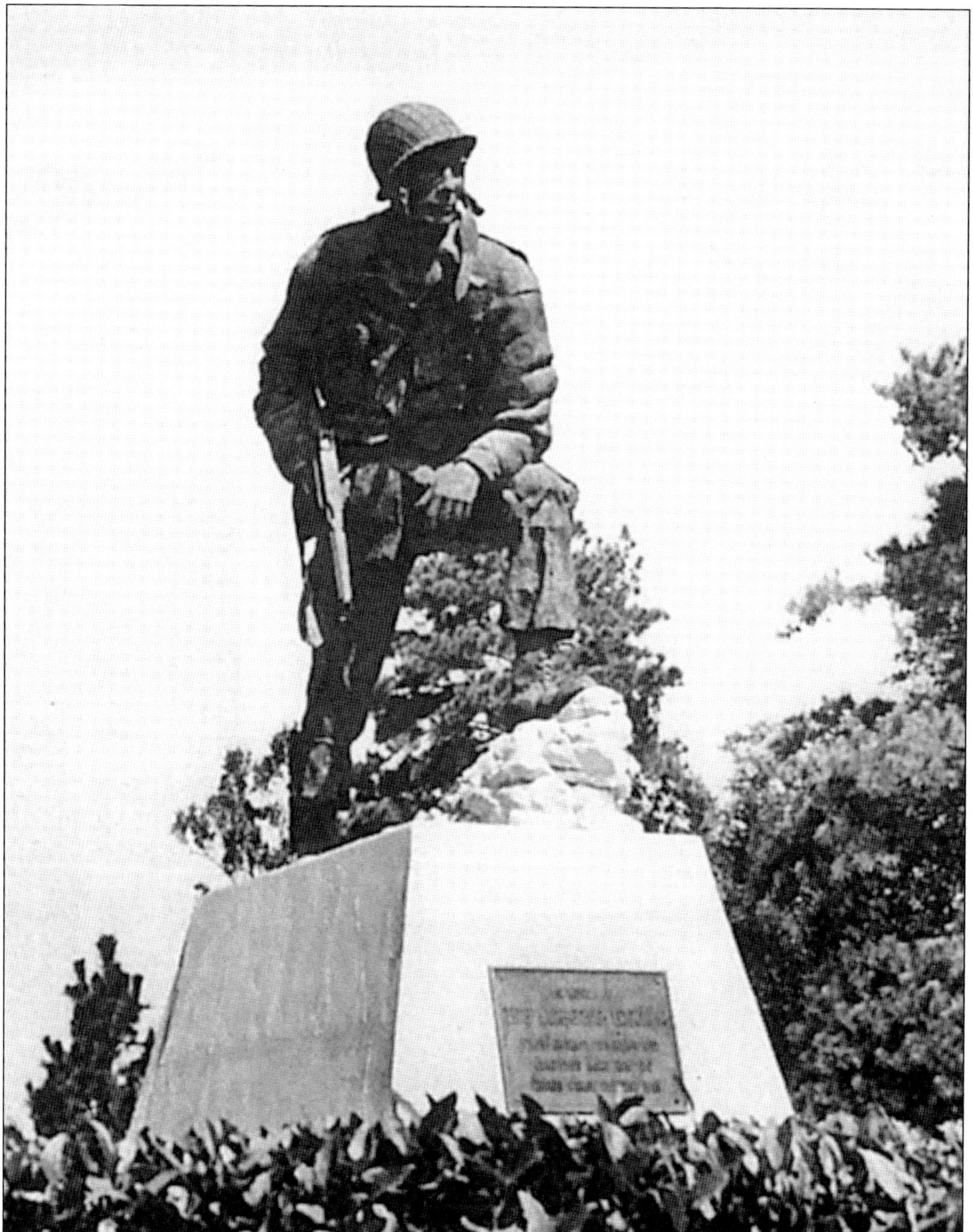

Iron Mike, a statue of a paratrooper, greets visitors to Fort Bragg.

Four

Historic Buildings

Historic structures abound in Cumberland County. Whether it is homes, ranging from the ornate to crude one-room cabins, churches, public buildings, or places of commerce, Cumberland has a wide range of buildings constructed in an earlier era, many of which are in excellent condition.

One early notable structure was the State House, which hosted a meeting of the North Carolina Legislature in November 1789. Two significant historical events occurred while this legislative body met there—North Carolina's ratification of the Unites States Constitution, and the chartering of the University of North Carolina, which opened six years later in Chapel Hill.

The State House was destroyed during the great Fayetteville fire of 1831. In 1838, a new structure was constructed on its site. Named the Market House, this building continues to serve as a symbol for the city of Fayetteville.

There are several old homes still standing throughout the county. Many that have been cared for, maintained, and restored continue to serve as residences.

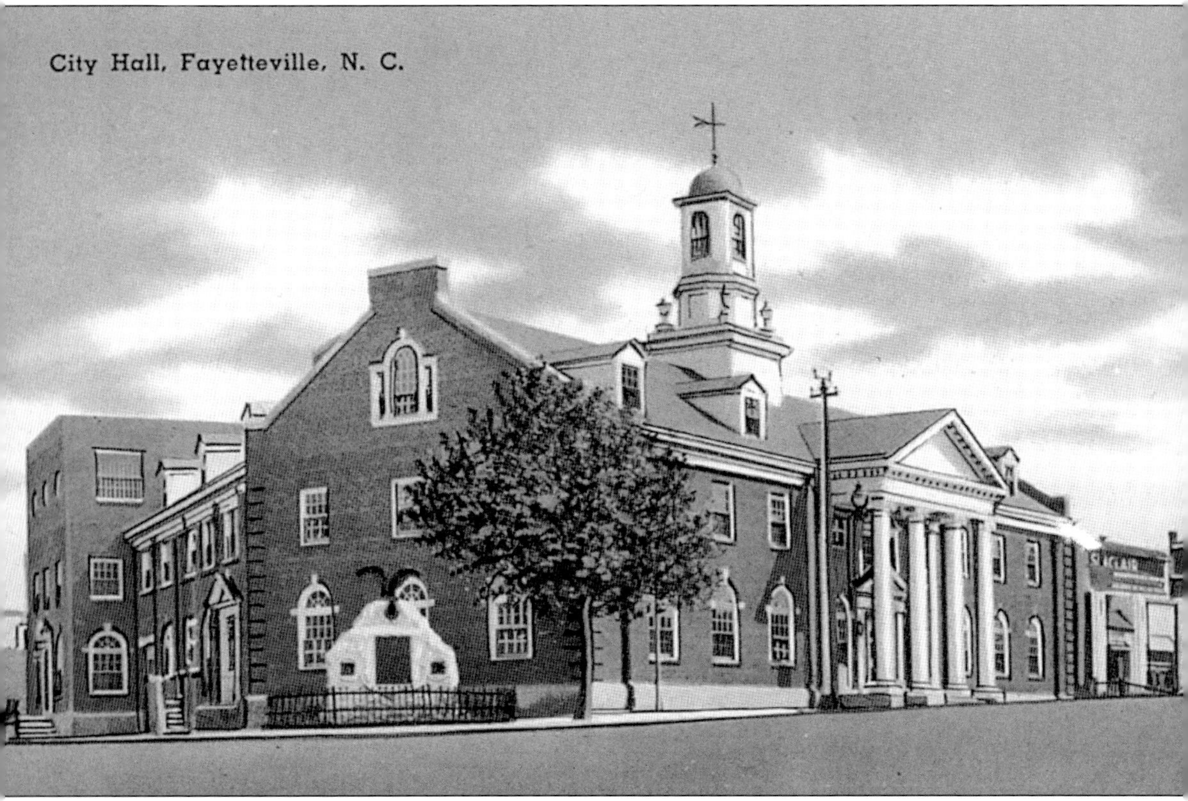

A postcard depicts the former Fayetteville City Hall, at the corner of Green and Bow Streets, c. 1935. This structure is now the site of a children's museum.

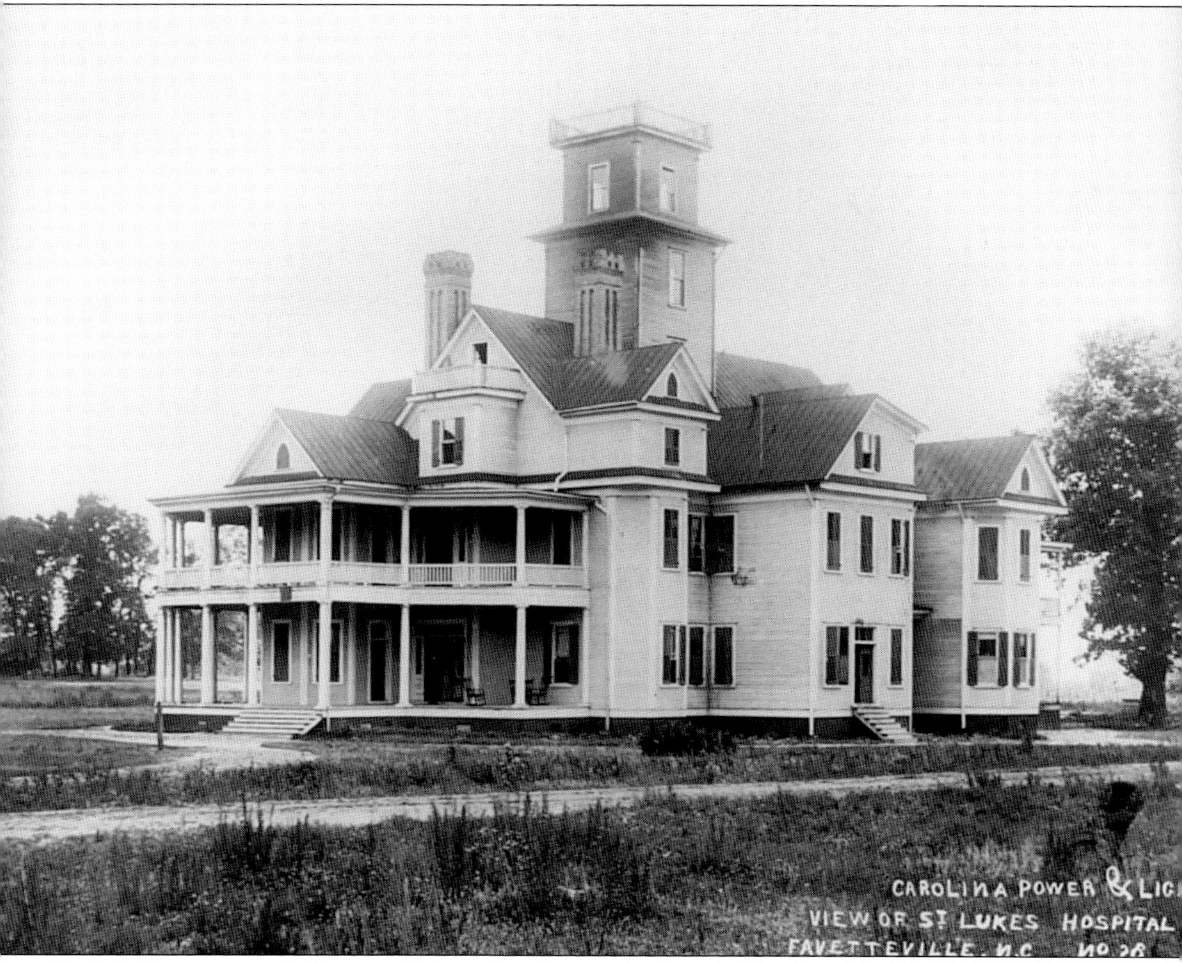

St. Luke's was one of Fayetteville's earliest hospitals, founded by Dr. John Henry Marsh in 1904. This 1910 photo shows the structure that stood atop Haymount Hill. (Courtesy N.C. Department of Archives and History.)

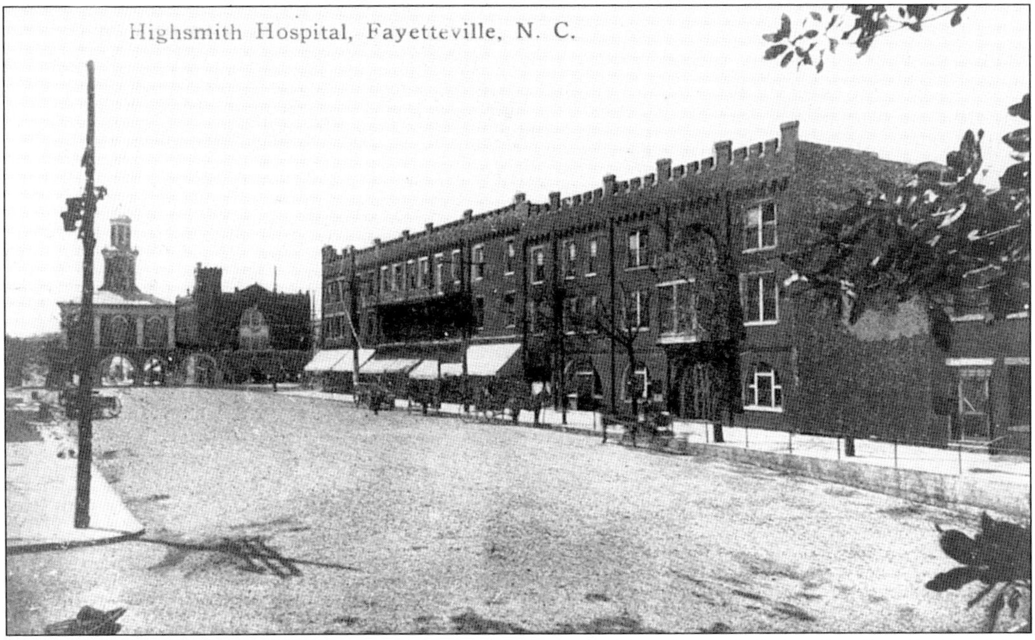

Highsmith Hospital was built on Green Street in 1899. Founded by Dr. Jacob Franklin Highsmith, it has the distinction of being the first privately owned hospital in North Carolina. (Courtesy N.C. Department of Archives and History.)

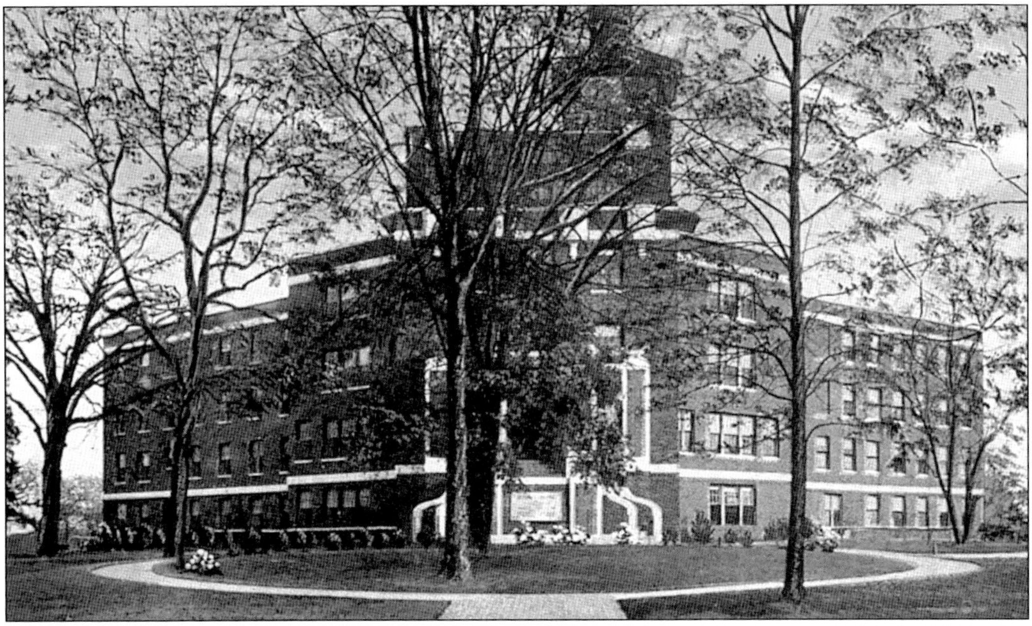

Due to inadequate space, Highsmith Hospital moved to this new facility in 1926. In 1963, the name was changed to Highsmith-Rainey Hospital to honor Dr. William Rainey.

The Prince Charles Hotel, located on Hay Street, was built in 1924. Funding for its construction was raised by a public offering of stock. This image was cropped from original letterhead used when the hotel opened. (Courtesy N.C. Department of Archives and History.)

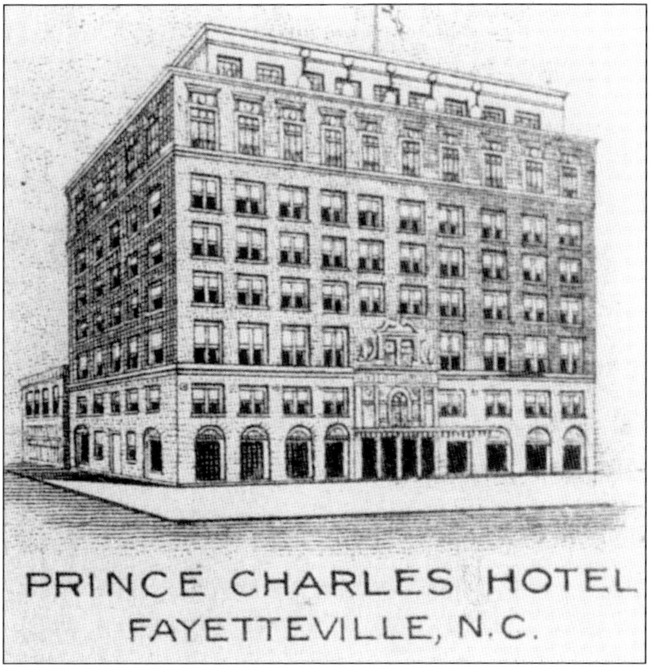

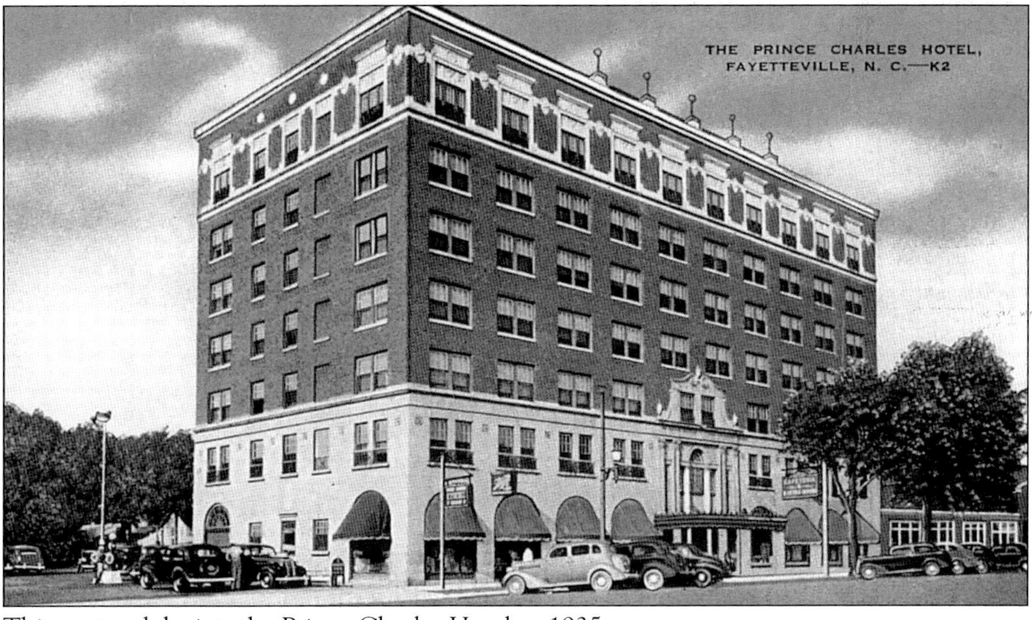

This postcard depicts the Prince Charles Hotel, *c.* 1935.

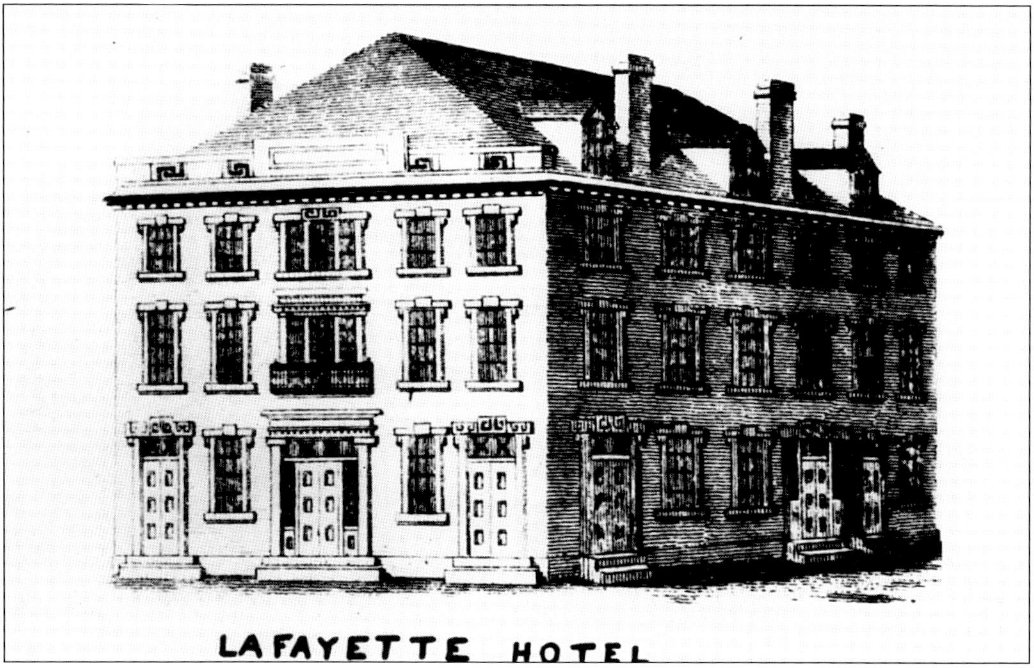

This drawing of the newly constructed Lafayette Hotel was included on McRae's Map of Fayetteville in 1825. The hotel was the setting of the ball honoring the Marquis de Lafayette during his visit to Fayetteville that year. The building was destroyed by fire in 1831. (Courtesy N.C. Department of Archives and History.)

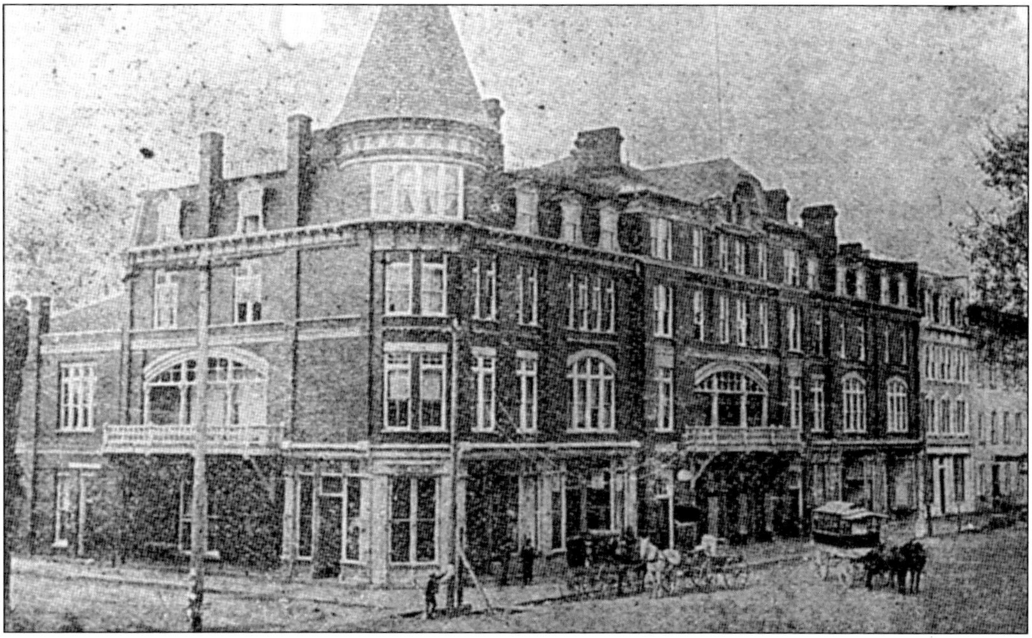

This picture of the Lafayette Hotel was taken in October of 1893. The third in a series of Lafayette Hotels, this structure replaced the second hotel, which was destroyed by fire in 1885. (Courtesy N.C. Department of Archives and History.)

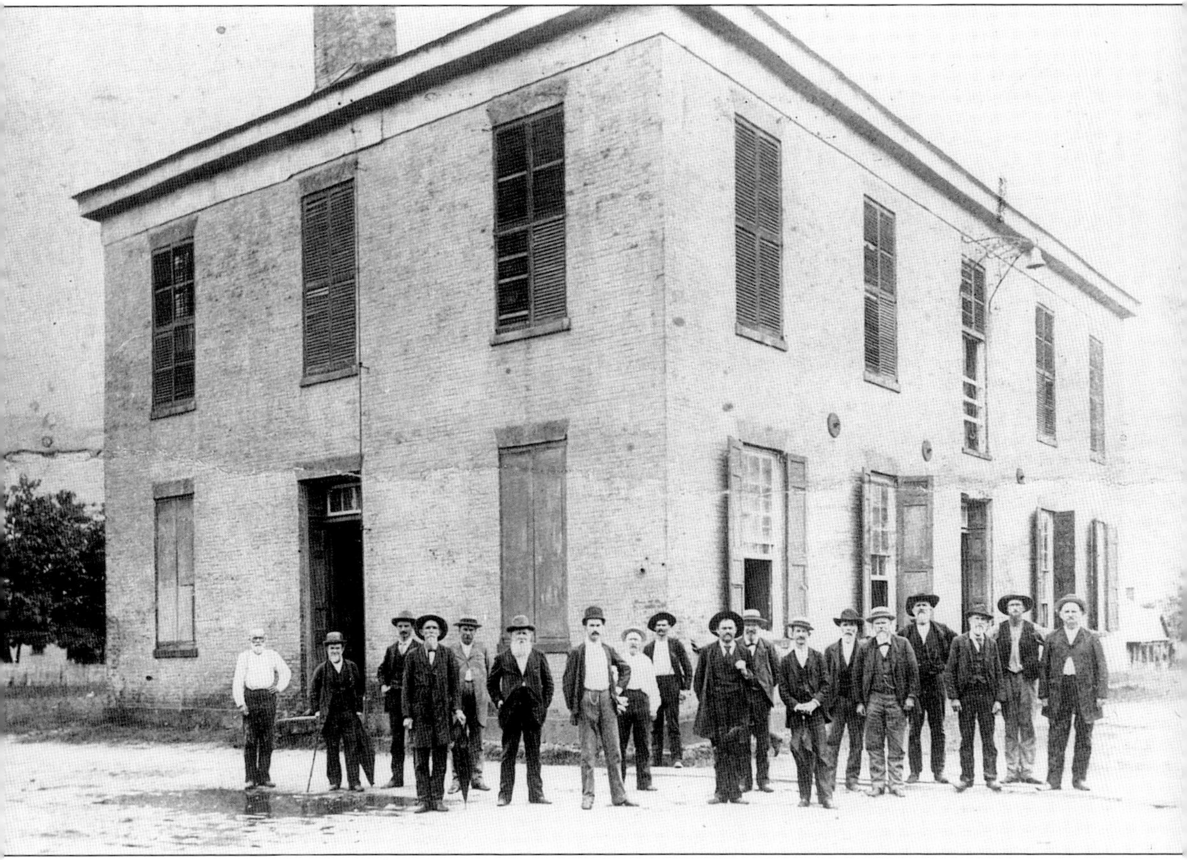

The Cumberland County Courthouse on St. James Square is seen in 1890. This structure was built in 1790 and served until a newer courthouse was built on Gillespie Street in 1893, supposedly because local attorneys thought the walk from their downtown offices to St. James Square too long. This was Cumberland's third courthouse; the first was a log structure built in the original county seat of Choeffington, which was located near present-day Linden. When the county seat moved, a second courthouse was built in Campbellton in the late 1770s and served until the completion of the pictured structure. (Courtesy N.C. Department of Archives and History.)

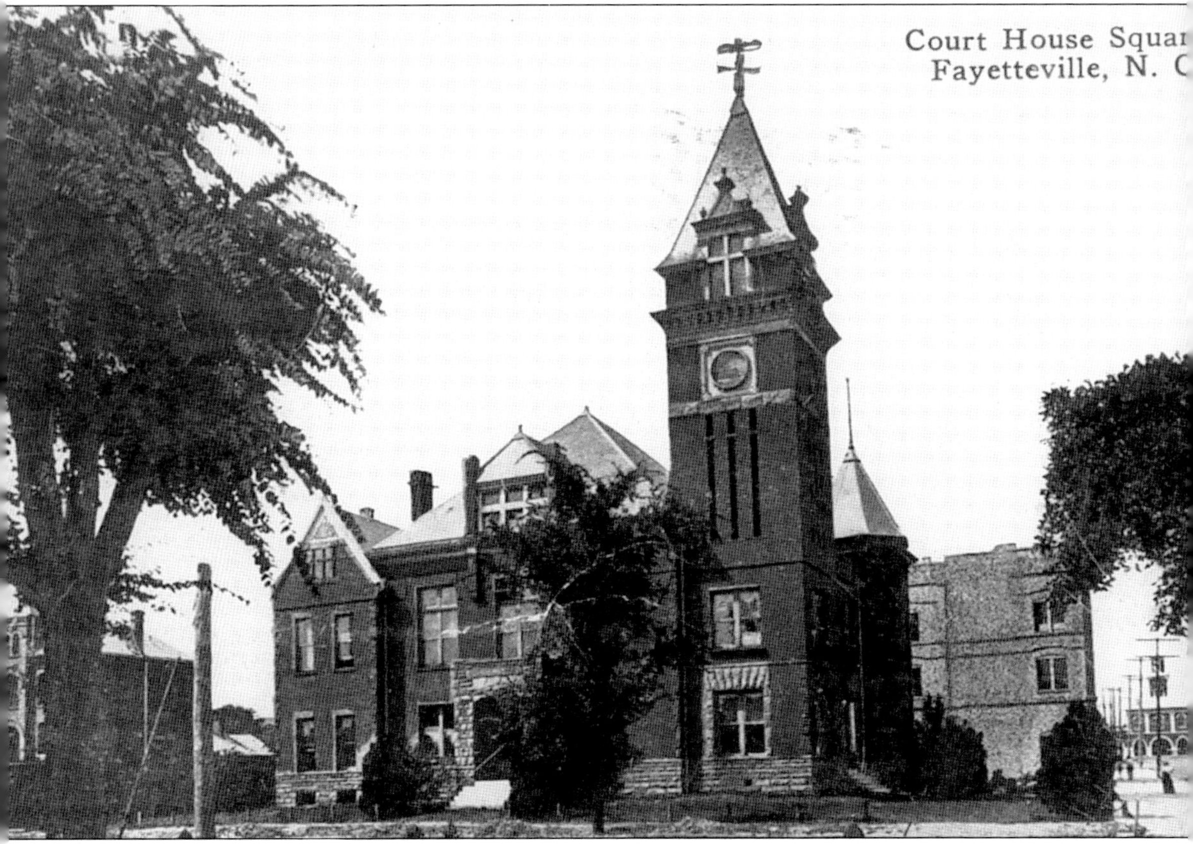

The courthouse square is seen in 1910. This was the fourth Cumberland County Courthouse, built in 1893 to replace the courthouse on St. James Square. It was located on the corner of Gillespie and Russell Streets. (Courtesy N.C. Department of Archives and History.)

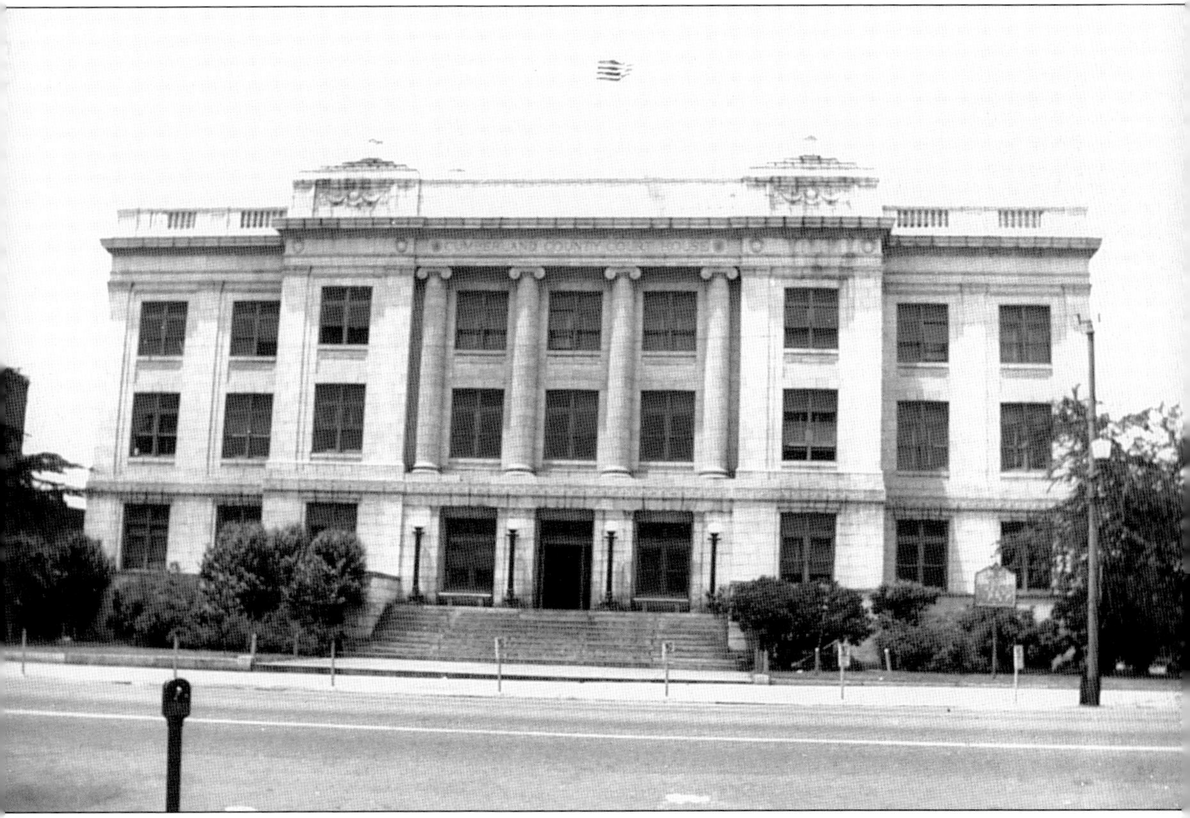

Built in 1924, this was the fifth courthouse to serve the county, pictured on Gillespie Street in 1948. It was used until the present courthouse was completed on Person Street in 1978. (Courtesy N.C. Department of Archives and History.)

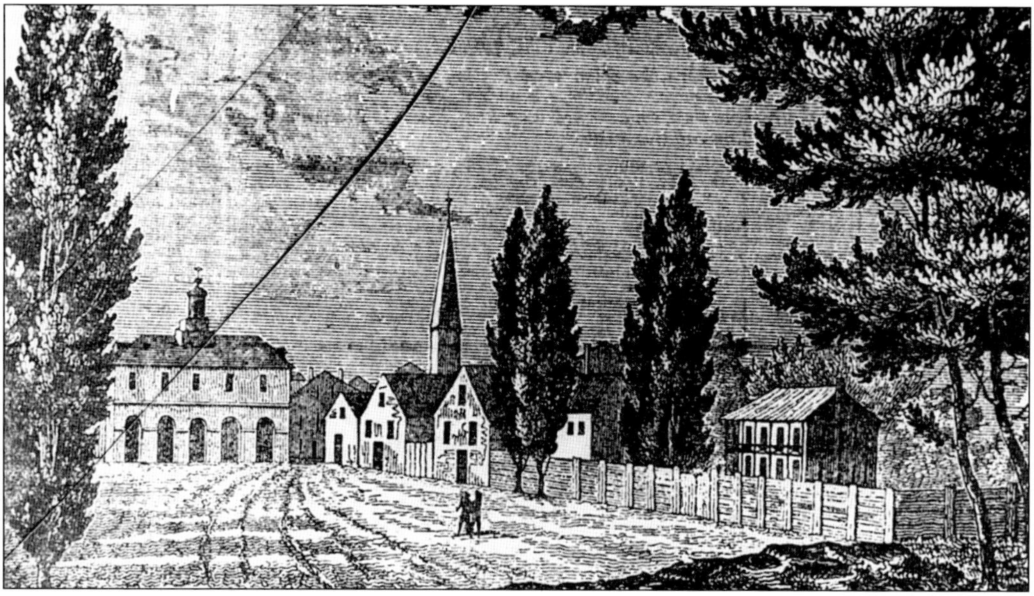

This 1814 engraving by Horace Say shows the State House, also known as the Constitution House, which stood on the present site of the Market House. It was destroyed by fire in 1831. During a November 1789 session of the North Carolina Legislature, two significant historic events occurred: the Ratification of the United States Constitution and the chartering of the University of North Carolina. (Courtesy N.C. Department of Archives and History.)

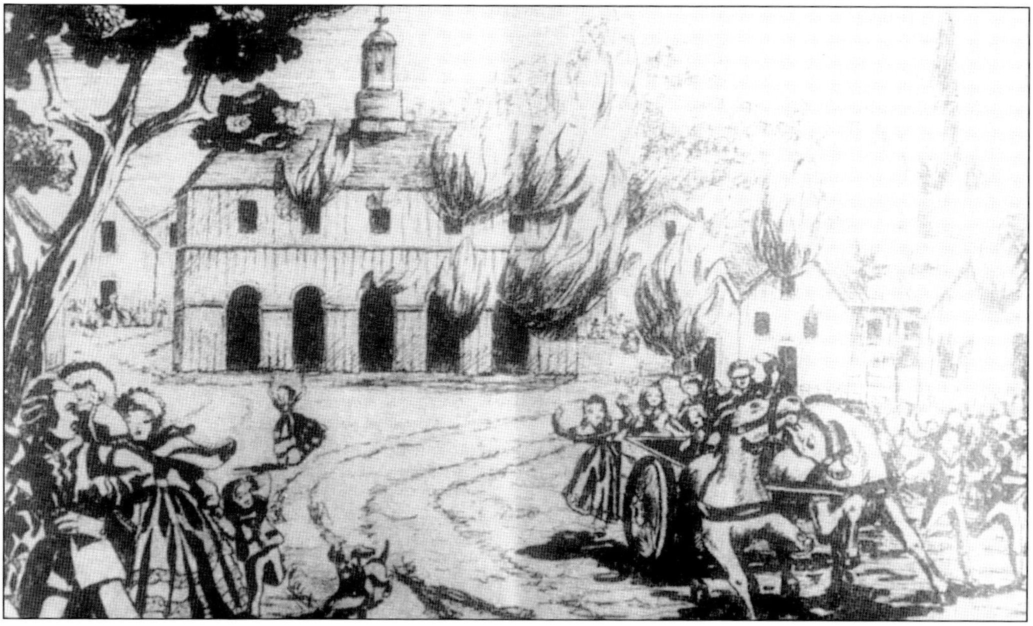

This 1831 drawing depicts the State House burning during the great Fayetteville fire of 1831. Seven years later the Market House was built on the site. (Courtesy N.C. Department of Archives and History.)

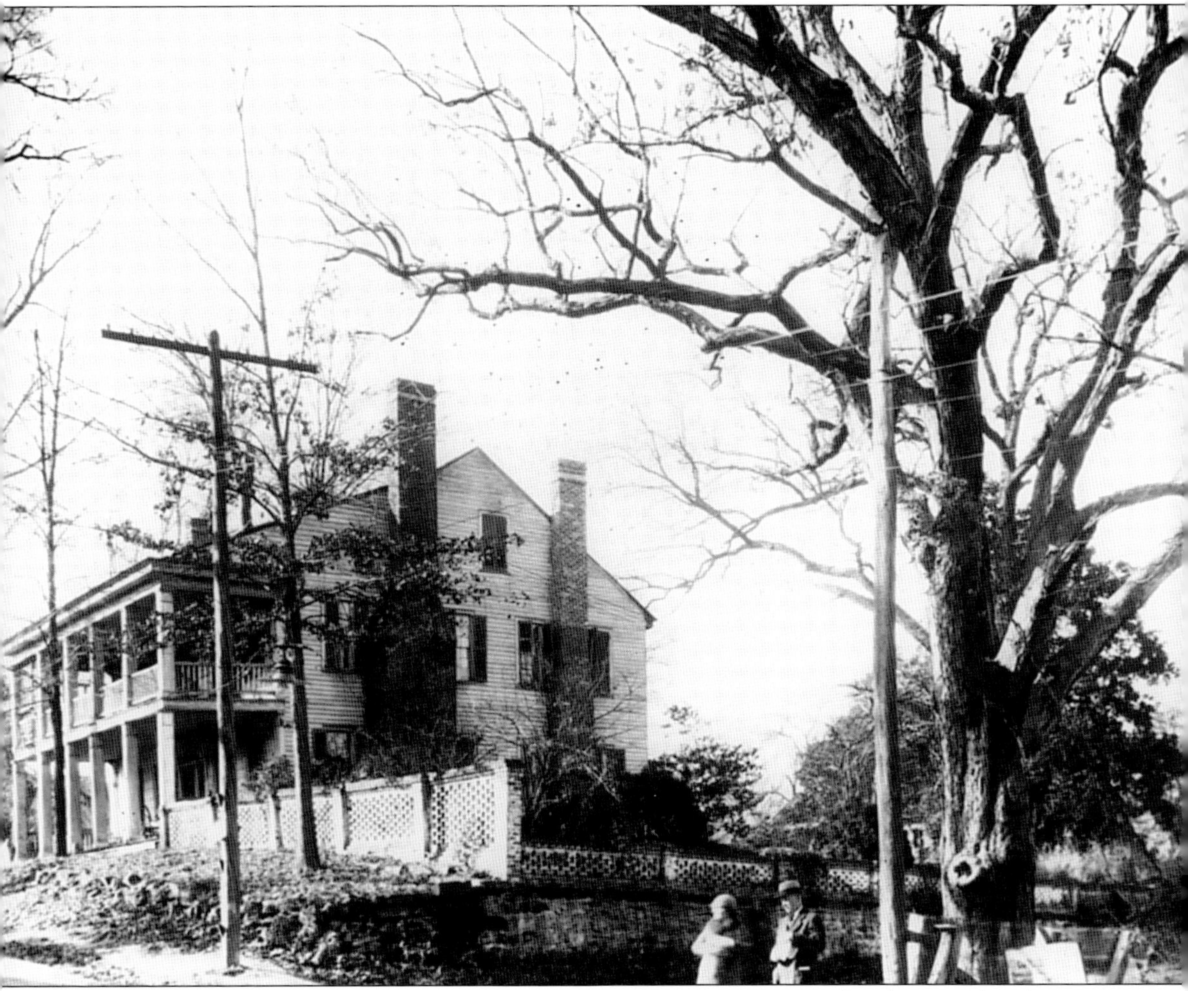

Cool Spring Tavern opened for business in 1789, supposedly to quench the thirsts of legislators meeting in Fayetteville. It stood adjacent to the Loyalist mustering ground, where legend has it that Flora MacDonald mounted a white horse and rallied Loyalist troops prior to the Battle of Moore's Creek 13 years earlier. (Courtesy N.C. Department of Archives and History.)

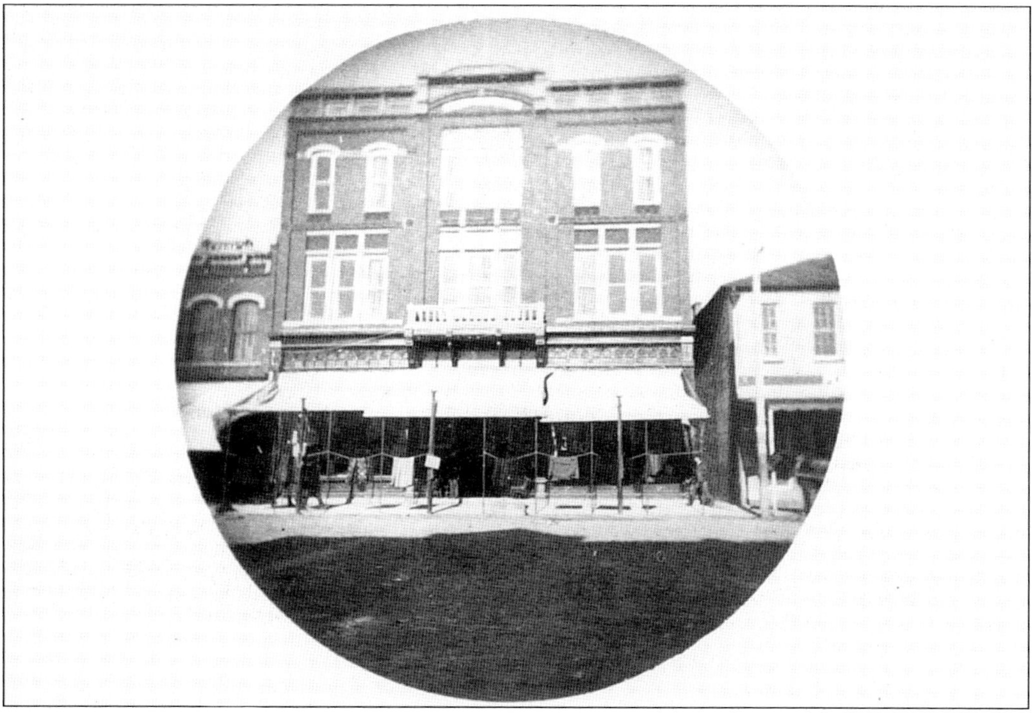

Pictured is a view of a downtown Fayetteville business in December of 1888. (Courtesy N.C. Department of Archives and History.)

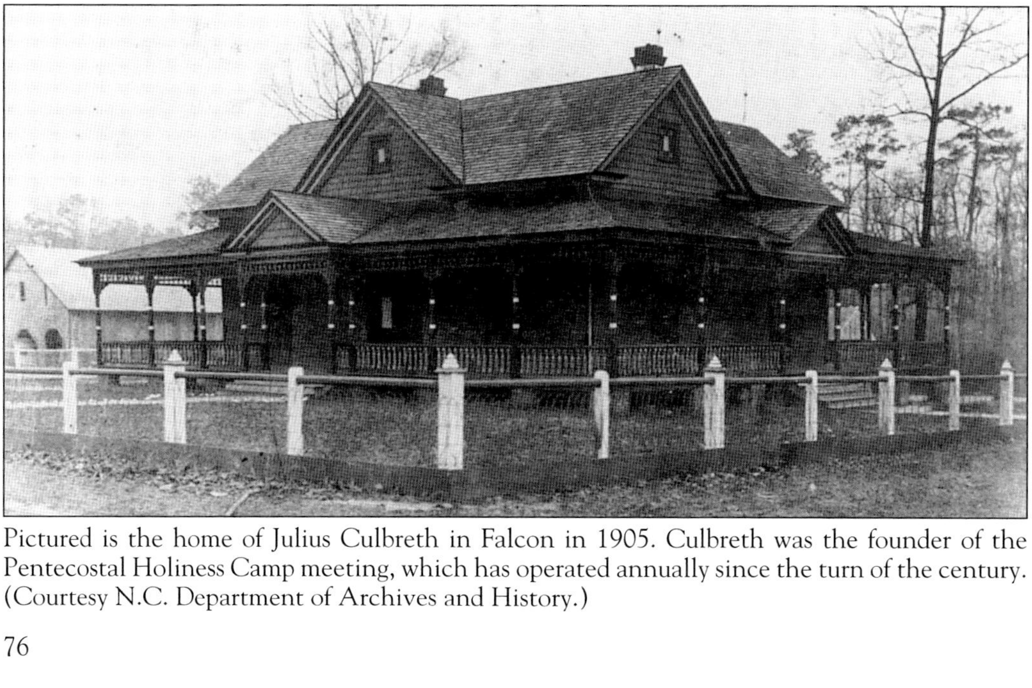

Pictured is the home of Julius Culbreth in Falcon in 1905. Culbreth was the founder of the Pentecostal Holiness Camp meeting, which has operated annually since the turn of the century. (Courtesy N.C. Department of Archives and History.)

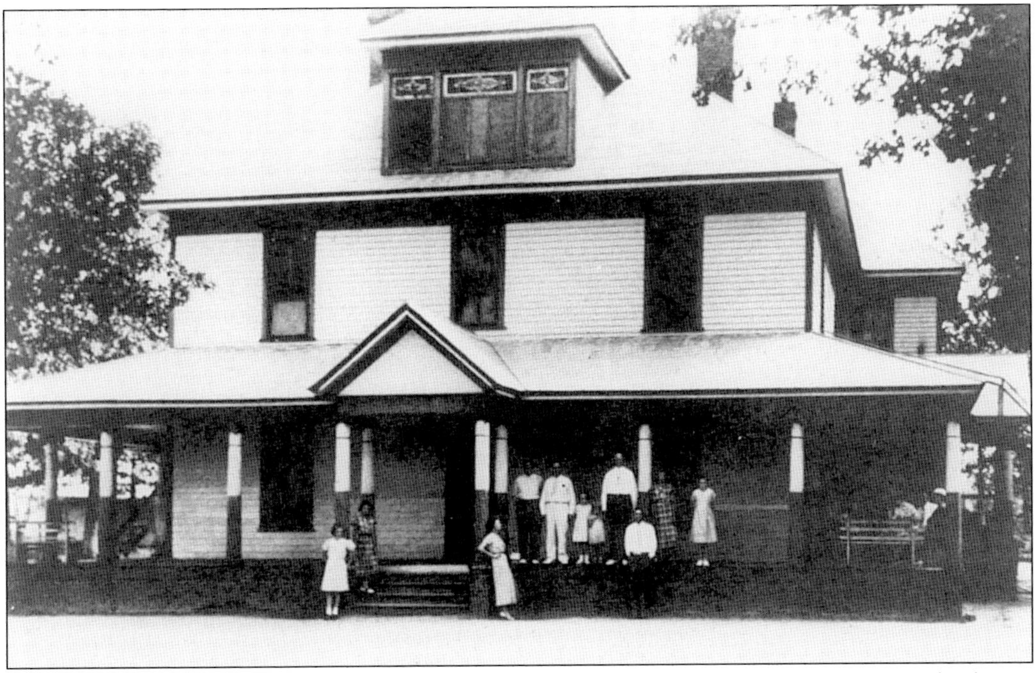

The first dormitory building of the Falcon Children's Home is pictured in 1930. The home is operated by the Pentecostal Holiness Church. (Courtesy N.C. Department of Archives and History.)

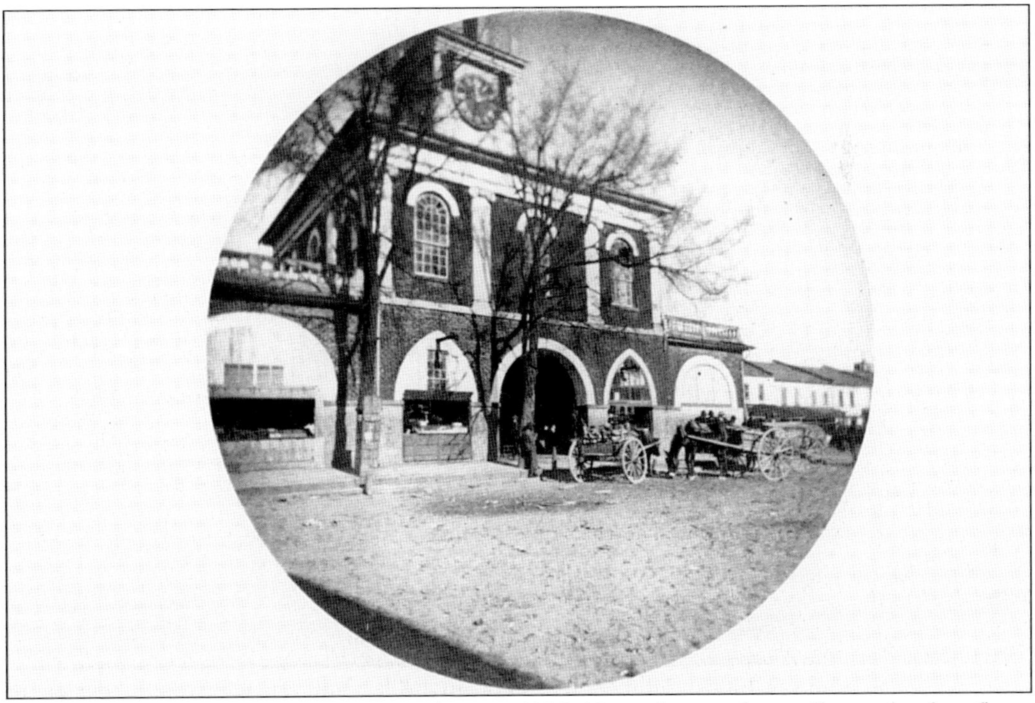

This view of the Market House was taken in 1888. Note the vendor stalls on the first floor. (Courtesy N.C. Department of Archives and History.)

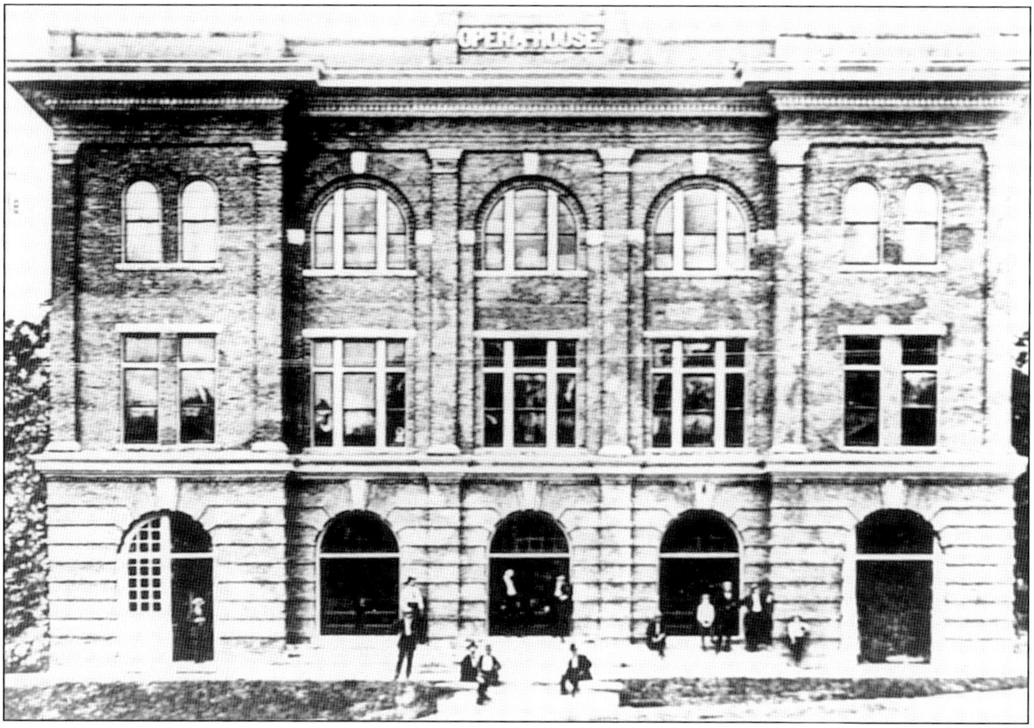

The Opera House on Person Street was built in 1908. Famed orator and presidential candidate William Jennings Bryan spoke there, and playwright Paul Green's drama *Highland Call* premiered there in November of 1939. The Opera House was destroyed by fire in 1950. (Courtesy N.C. Department of Archives and History.)

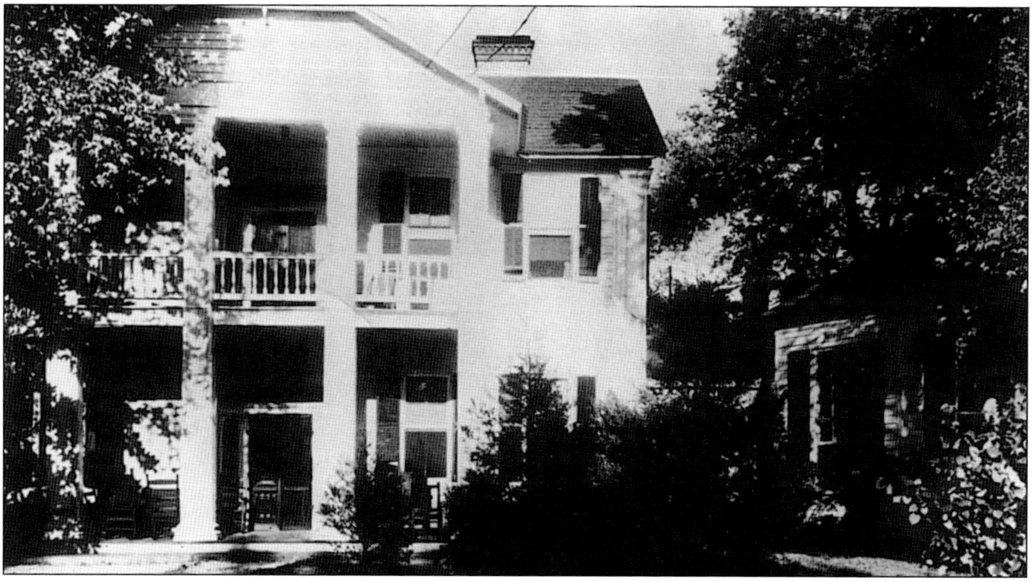

The Halliday-Williams House on Gillespie Street was built by Robert Halliday, c. 1810. This was the original site of the Oval Ballroom, which was constructed for the wedding reception of Margaret Halliday and John Sandford in June of 1830. (Courtesy N.C. Department of Archives and History.)

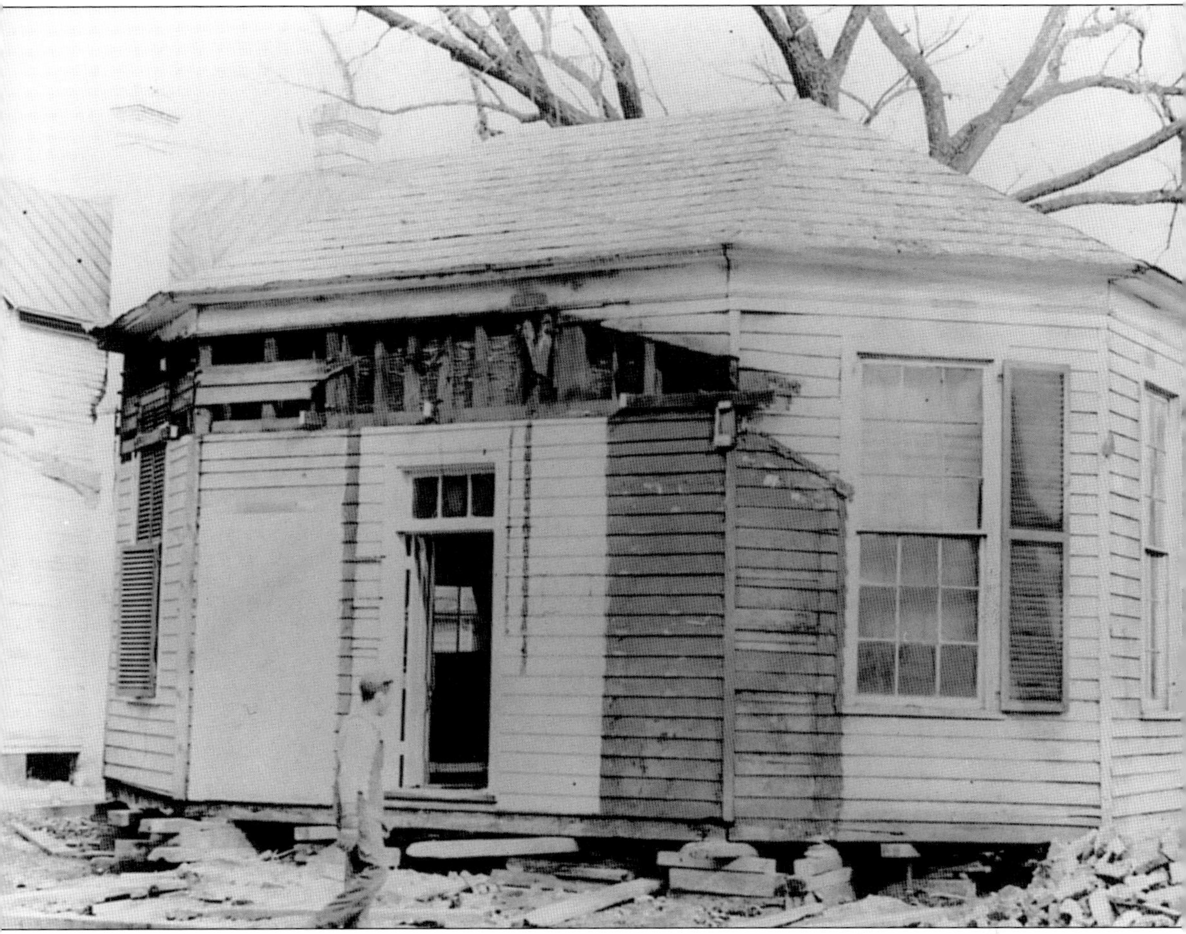

This 1956 photo shows the moving and renovation of the Oval Ballroom. This structure was donated to the Fayetteville Women's Club and was moved to their Heritage Square site when the Halliday-Williams House was torn down. (Courtesy N.C. Department of Archives and History.)

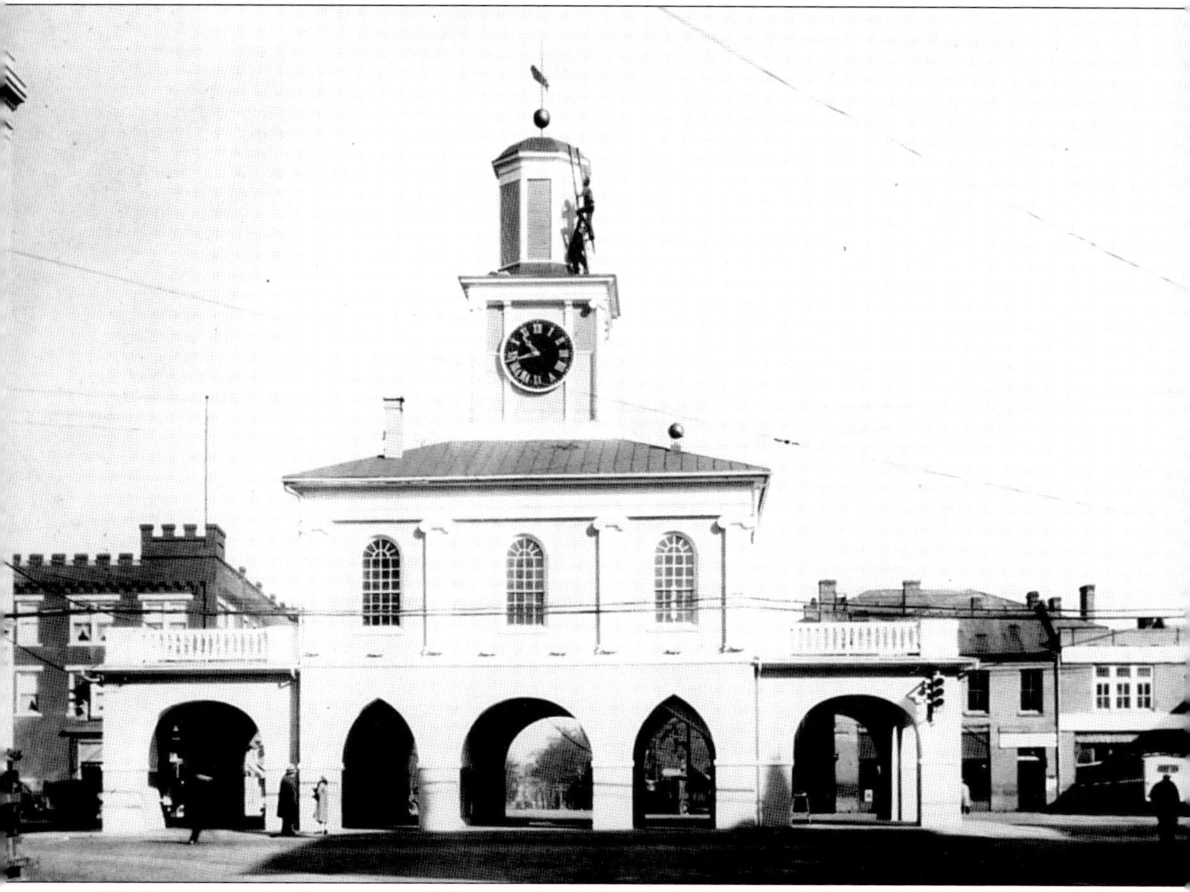

Workmen use a ladder to ascend the cupola of the Market House in this *c.* 1935 photo. (Courtesy N.C. Department of Archives and History.)

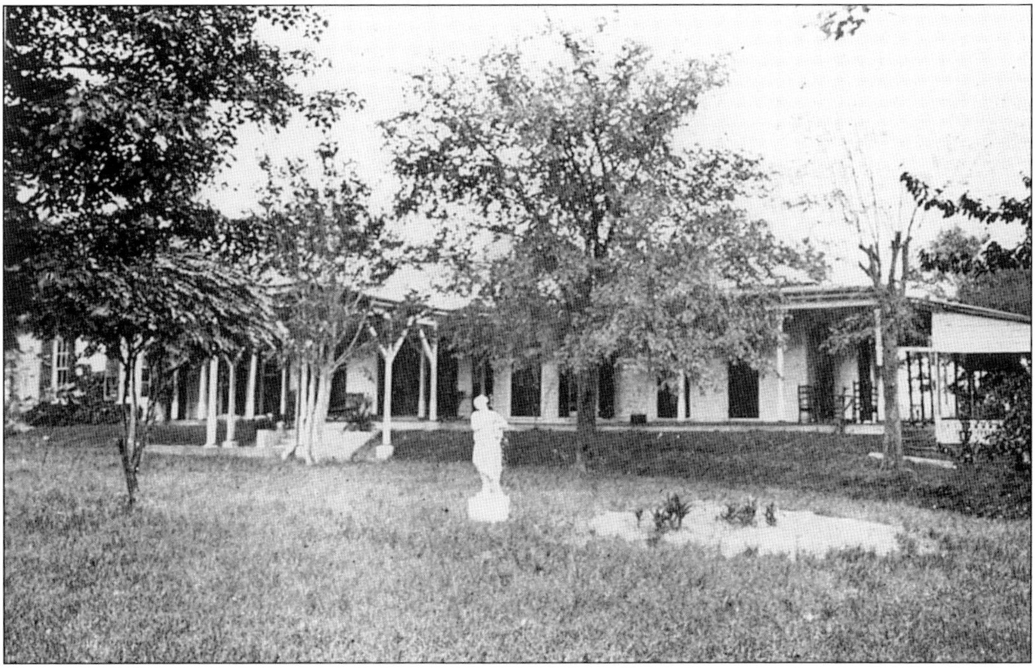

"Tokay," the home of Colonel Wharton Green, is seen in 1906. Located north of Fayetteville, the Tokay Vineyard at the turn of the century was reportedly the largest vineyard in the United States east of the Rocky Mountains. (Courtesy N.C. Department of Archives and History.)

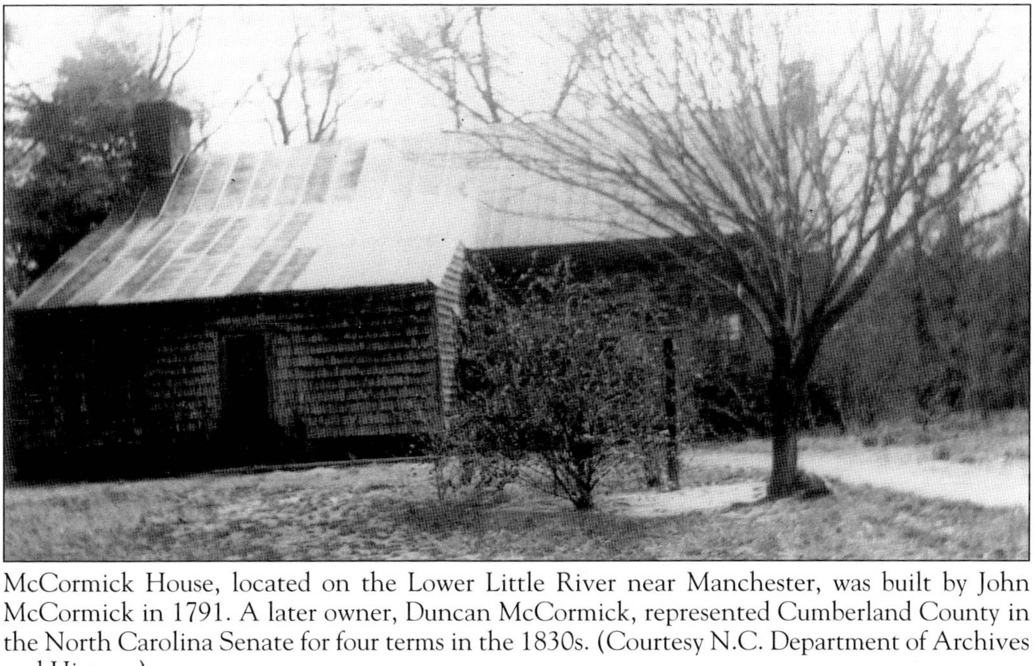

McCormick House, located on the Lower Little River near Manchester, was built by John McCormick in 1791. A later owner, Duncan McCormick, represented Cumberland County in the North Carolina Senate for four terms in the 1830s. (Courtesy N.C. Department of Archives and History.)

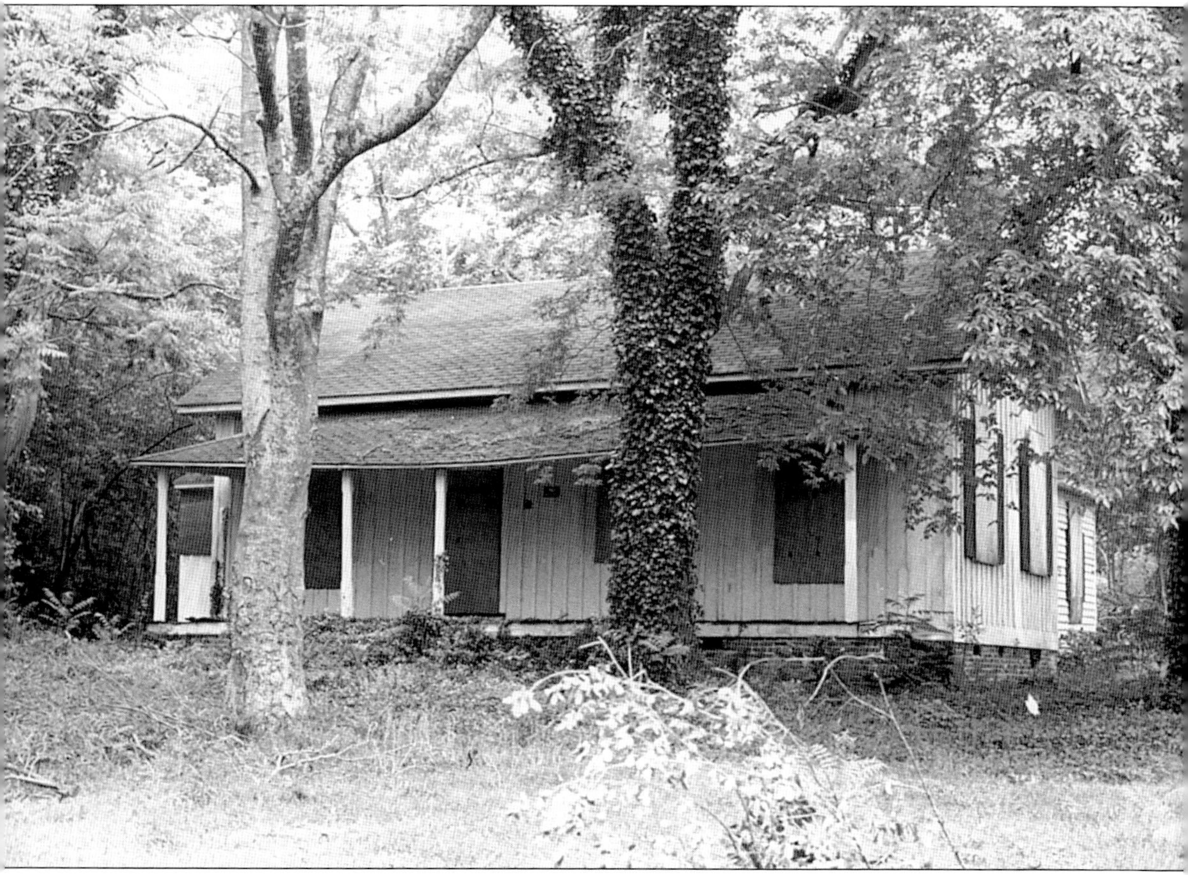

The Arsenal House was built in 1838 on Branson Street. The house, which is listed on the National Register of Historic Places, was moved to its present location on Arsenal Avenue in 1976. (Courtesy N.C. Department of Archives and History.)

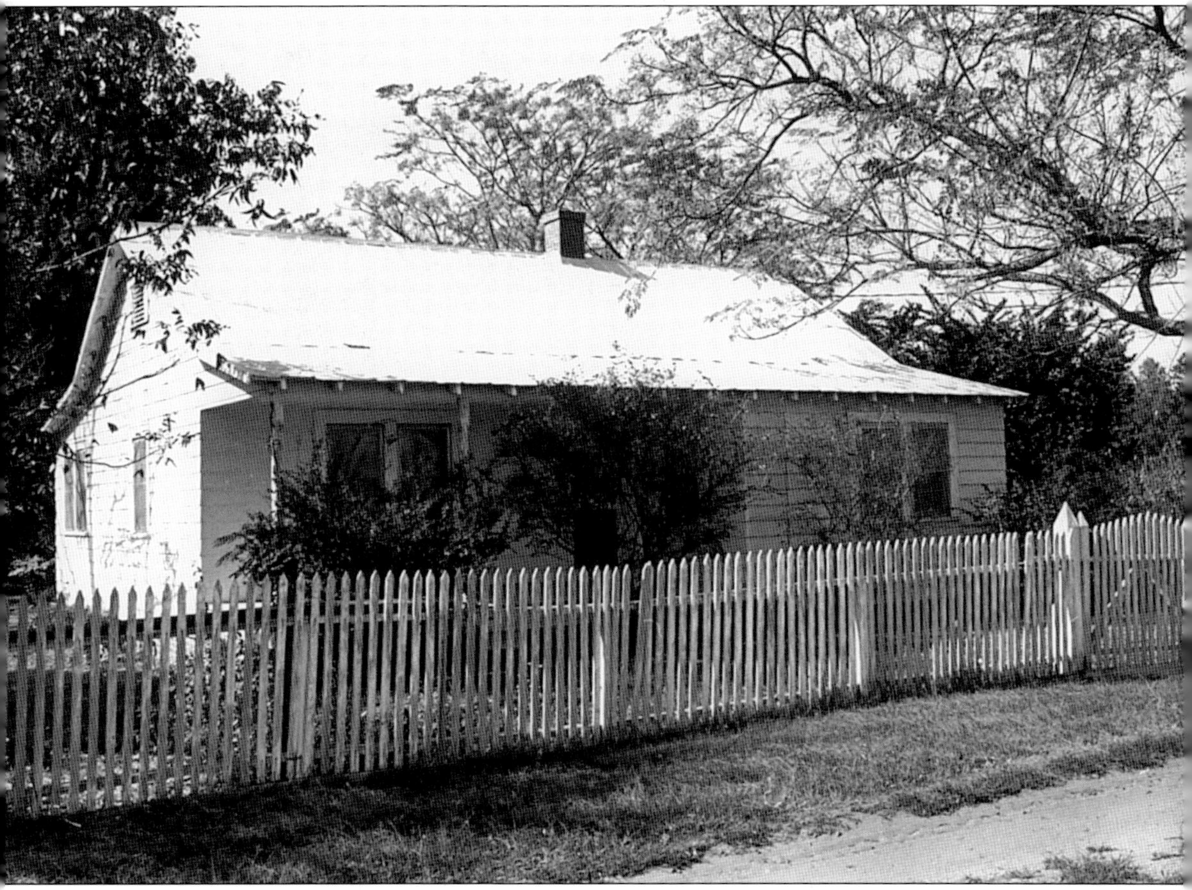

Pictured is the David Marshall "Carbine" Williams home near Godwin. Born in 1900, Williams held many firearms patents, including the floating chamber; his improvements to the carbine rifle, making it lighter, were of major importance to the success of U.S. troops in World War II. His workshop is now on permanent display at the North Carolina Museum of History in Raleigh. (Courtesy N.C. Department of Archives and History.)

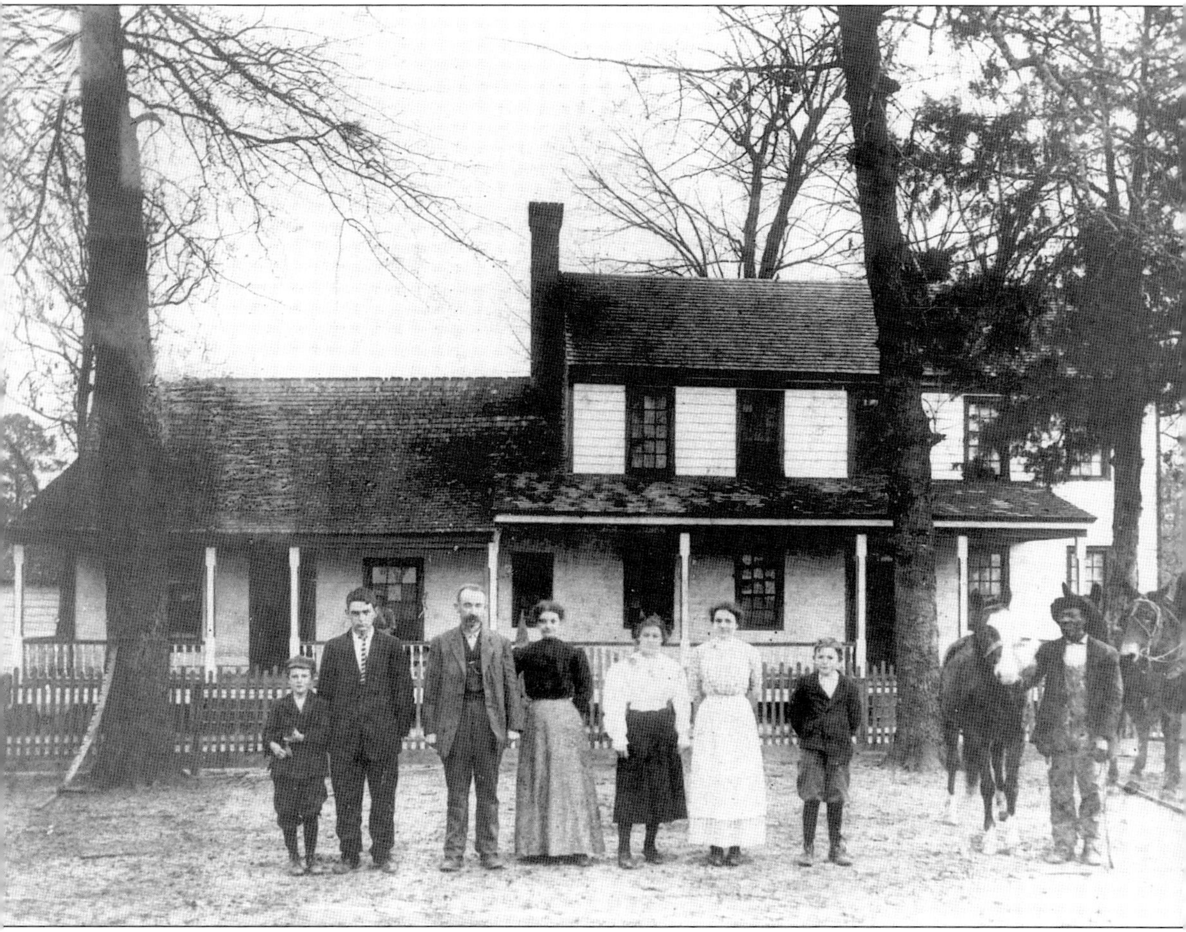

The Daniel Maxwell family is pictured in front of the family's home, the Maxwell House, near Stedman *c.* 1910. The home was built in 1806 and stands on Highway 24. (Courtesy N.C. Department of Archives and History.)

Five

Religion and Education

Cumberland is the home of many churches of different denominations. The oldest, Old Bluff Presbyterian, was built in 1758 and stands stately among a grove on bluffs high above the Cape Fear River near Wade.

Cumberland is also the birthplace of a large Christian denomination. The Pentecostal Holiness Church was founded in Falcon in 1911. A camp meeting established there in 1900 continues to meet annually in July.

Quality education is a priority for the citizens of Cumberland County. Several excellent academies educated students in the 1800s, including the Donaldson Academy in Fayetteville and the Little River Academy in Linden. A strong county public school system educates students today using both traditional means and the newest technological advancements, a distinct difference from the many one-room schools that once existed.

Higher education is readily available in the area. Methodist College, Fayetteville State University, and Fayetteville Technical Community College have excellent academic programs. Others, including Campbell University, East Carolina University, and Central Texas College, offer extension degree programs at Fort Bragg and Pope Air Force Base.

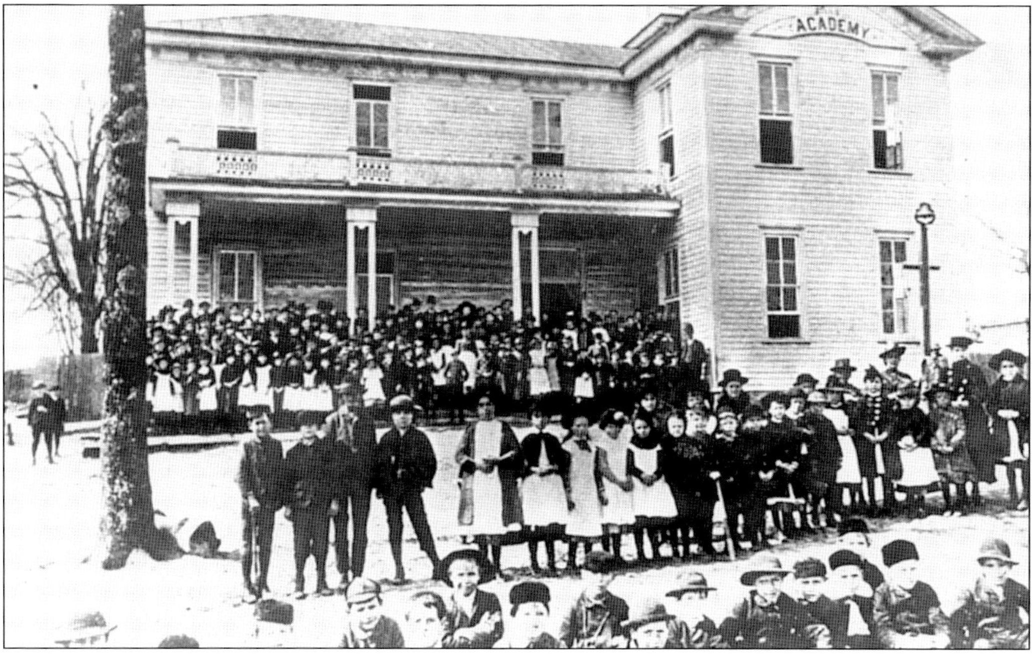

Pictured is the student body of Donaldson Academy on Hay Street in Fayetteville. The Academy was chartered in 1833. The first principal was Rev. Dr. Simeon Colton, who later moved to Harnett County to serve as principal of Summerville Academy. (Courtesy N.C. Department of Archives and History.)

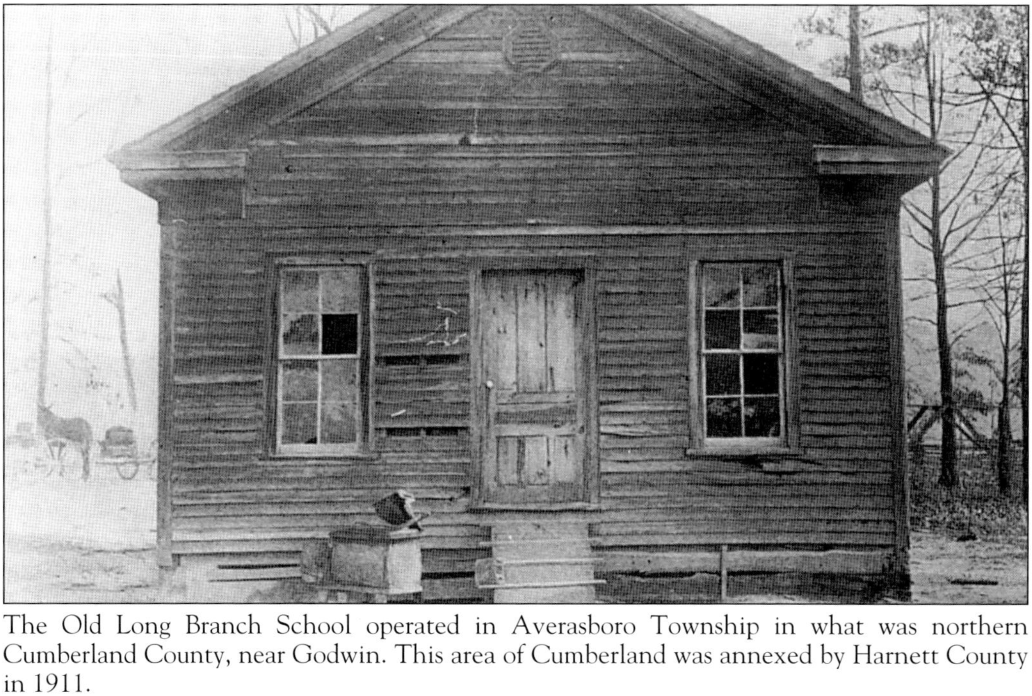

The Old Long Branch School operated in Averasboro Township in what was northern Cumberland County, near Godwin. This area of Cumberland was annexed by Harnett County in 1911.

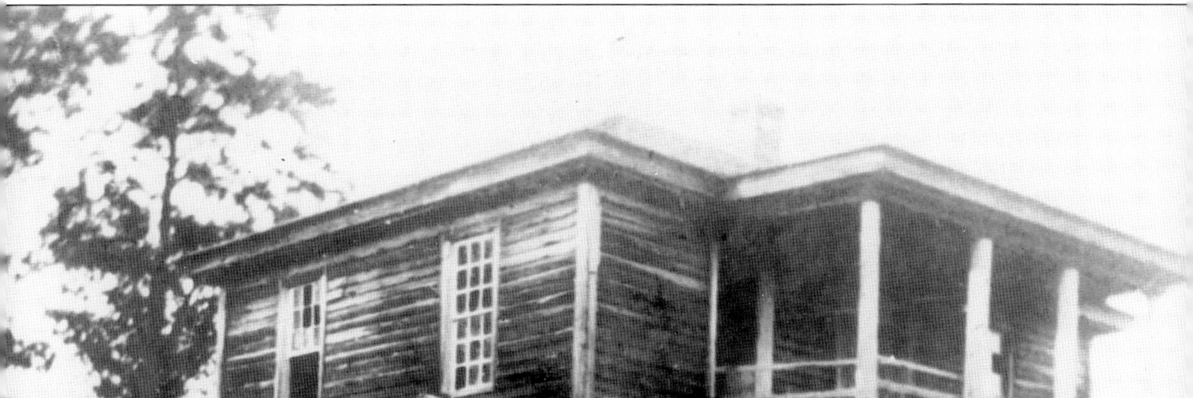

Little River Academy was established in Linden in 1867. Founded by Rev. D.D. McBryde, pastor of Sardis Presbyterian Church, the two-story structure stood less than 100 yards from Lower Little River. According to newspaper advertisements of the time, the tuition-charging private academy was a co-education institute of high academic quality. (Courtesy N.C. Department of Archives and History.)

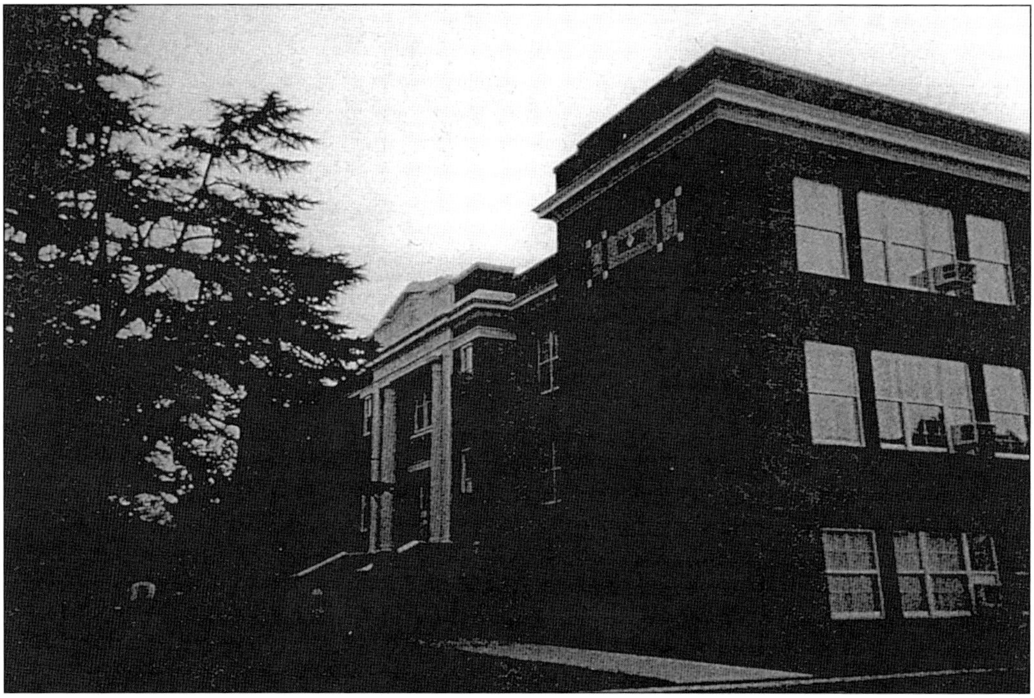

Massey Hill High School was built in 1925, although a public school began operating in the community in 1897. The building now houses Massey Hill Classical Academy.

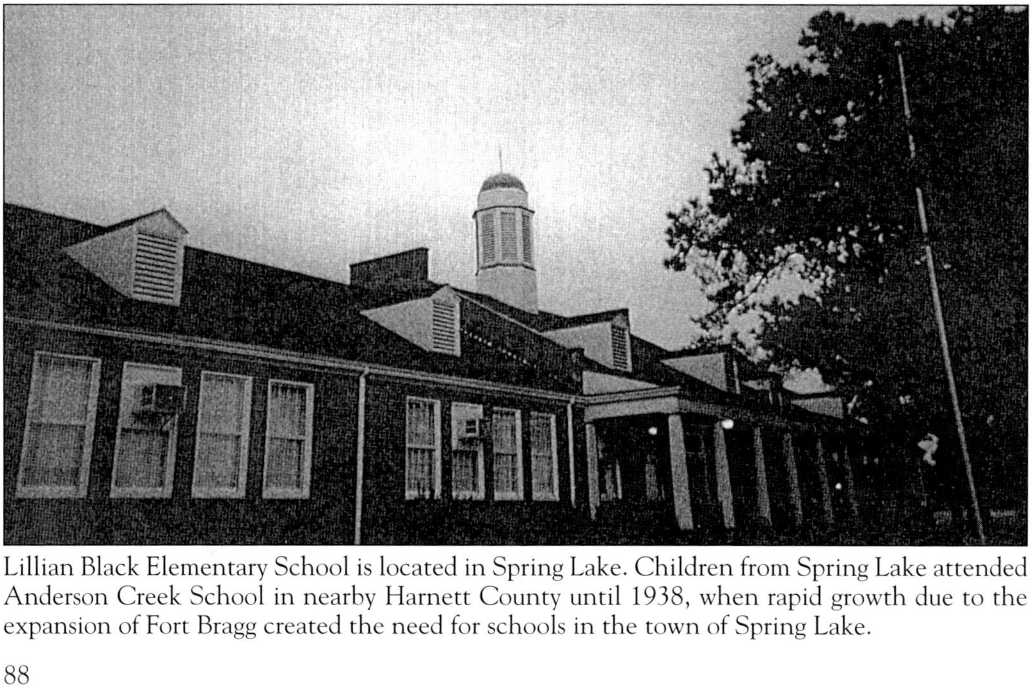

Lillian Black Elementary School is located in Spring Lake. Children from Spring Lake attended Anderson Creek School in nearby Harnett County until 1938, when rapid growth due to the expansion of Fort Bragg created the need for schools in the town of Spring Lake.

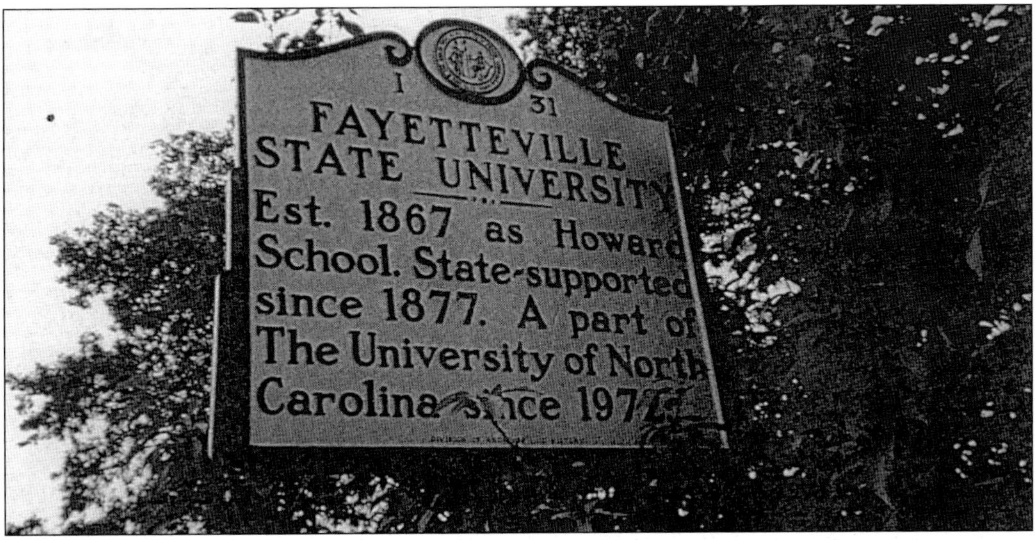

Fayetteville State University was founded in 1867 as the Howard School, named in honor of General O.O. Howard, who built the first building. A member of the University of North Carolina system, the school had its beginnings as a teacher-training institution for African Americans.

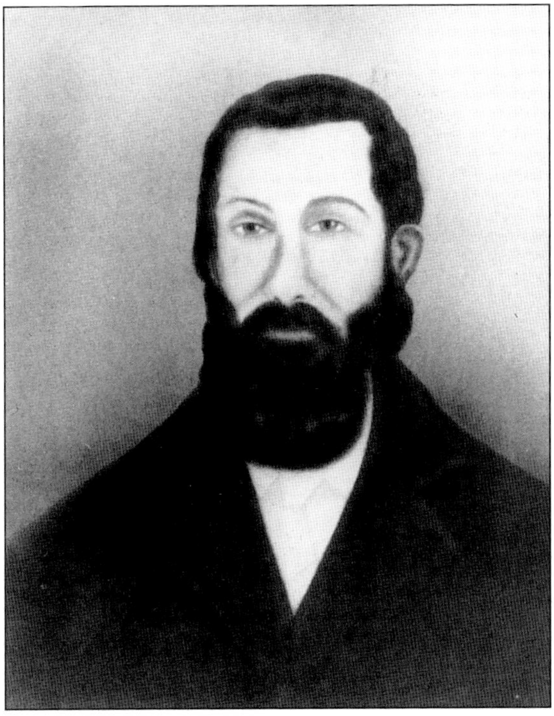

Robert Harris was the first principal of the Howard School. Under his leadership, the school became state supported in 1877. He died in 1880 and was succeeded by Charles W. Chestnutt. (Courtesy N.C. Department of Archives and History.)

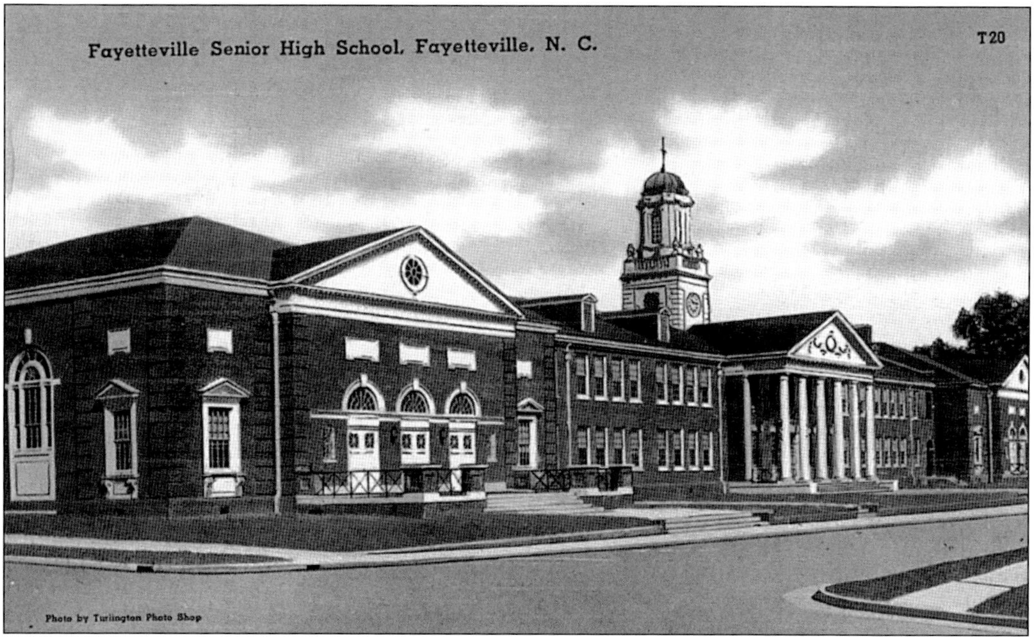

Fayetteville High School was located on Robeson Street in downtown Fayetteville. It later moved to a new location on Fort Bragg Road and was renamed Terry Sanford High School in honor of a North Carolina governor and U.S. senator who lived in Fayetteville.

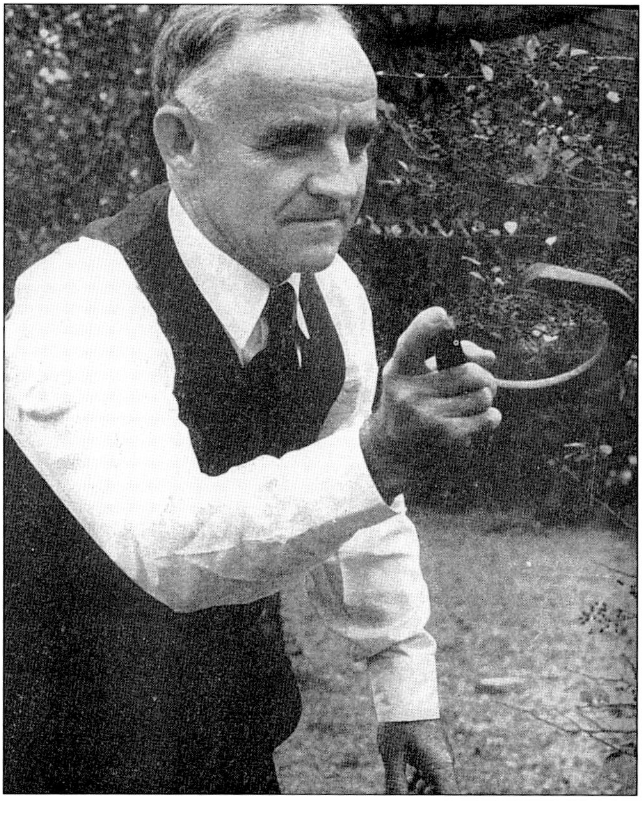

Dr. Frank Porter Graham was born in Fayetteville in 1886. He was the son of Dr. Alexander Graham, the first superintendent of the Fayetteville Public Schools. Frank Porter Graham served as the longtime president of the University of North Carolina, and was appointed to the U.S. Senate by Governor Kerr Scott in 1949. He filled the unexpired term of the late Senator J. Melville Broughton.

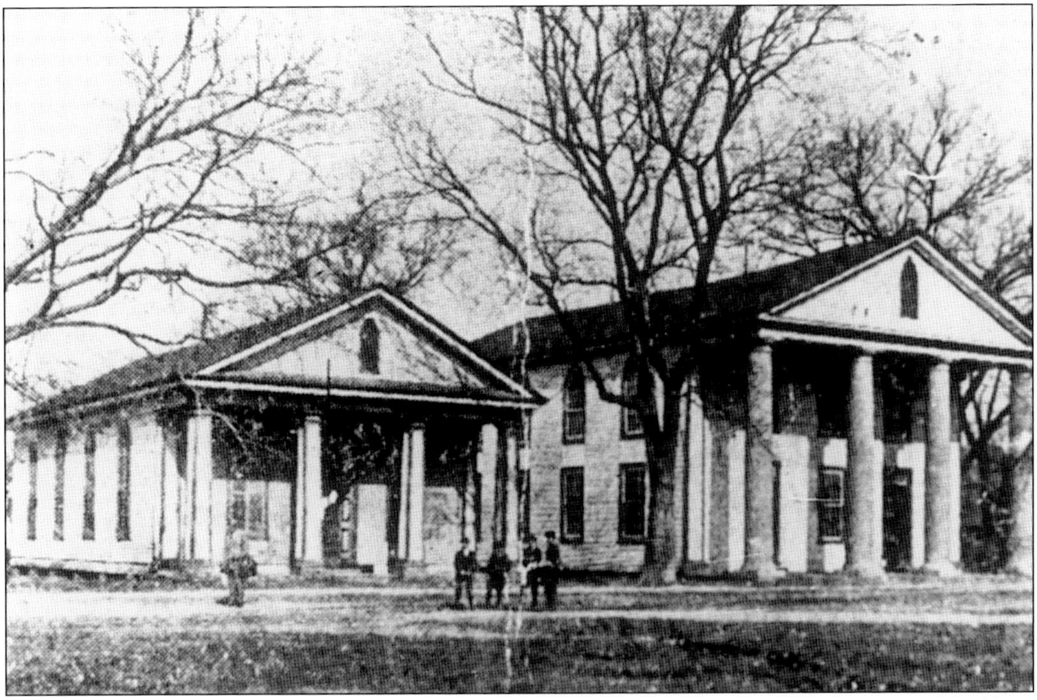

Hay Street Methodist Church is pictured in 1890. Built in the 1830s, the sanctuary is the building on the right, while the Sunday school building is on the left. (Courtesy N.C. Department of Archives and History.)

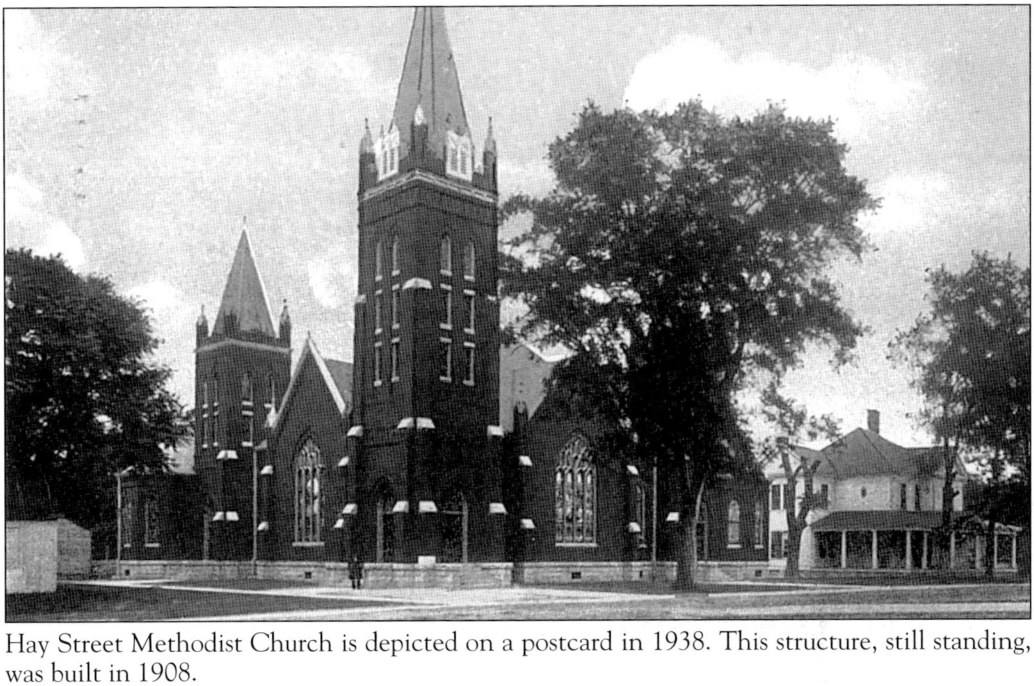

Hay Street Methodist Church is depicted on a postcard in 1938. This structure, still standing, was built in 1908.

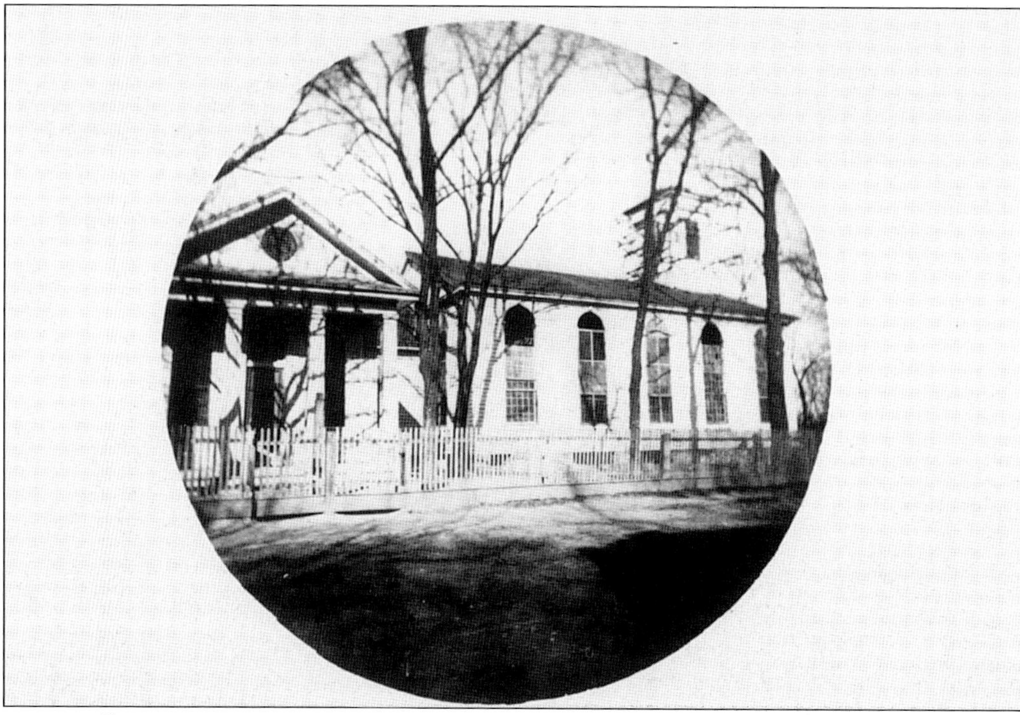

Fayetteville's First Baptist Church was built in 1837. Rev. James McDaniel was the first pastor. This is how the church appeared in 1888. (Courtesy N.C. Department of Archives and History.)

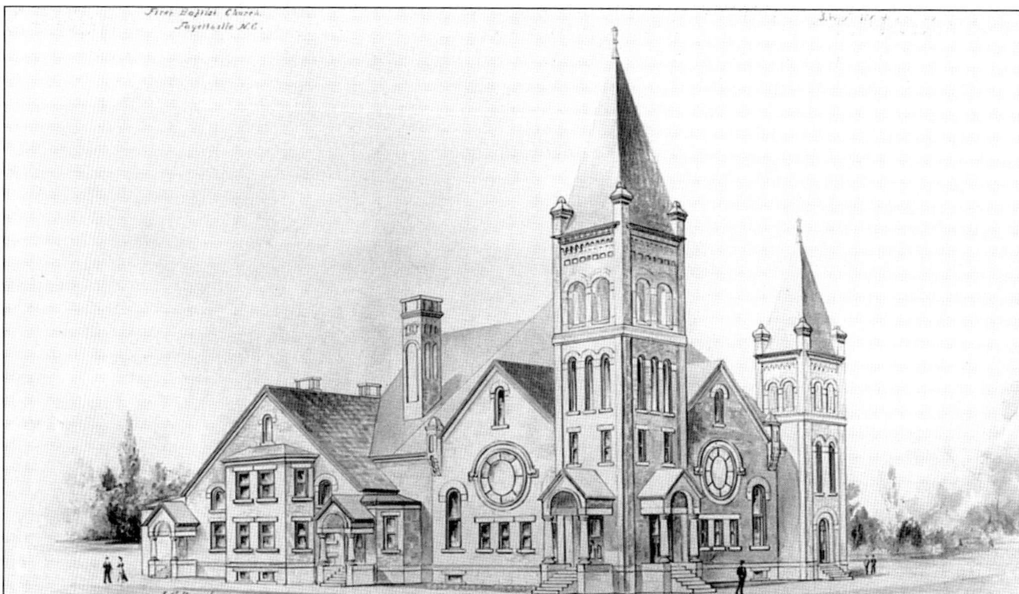

This drawing of Fayetteville's First Baptist Church was made in 1906. This church building was constructed on the site of the original wooden structure, which was torn down. The church is located on Old Street in downtown Fayetteville. (Courtesy N.C. Department of Archives and History.)

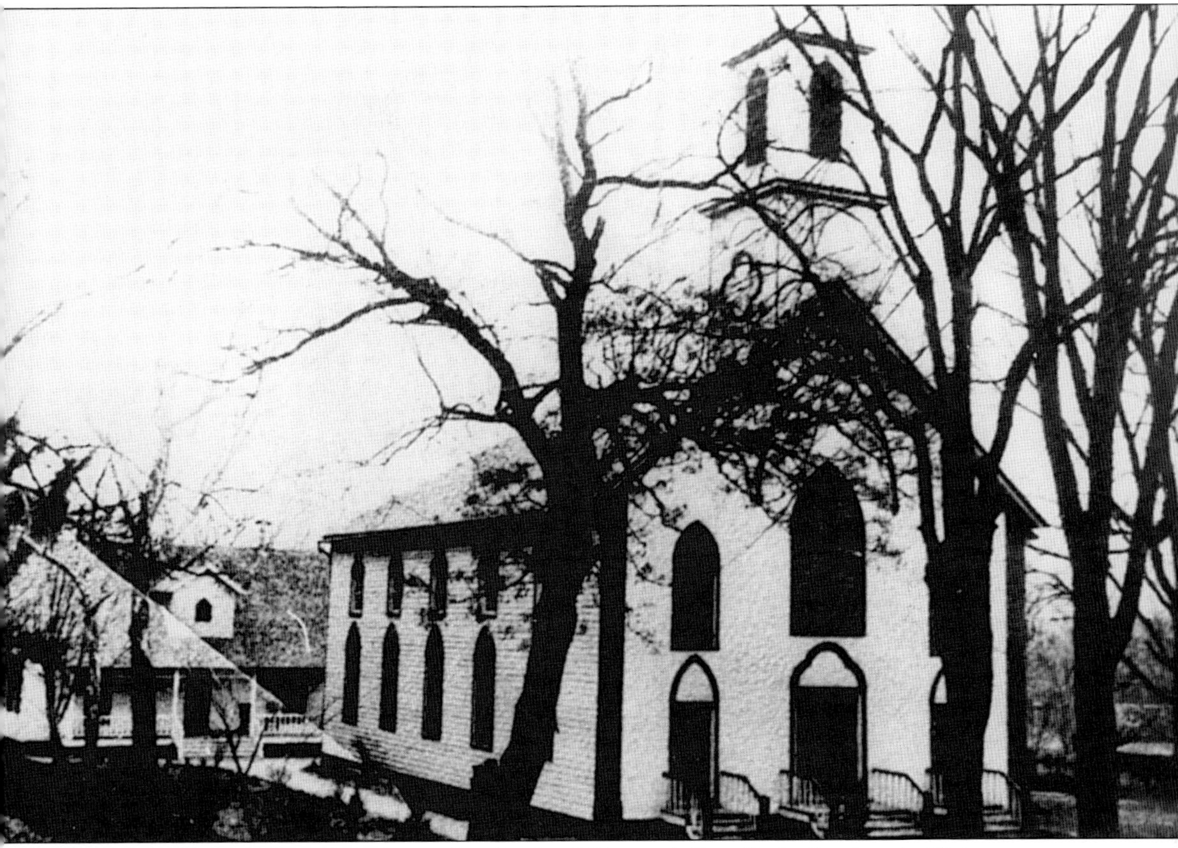

Saint Patrick's Catholic Church was Cumberland County's first Catholic church. This structure was built in 1832 and stood on Bow Street near Liberty Point. (Courtesy N.C. Department of Archives and History.)

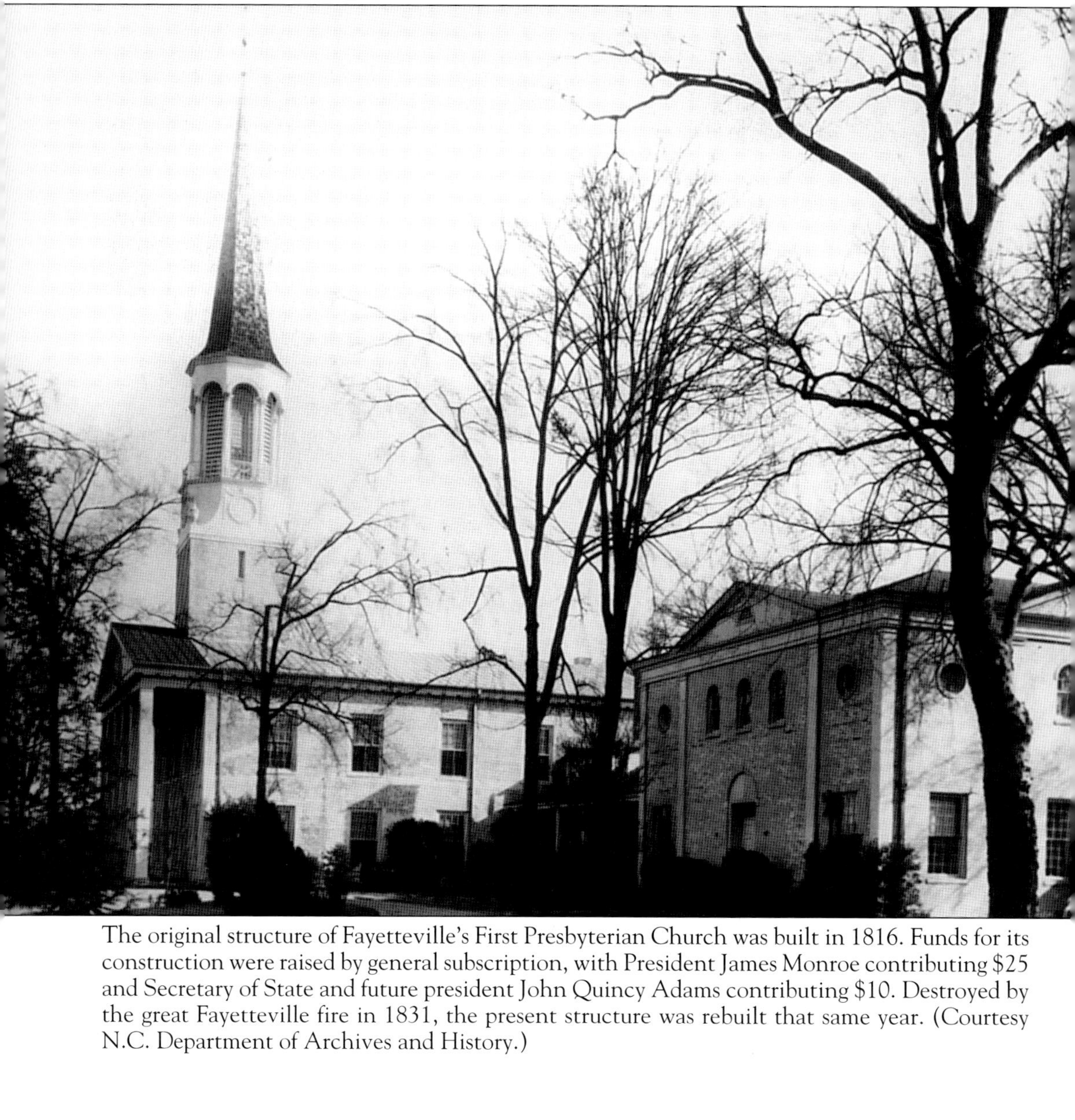

The original structure of Fayetteville's First Presbyterian Church was built in 1816. Funds for its construction were raised by general subscription, with President James Monroe contributing $25 and Secretary of State and future president John Quincy Adams contributing $10. Destroyed by the great Fayetteville fire in 1831, the present structure was rebuilt that same year. (Courtesy N.C. Department of Archives and History.)

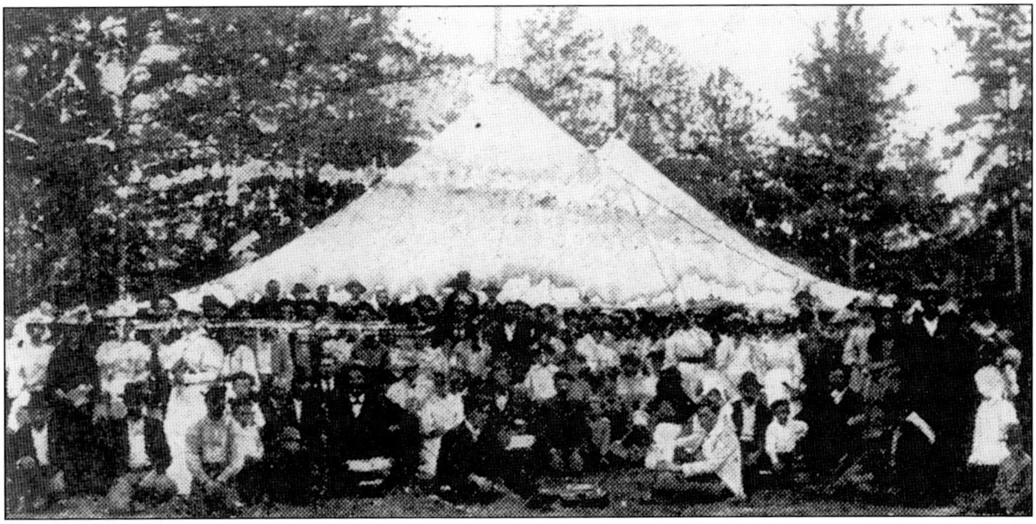

These people attended the first Falcon Camp Meeting in July of 1900. The meetings were held in tents until a structure was built to hold the services. (Courtesy N.C. Department of Archives and History.)

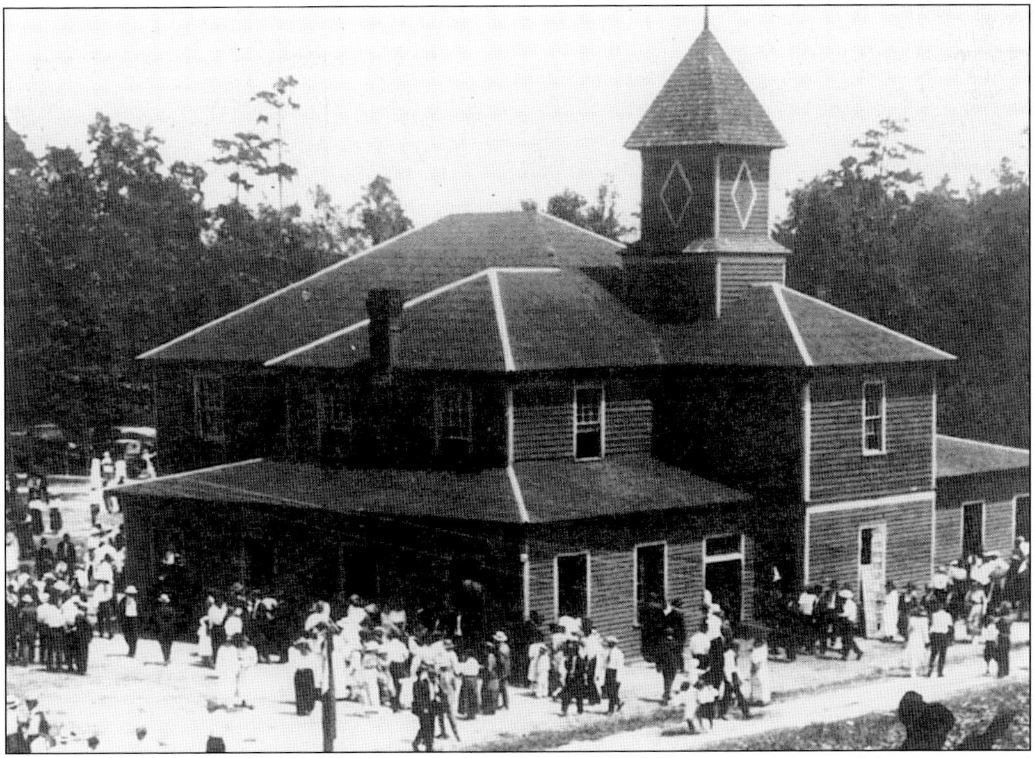

Camp meeting services were held in the Falcon tabernacle in 1915. Now part of the Pentecostal Holiness Church, the camp meeting has been held continuously since 1900. (Courtesy N.C. Department of Archives and History.)

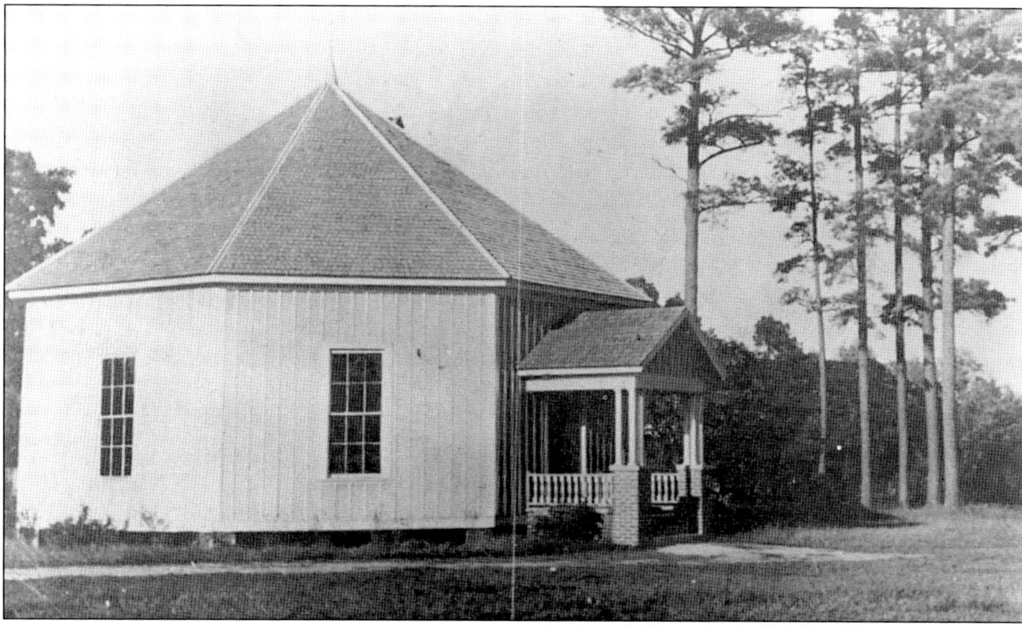

Falcon's Octagonal Tabernacle was the birthplace of the Pentecostal Holiness Church. (Courtesy N.C. Department of Archives and History.)

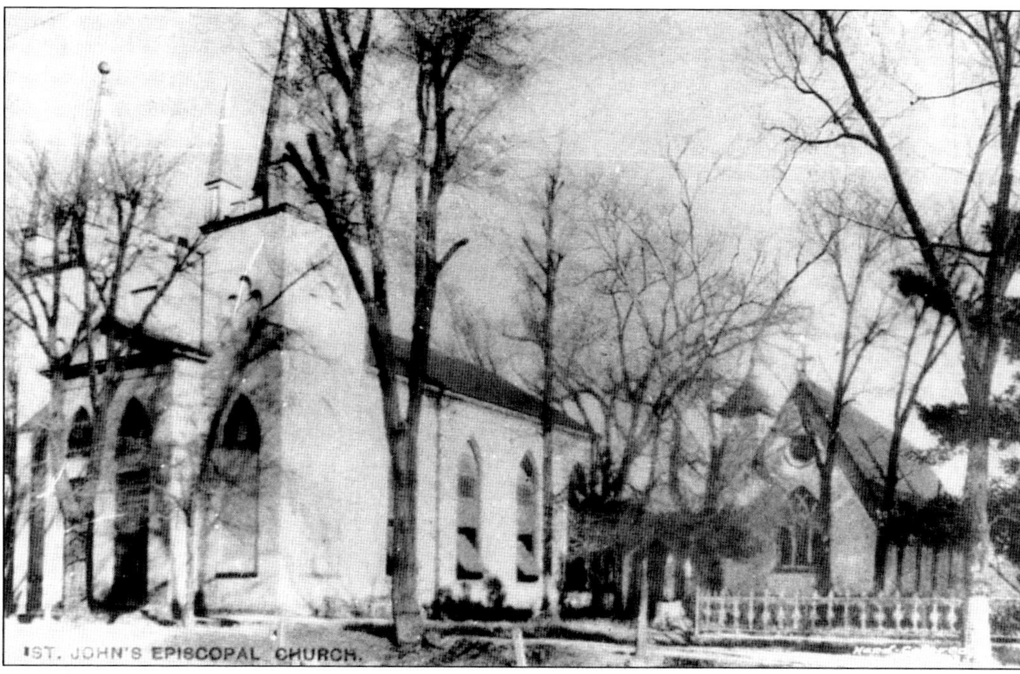

St. John's Episcopal Church is located on Green Street in Fayetteville. Built in 1818, the original structure was destroyed by the great Fayetteville fire of 1831. The present structure was rebuilt on site and was consecrated in 1833. (Courtesy N.C. Department of Archives and History.)

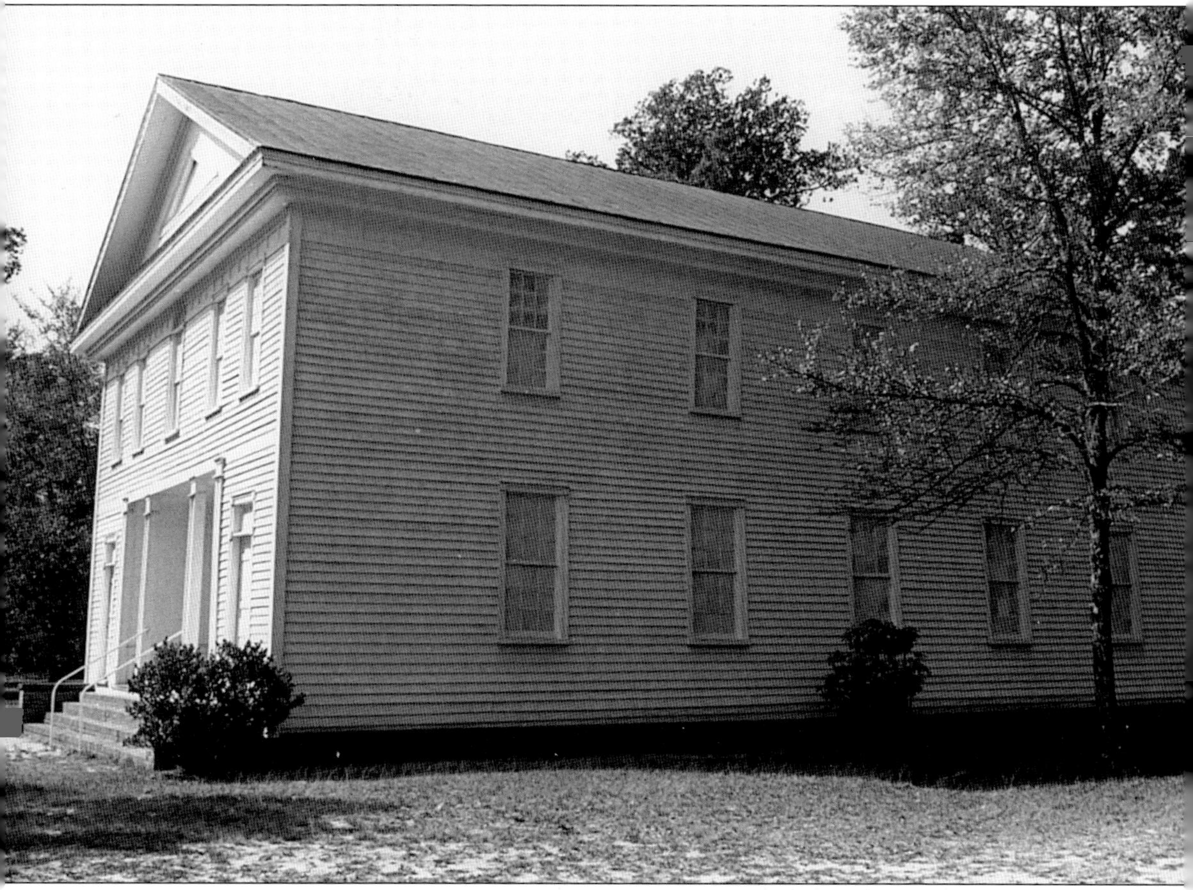

Old Bluff Presbyterian Church, located near Wade, was established in 1758 by Scottish minister James Campbell to minister to a colony of Scots that had settled along the high bluffs of the Cape Fear River in the 1730s. This structure, built in 1858, is the third church building on the site, and was used until a new church was built in Wade in 1908. A large homecoming service is held at Old Bluff each year. (Courtesy N.C. Department of Archives and History.)

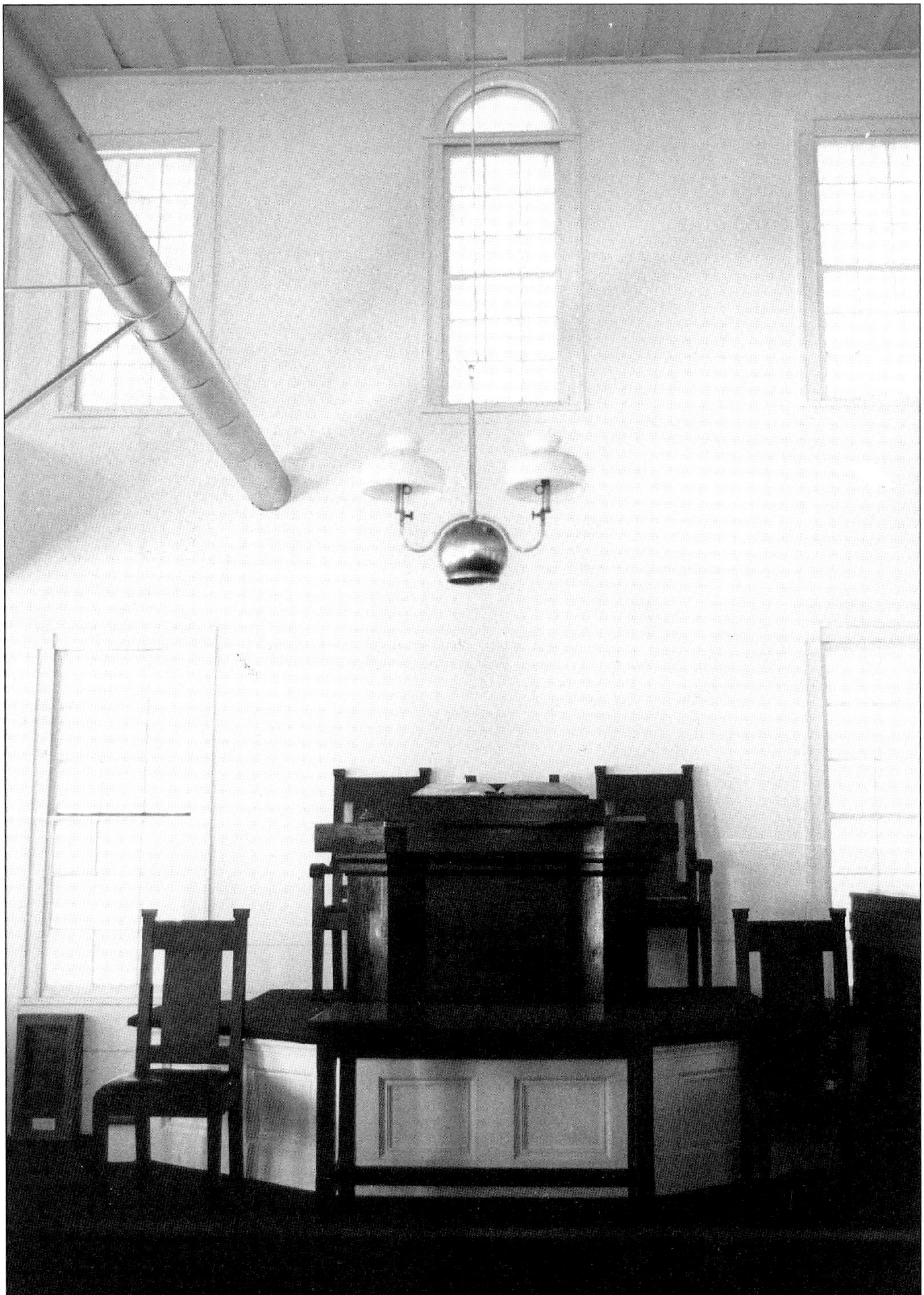

Seen here is the interior of Old Bluff Church. (Courtesy N.C. Department of Archives and History.)

A marker honoring Rev. James Campbell is located on the grounds of Old Bluff Church. Campbell founded two other churches, Barbecue and Longstreet, in what was then Cumberland County.

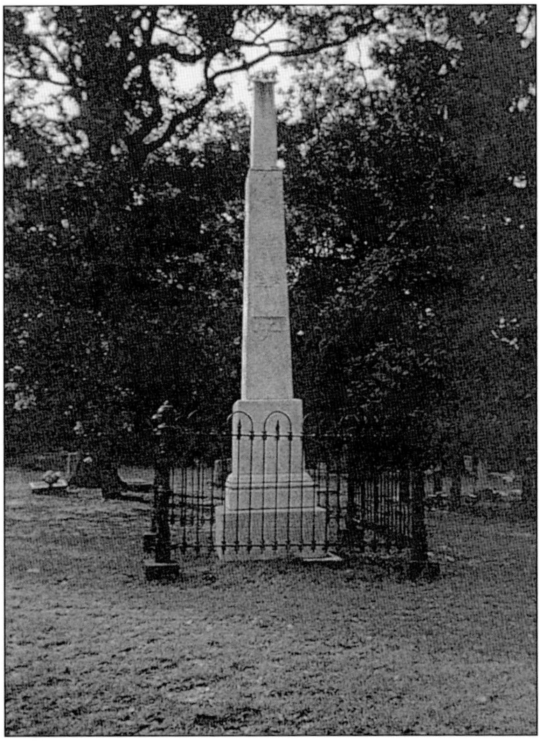

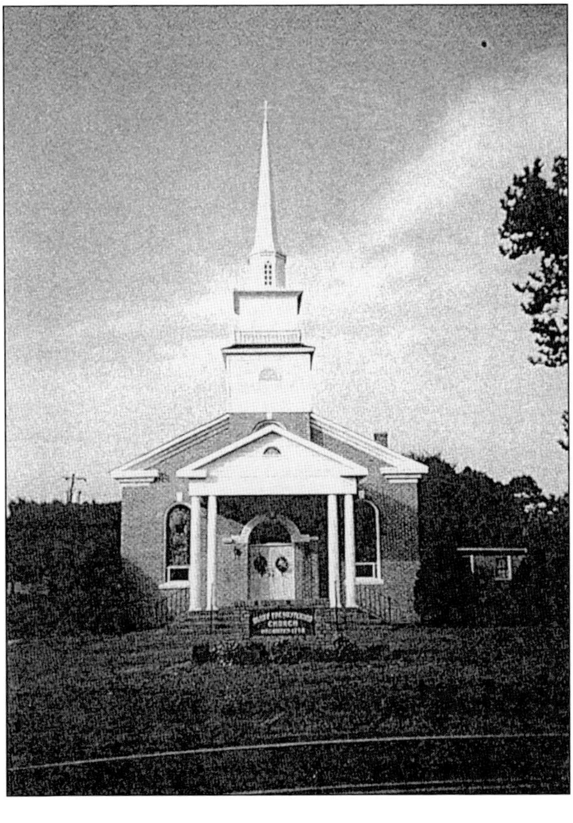

Bluff Presbyterian Church in Wade was built in 1908. The church moved from its former site to a new building in Wade because most of its members resided there.

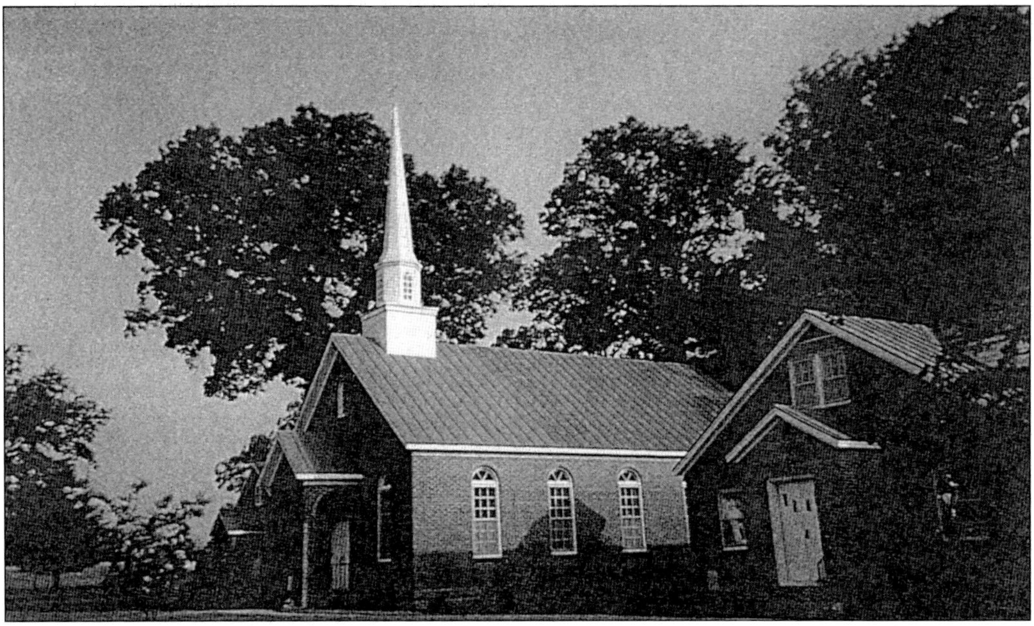

Godwin Presbyterian Church was founded in 1904. Eighty-six members of Old Bluff lived in Godwin and desired to be closer to their church, so they withdrew and became charter members of Godwin Presbyterian Church. A Presbyterian Sunday school was established here in 1889.

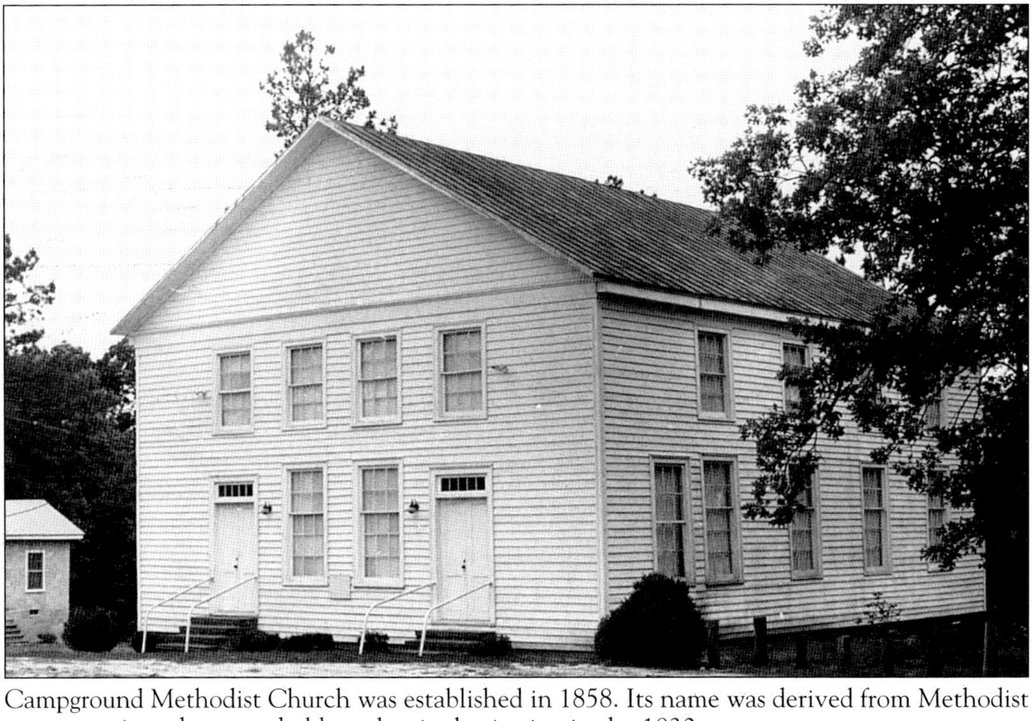

Campground Methodist Church was established in 1858. Its name was derived from Methodist camp meetings that were held on the site beginning in the 1830s.

Sardis Presbyterian Church was founded in Linden in May of 1816. Scottish minister Rev. Colin McIver was the first pastor, and served until 1821. The present church building was constructed in 1916.

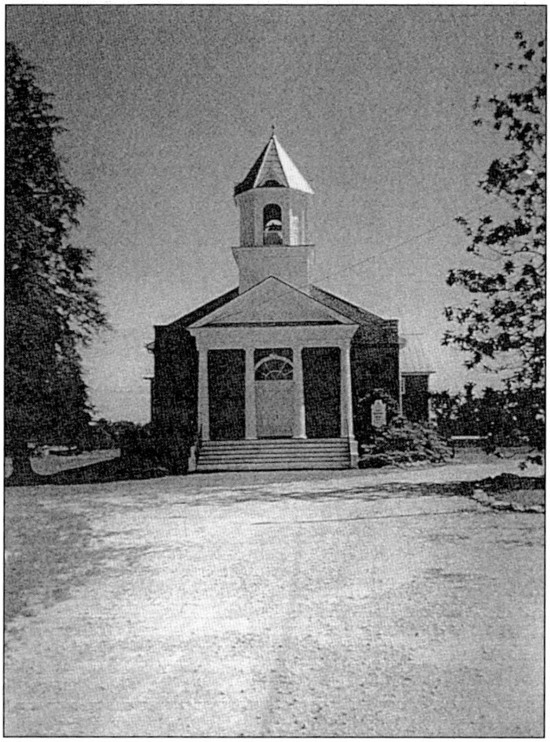

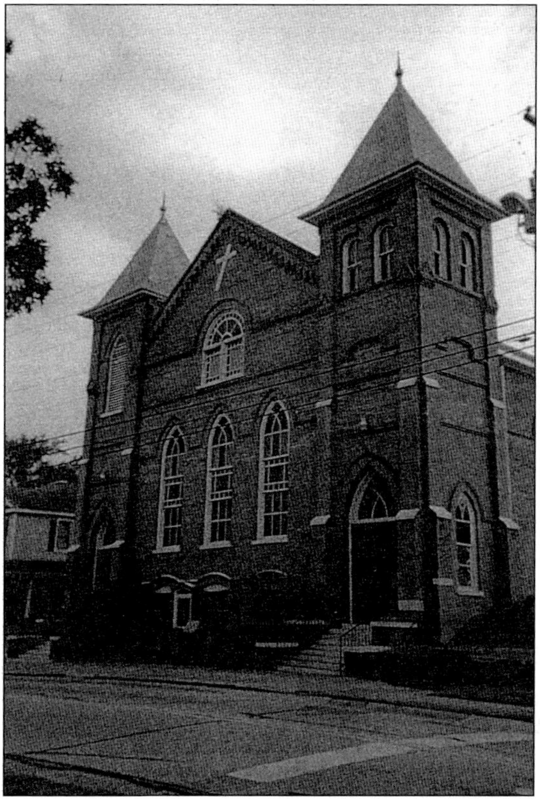

Evans Metropolitan AME Zion Church was established *c.* 1803 by Henry Evans, a free black preacher and shoemaker. The original structure was Fayetteville's first church building. Evans originally was forbidden to preach in town, but his large following influenced the town leaders to allow him to build a church that was attended by both blacks and whites.

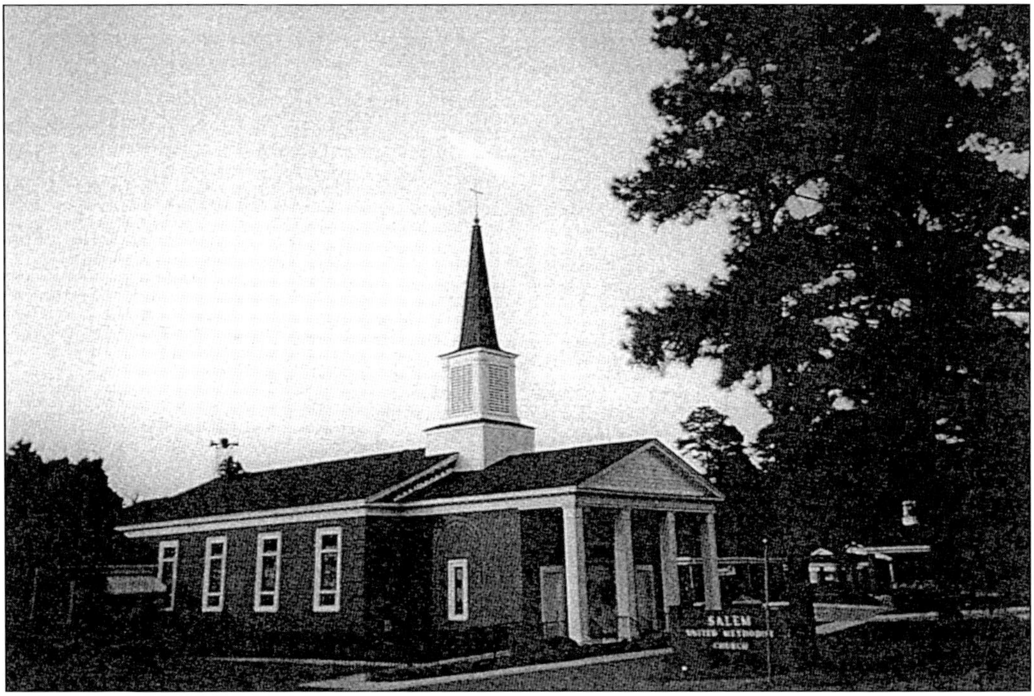

Salem United Methodist Church, one of Cumberland County's oldest Methodist churches, was established in 1848. It is located in Eastover, which was formerly called Flea Hill and received its name due to its proximity to Fayetteville, over the river and to the east.

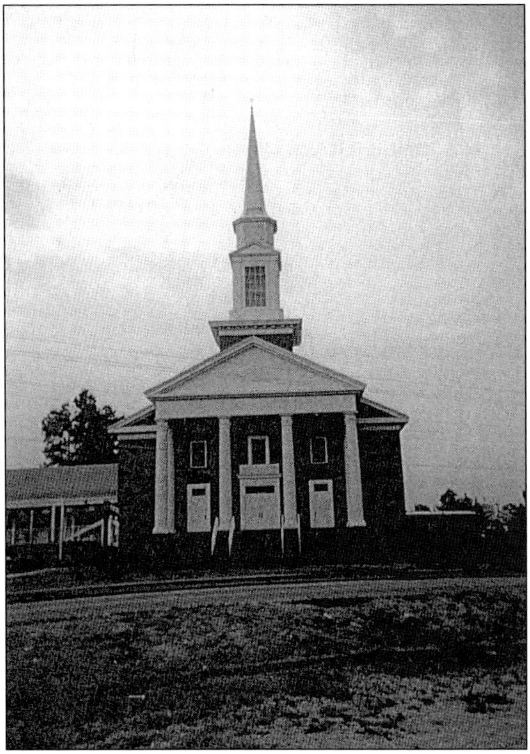

Spring Lake First Baptist Church, one of that towns largest churches, is located one block off Bragg Boulevard just east of downtown Spring Lake.

Six

PEOPLE

From the earliest Scottish settlers of the 1730s to today's longtime residents, many people have played huge roles in the development of Cumberland County into one of the largest metropolitan areas in the state. Cumberland has produced many leaders, several of whom have served the state and nation in political and military leadership roles. The majority of Cumberland's residents through the years, although not famous, have been the backbone of the county, working hard and providing responsible family leadership, helping it to become the modern county it is today.

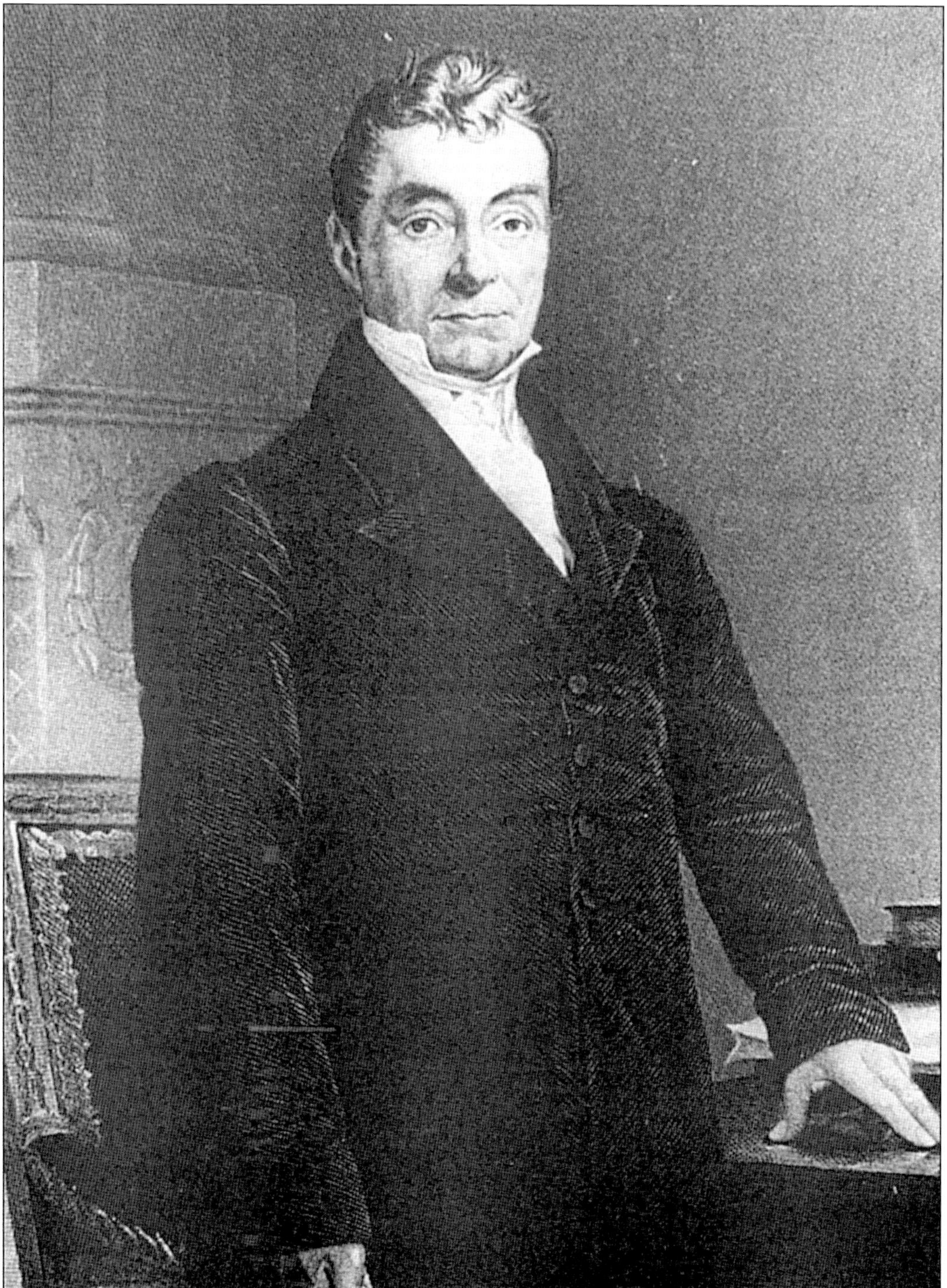

This portrait of Marquis de Lafayette was done in 1824. The following year he visited Fayetteville, the first American town named in his honor. A grand ball was held in his honor at the Lafayette Hotel, with an estimated attendance of 400. (Courtesy *The Return of Lafayette, 1824–1825*, by Marian Klamkin.)

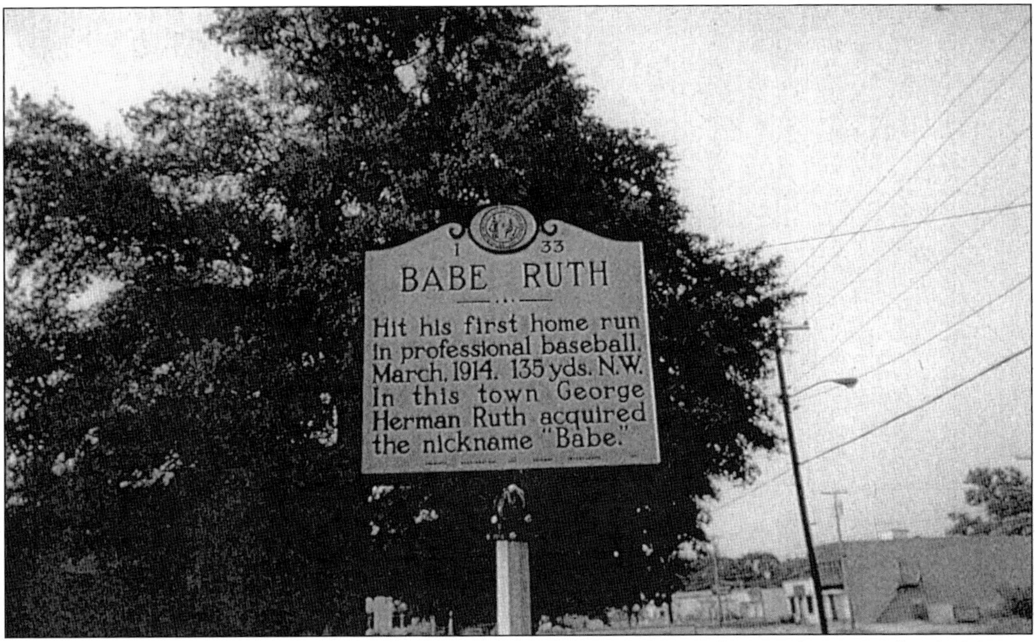

New York Yankee great Babe Ruth hit his first home run as a professional in March of 1914, at the old ballpark on Gillespie Street in Fayetteville. Ruth was in Fayetteville playing for a minor league team, the Baltimore Orioles, during spring training. He was later sold to the Yankees. Ruth also received his nickname, "Babe," during his stay in Fayetteville.

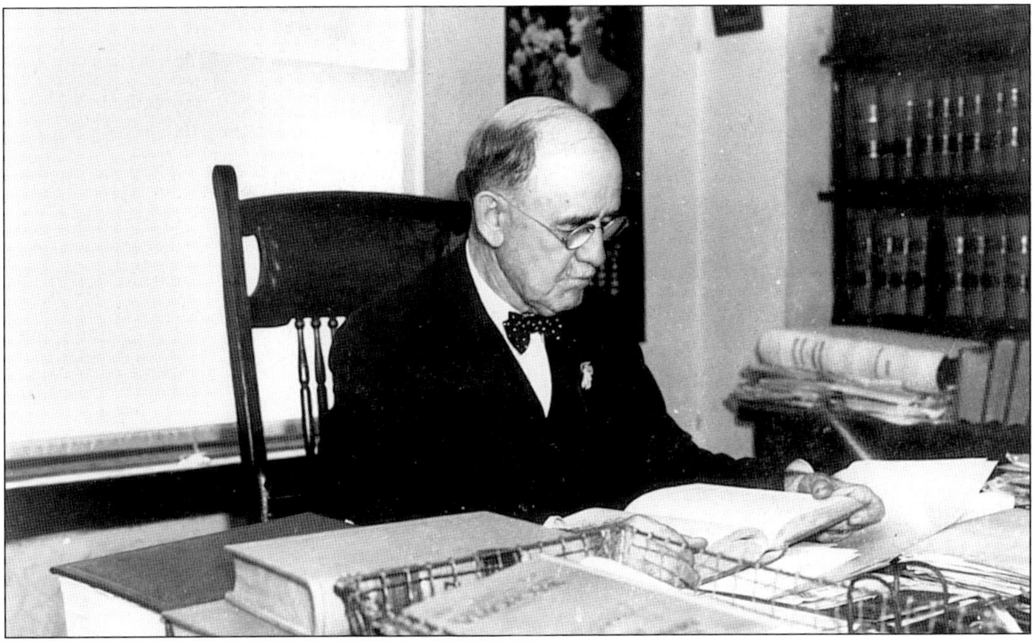

John A. Oates is pictured in his office in November of 1939. He served in many civic capacities, including chairman of the Cumberland County School Board and member of the state legislature. He is best known as author of *The Story of Fayetteville and The Upper Cape Fear*, an 868-page history of Fayetteville, Cumberland County, and the surrounding counties making up the Cape Fear region. (Courtesy N.C. Department of Archives and History.)

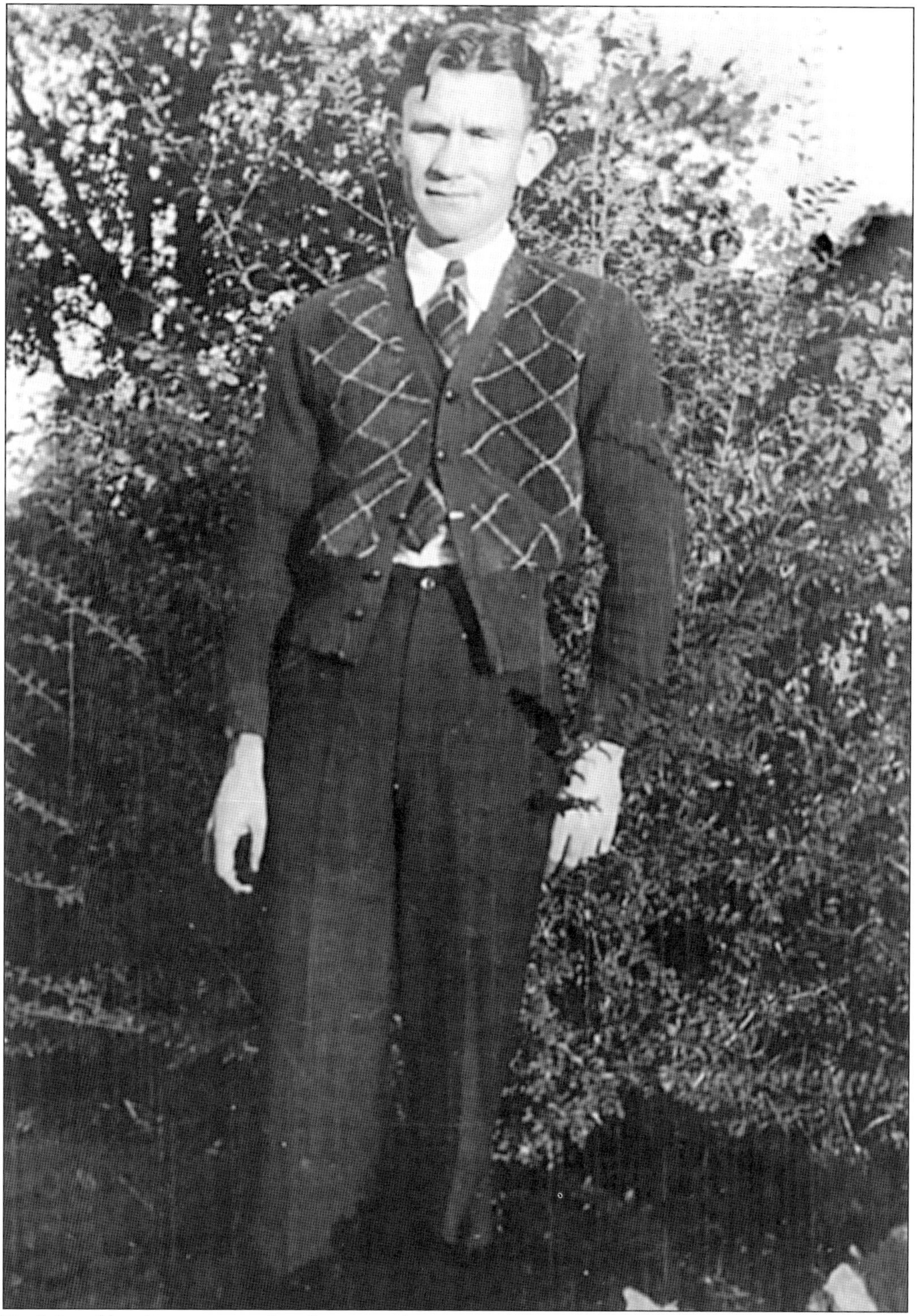

Fred Strickland, manager of Holmes Hardware and Grocery, posed for this picture in Linden in 1939.

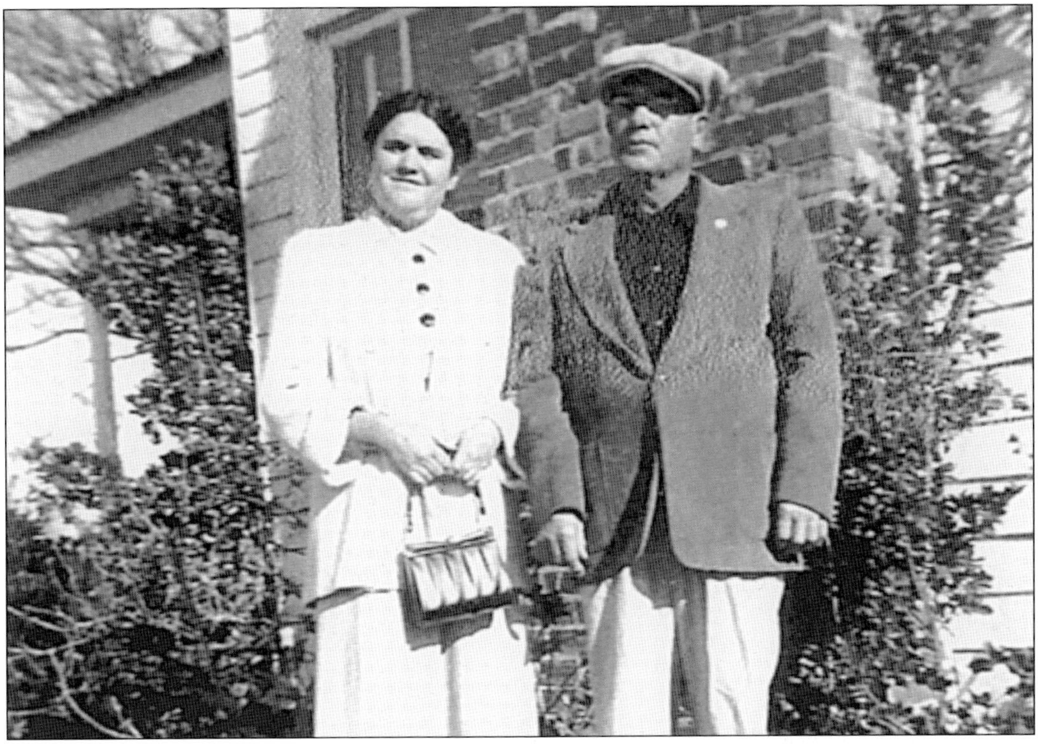

Coleman and Eva Lucas are seen at their home near Godwin in 1955. Coleman was the owner of the Old Roberson Mill on Silver Run, which was built in 1757 by Scotch immigrant "Bluff" Hector McNeill, and is mentioned in both Confederate and Yankee reports prior to the Battle of Averasboro.

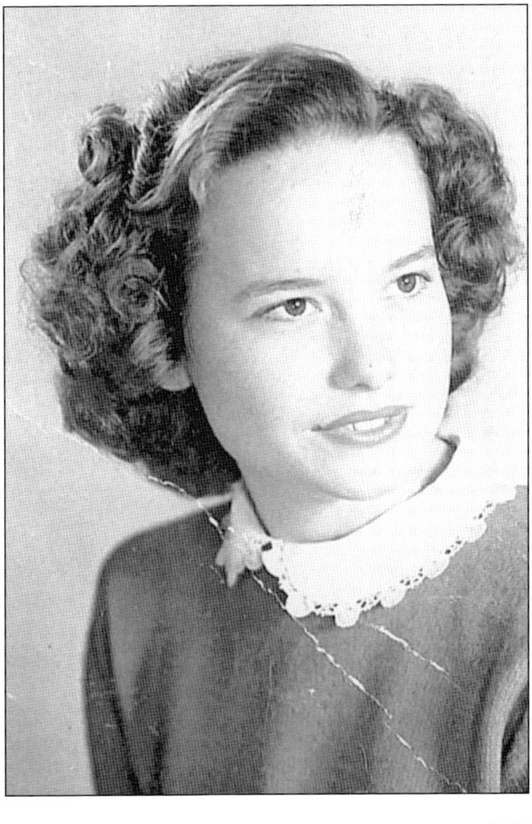

Pictured is Peggy Lucas, a senior at Central High School near Eastover in 1949.

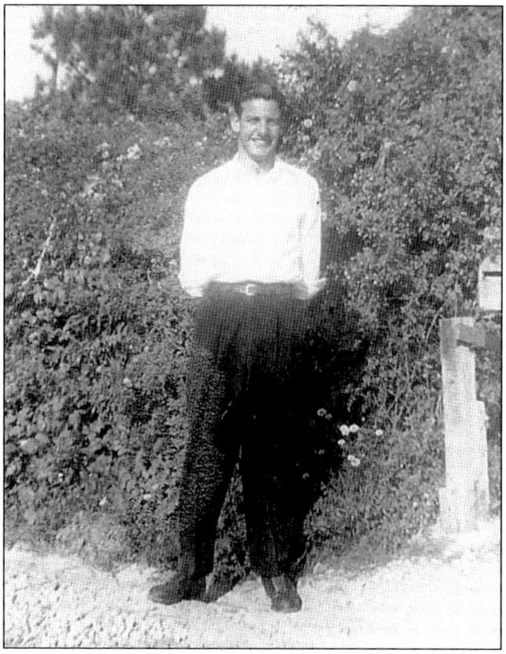

Seventeen-year-old Joe Powell is pictured near Godwin in 1948.

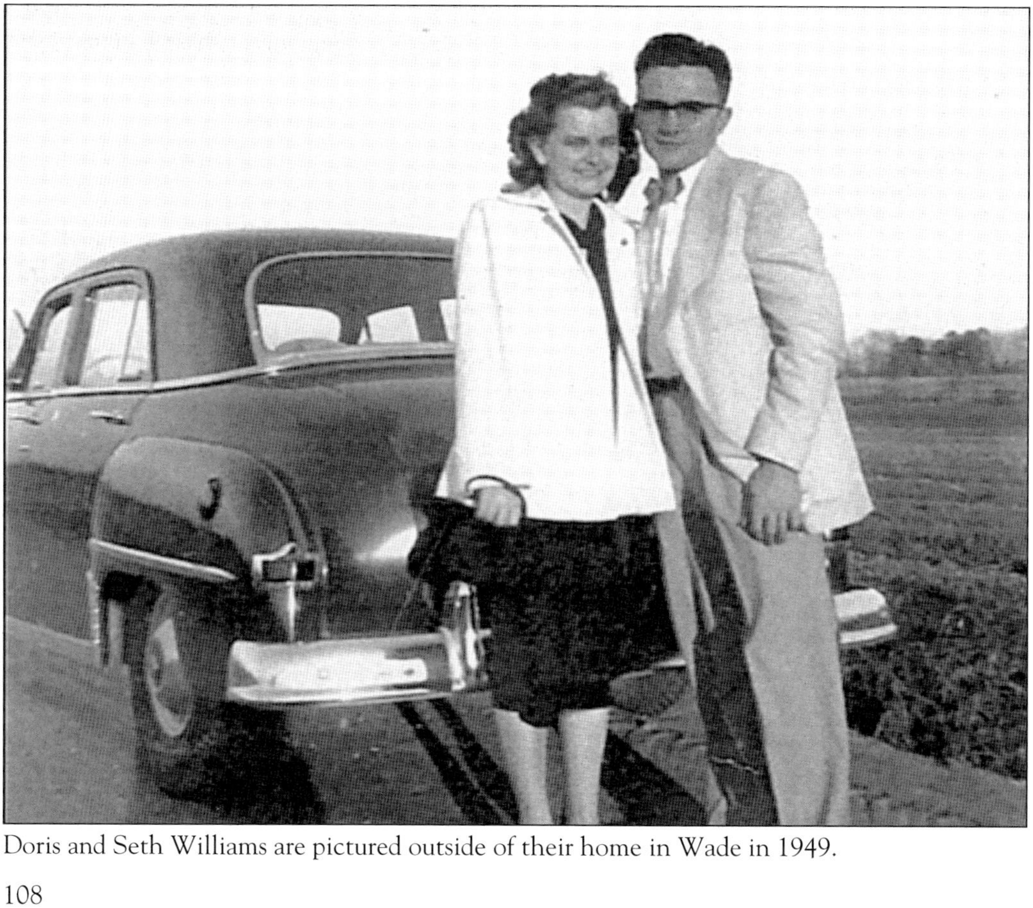

Doris and Seth Williams are pictured outside of their home in Wade in 1949.

Two unidentified men caught this large catfish at the mouth of Lower Little River near Linden in 1947.

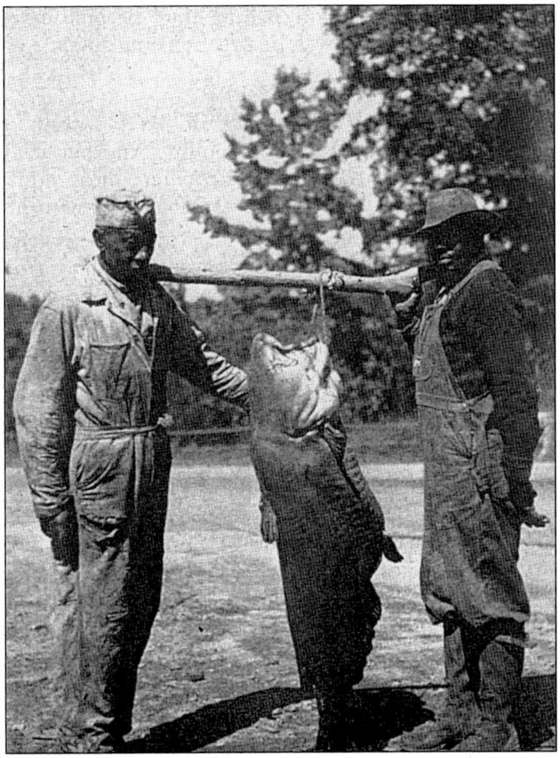

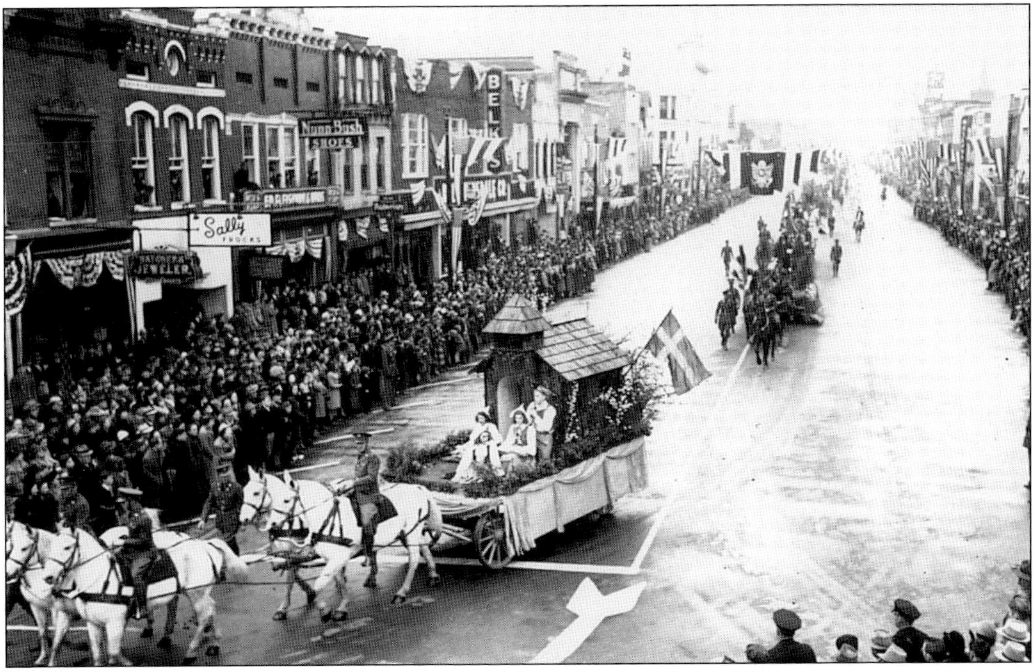

On November 21, 1939, a celebration was held in honor of the 150th anniversary of North Carolina's ratification of the United States Constitution in Fayetteville. Despite cold, rainy weather, a large crowd turned out to watch the parade advance along Hay Street. (Courtesy N.C. Department of Archives and History.)

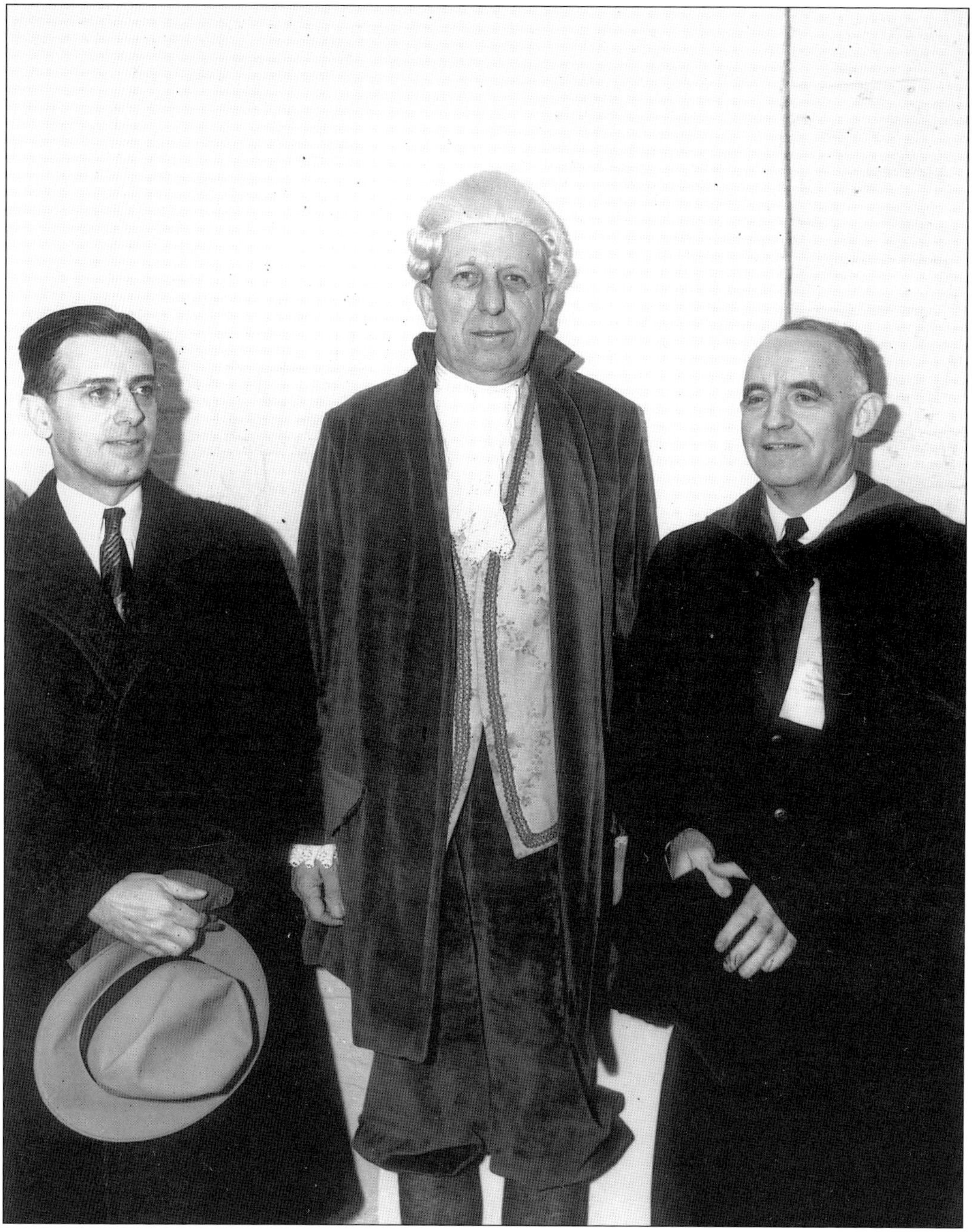

Among the dignitaries present at the commemoration of the ratification of the Constitution on November 21, 1939, were, from left to right: Governor Prentice Cooper of Tennessee, Governor Clyde Hoey of North Carolina, and University of North Carolina President and Fayetteville native Frank Porter Graham, who later served in the U.S. Senate. Graham delivered the keynote address at Hay Street Methodist Church. (Courtesy N.C. Department of Archives and History.)

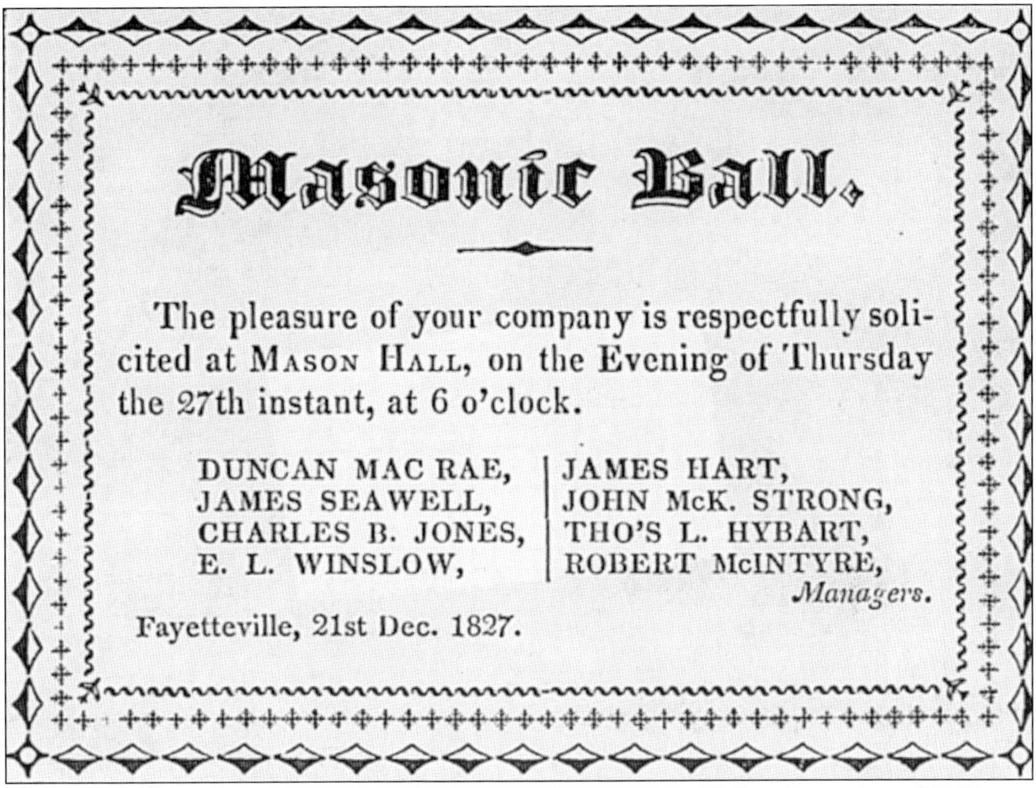

Masonic Ball.

The pleasure of your company is respectfully solicited at MASON HALL, on the Evening of Thursday the 27th instant, at 6 o'clock.

DUNCAN MAC RAE,	JAMES HART,
JAMES SEAWELL,	JOHN McK. STRONG,
CHARLES B. JONES,	THO'S L. HYBART,
E. L. WINSLOW,	ROBERT McINTYRE,

Managers.

Fayetteville, 21st Dec. 1827.

Pictured is an invitation to a ball held at Fayetteville's Masonic Hall in December of 1827.

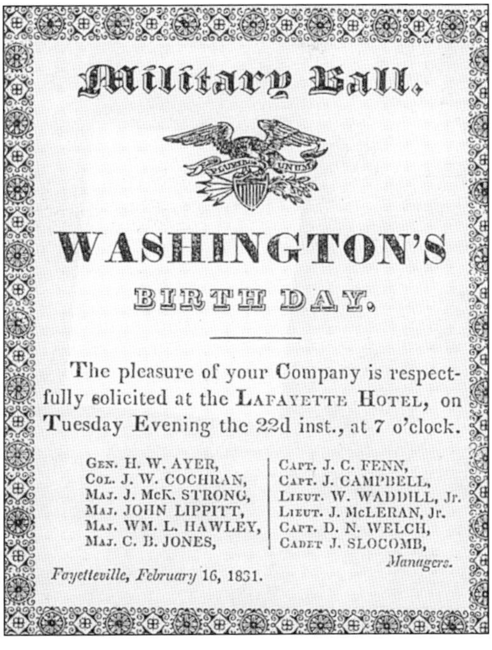

Military Ball.

WASHINGTON'S

BIRTH DAY.

The pleasure of your Company is respectfully solicited at the LAFAYETTE HOTEL, on Tuesday Evening the 22d inst., at 7 o'clock.

GEN. H. W. AYER,	CAPT. J. C. FENN,
COL. J. W. COCHRAN,	CAPT. J. CAMPBELL,
MAJ. J. McK. STRONG,	LIEUT. W. WADDILL, Jr.
MAJ. JOHN LIPPITT,	LIEUT. J. McLERAN, Jr.
MAJ. WM. L. HAWLEY,	CAPT. D. N. WELCH,
MAJ. C. B. JONES,	CADET J. SLOCOMB,

Managers.

Fayetteville, February 16, 1831.

This invitation was sent for a military ball honoring George Washington's birthday, held at the Lafayette Hotel in February of 1831.

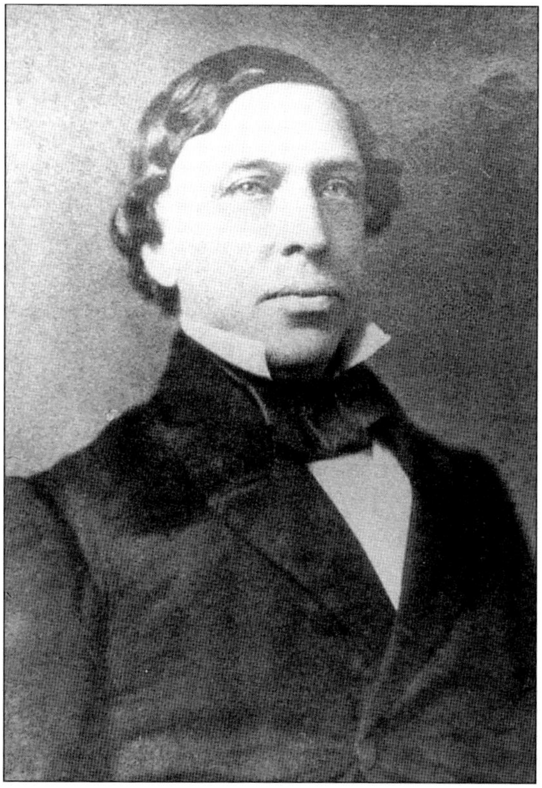

Warren Winslow of Fayetteville served as acting governor of North Carolina from December 6, 1854, to January 1, 1855, due to the resignation of Governor David S. Reid to enter the U.S. Senate. North Carolina had no lieutenant governor, so Winslow, as Speaker of the Senate, moved into the governor's office until elected Governor Thomas Bragg took over on January 1, 1855. (Courtesy N.C. Department of Archives and History.)

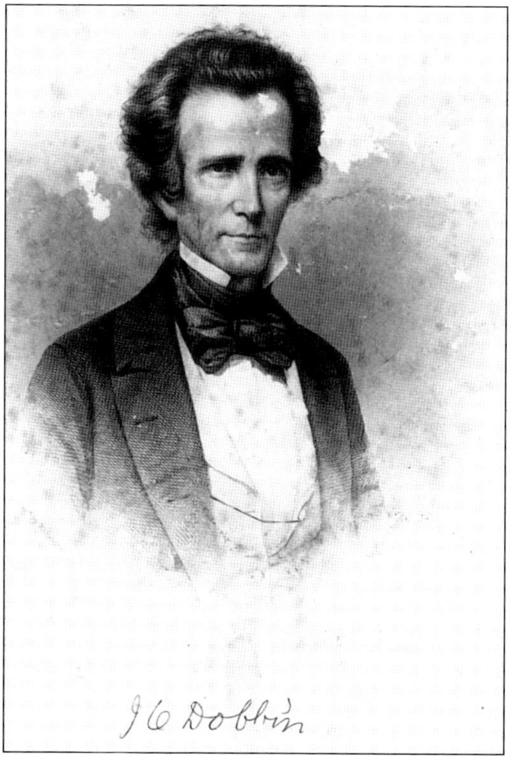

James Cochran Dobbin served as a state legislator and, in 1848, introduced a bill that established Dorothea Dix Hospital in Raleigh for the mentally ill. He also served as Secretary of the Navy in the administration of the 14th president, Franklin Pierce, from 1853 to 1857. (Courtesy N.C. Department of Archives and History.)

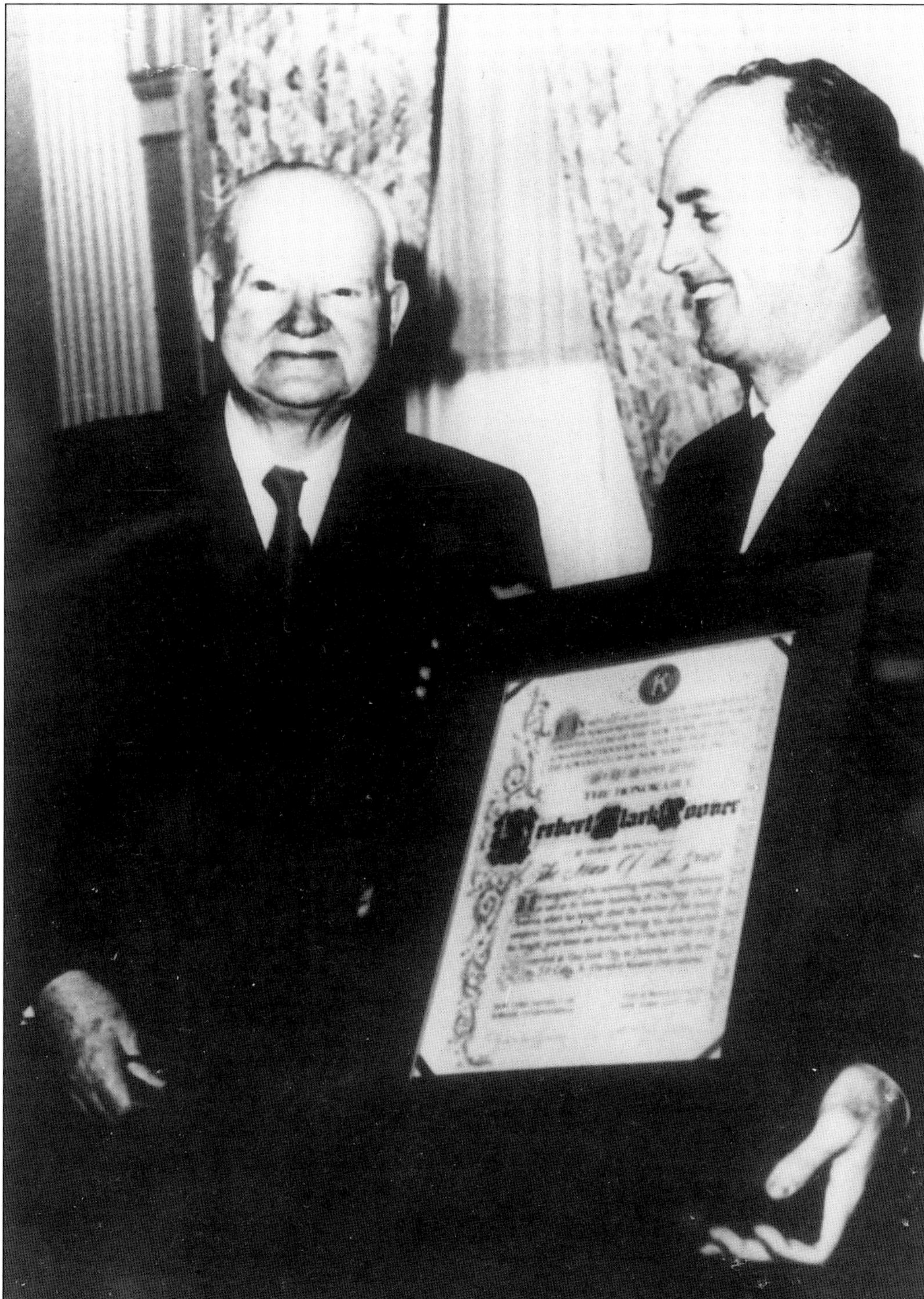

Joseph Tally of Fayetteville, president of Kiwanis International, presents a Kiwanis Man of the Year award to former President Herbert Hoover. (Courtesy N.C. Department of Archives and History.)

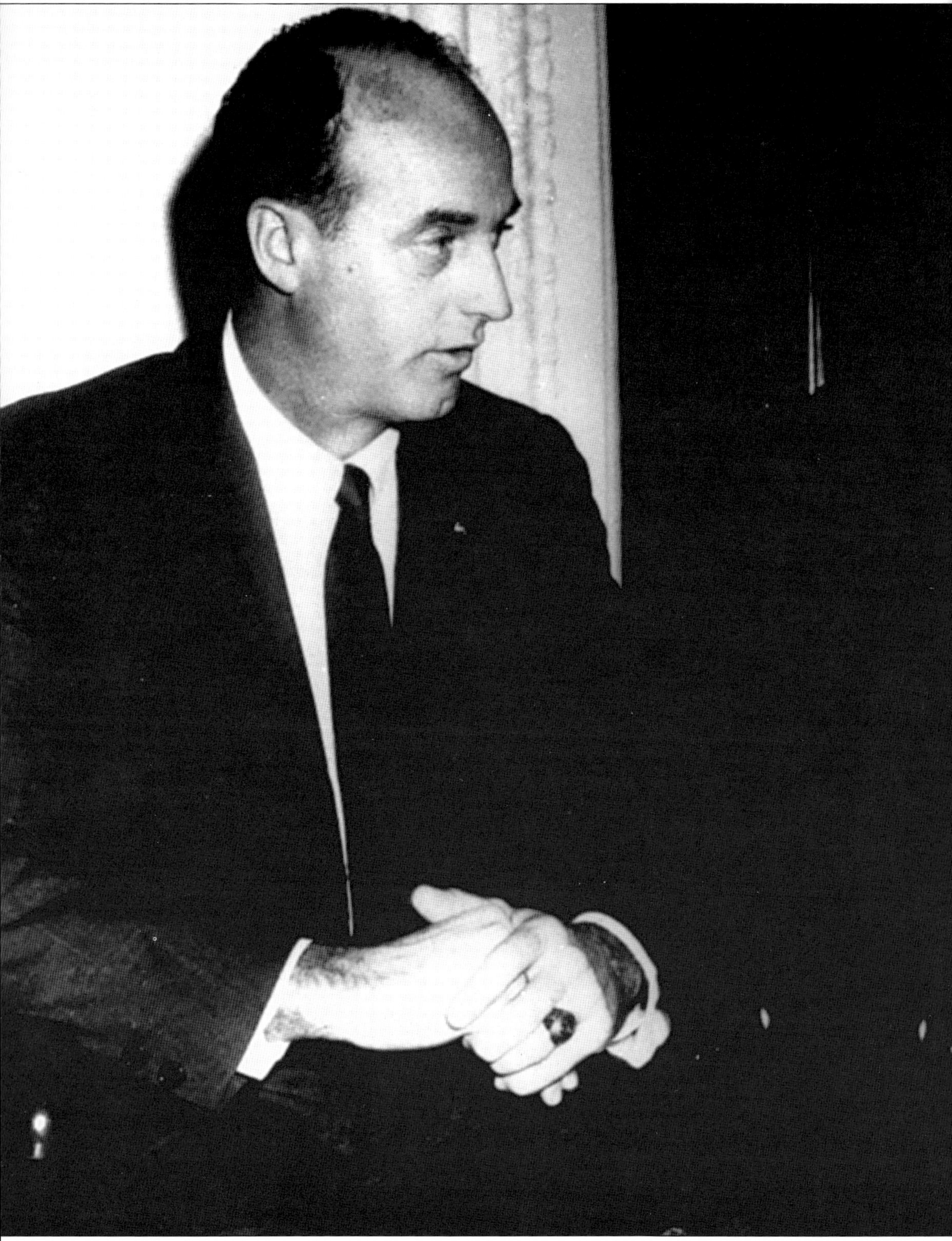

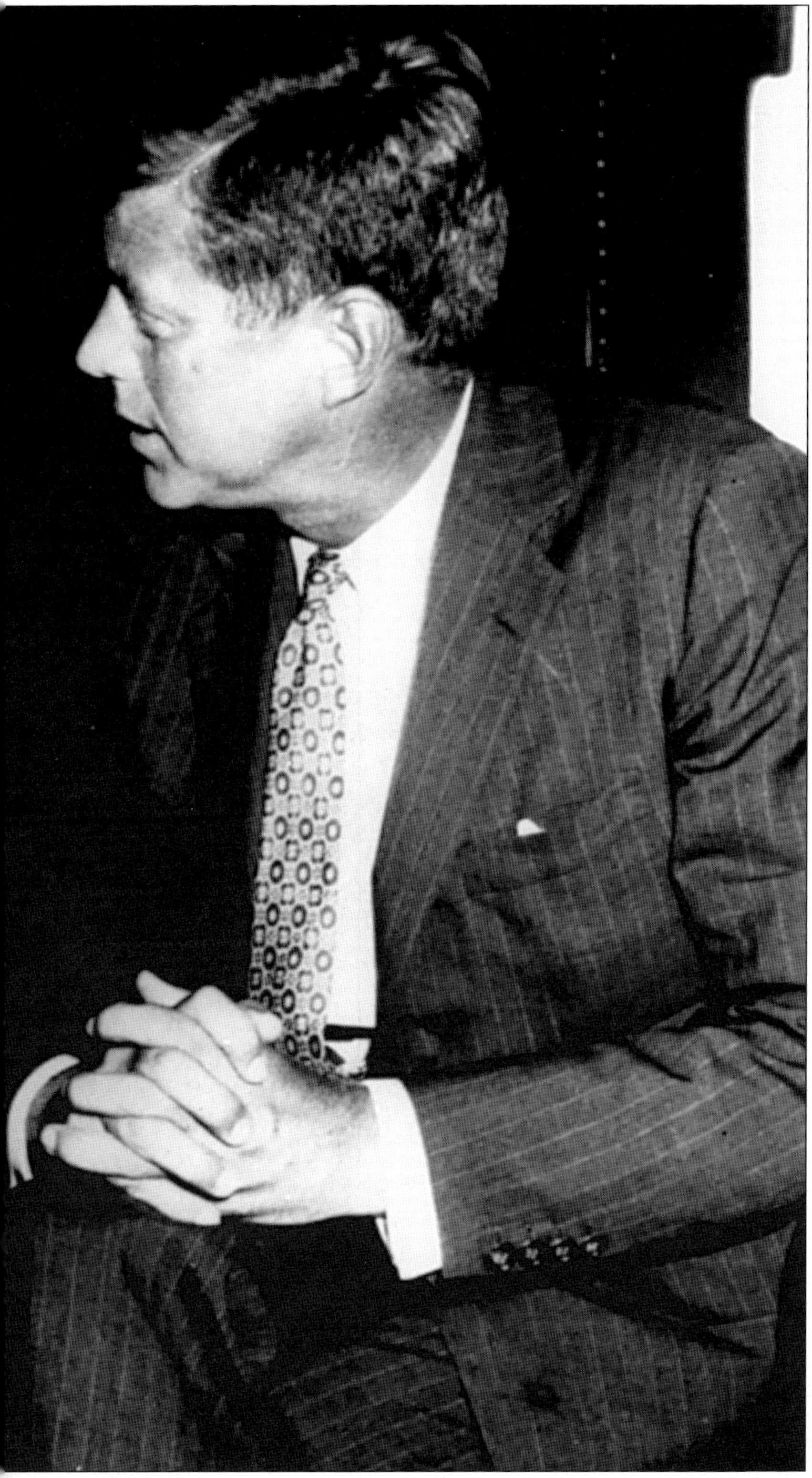

Joseph Tally meets with President John F. Kennedy in the early 1960s. (Courtesy N.C. Department of Archives and History.)

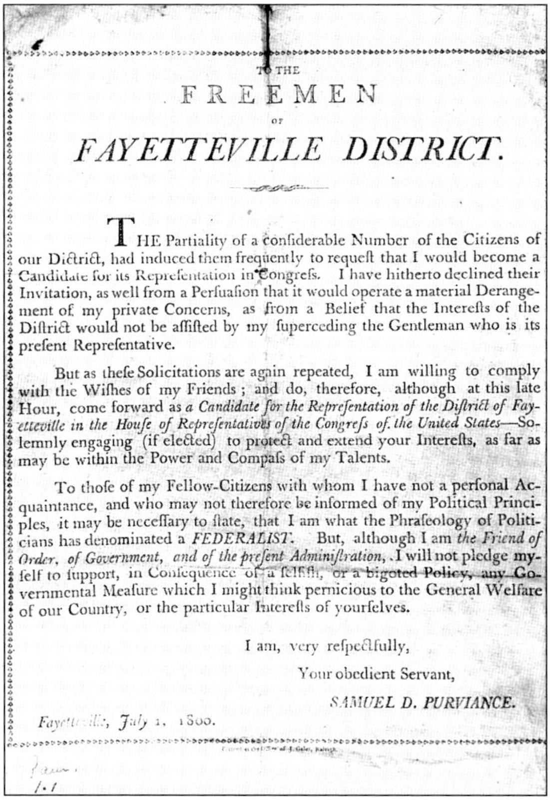

TO THE

FREEMEN

OF

FAYETTEVILLE DISTRICT.

THE Partiality of a conſiderable Number of the Citizens of our Diſtrict, had induced them frequently to requeſt that I would become a Candidate for its Repreſentation in Congreſs. I have hitherto declined their Invitation, as well from a Perſuaſion that it would operate a material Derangement of my private Concerns, as from a Belief that the Intereſts of the Diſtrict would not be aſſiſted by my ſuperceding the Gentleman who is its preſent Repreſentative.

But as theſe Solicitations are again repeated, I am willing to comply with the Wiſhes of my Friends; and do, therefore, although at this late Hour, come forward as *a Candidate for the Repreſentation of the Diſtrict of Fayetteville in the Houſe of Repreſentatives of the Congreſs of the United States*—Solemnly engaging (if elected) to protect and extend your Intereſts, as far as may be within the Power and Compaſs of my Talents.

To thoſe of my Fellow-Citizens with whom I have not a perſonal Acquaintance, and who may not therefore be informed of my Political Principles, it may be neceſſary to ſtate, that I am what the Phraſeology of Politicians has denominated a *FEDERALIST.* But, although I am *the Friend of Order, of Government, and of the preſent Adminiſtration,* I will not pledge myſelf to ſupport, in Conſequence of a ſelfiſh, or a bigoted Policy, any Governmental Meaſure which I might think pernicious to the General Welfare of our Country, or the particular Intereſts of yourſelves.

I am, very reſpectfully,

Your obedient Servant,

SAMUEL D. PURVIANCE.

Fayetteville, July 1, 1800.

Fayetteville resident Samuel Purviance, a Federalist, announces his candidacy for U.S. Congress on July 1, 1800. (Courtesy N.C. Department of Archives and History.)

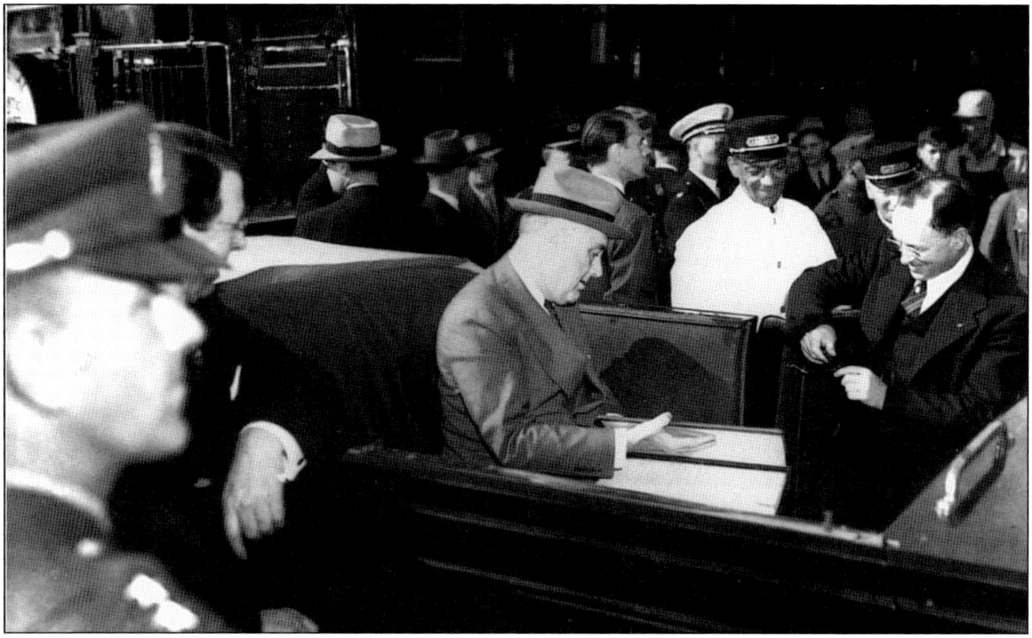

President Franklin Delano Roosevelt is shown here during his visit to Fayetteville and Fort Bragg in 1941. North Carolina Governor J. Melville Broughton is leaning against the car in the left of the picture. (Courtesy N.C. Department of Archives and History.)

Charles Manly Stedman was a congressman who served as lieutenant governor from 1885 to 1889, and ran unsuccessfully for governor in 1888 and 1904. He was also president of the North Carolina Railroad. The town of Stedman in eastern Cumberland County was named in his honor. (Courtesy *Biographical History of North Carolina* by Samuel A. Ashe.)

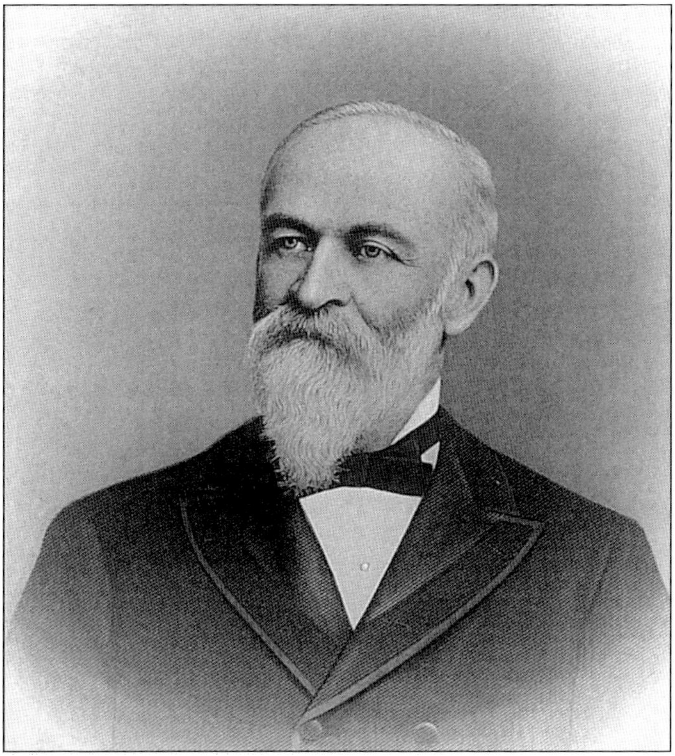

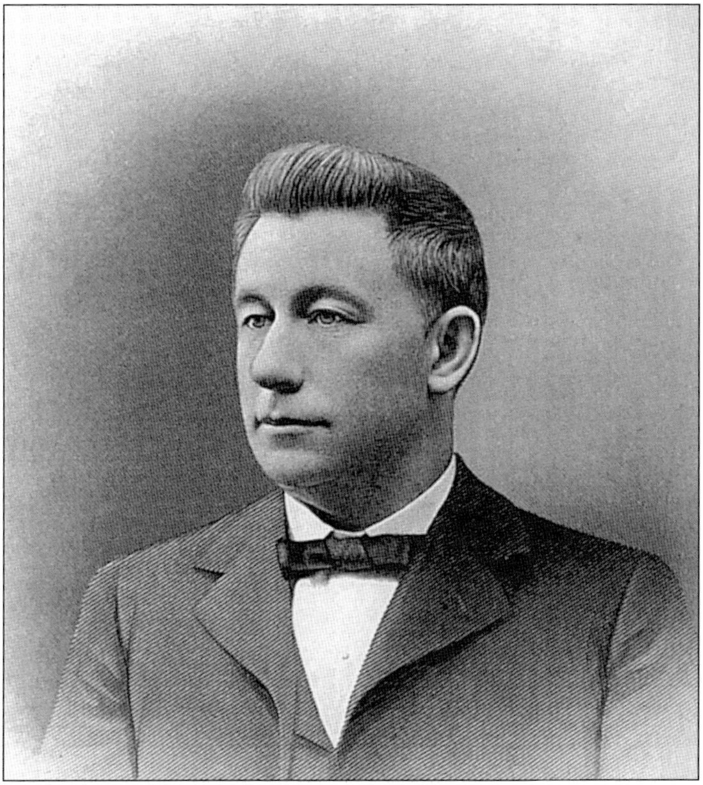

Dr. Jacob Franklin Highsmith, along with Dr. J.H. Marsh, founded Fayetteville's first hospital in 1899 at the age of 31. Marsh-Highsmith Hospital was a three-story brick building that stood at the corner of Green and Old Streets downtown. Highsmith became sole owner in 1905 and the name was changed to Highsmith Hospital. It was the first privately owned hospital in the state. (Courtesy *Biographical History of North Carolina* by Samuel A. Ashe.)

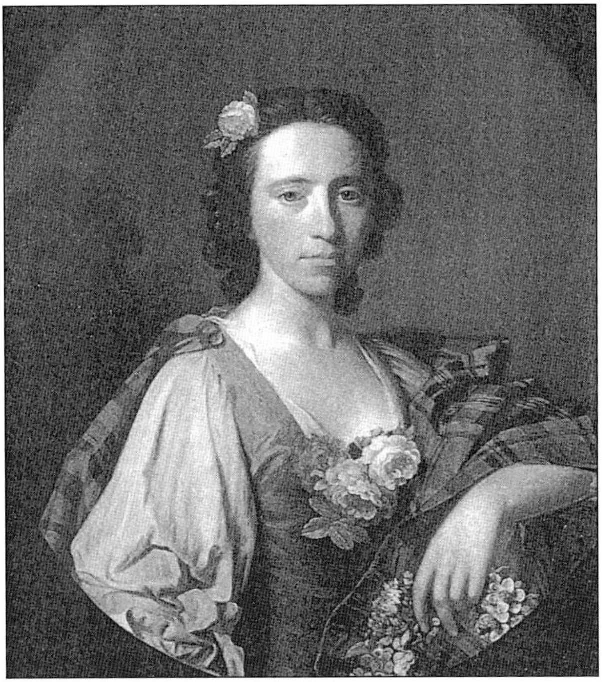

Flora MacDonald, the Scottish heroine who gained fame for helping Bonnie Prince Charles escape from the English following the Battle of Culloden, lived in Cross Creek for a short while after her arrival from Scotland. According to legend, she rallied Scottish troops in Fayetteville prior to their departure for Wilmington before the Battle of Moore's Creek Bridge. (Courtesy *Flora MacDonald* by Ruairidh MacLeod.)

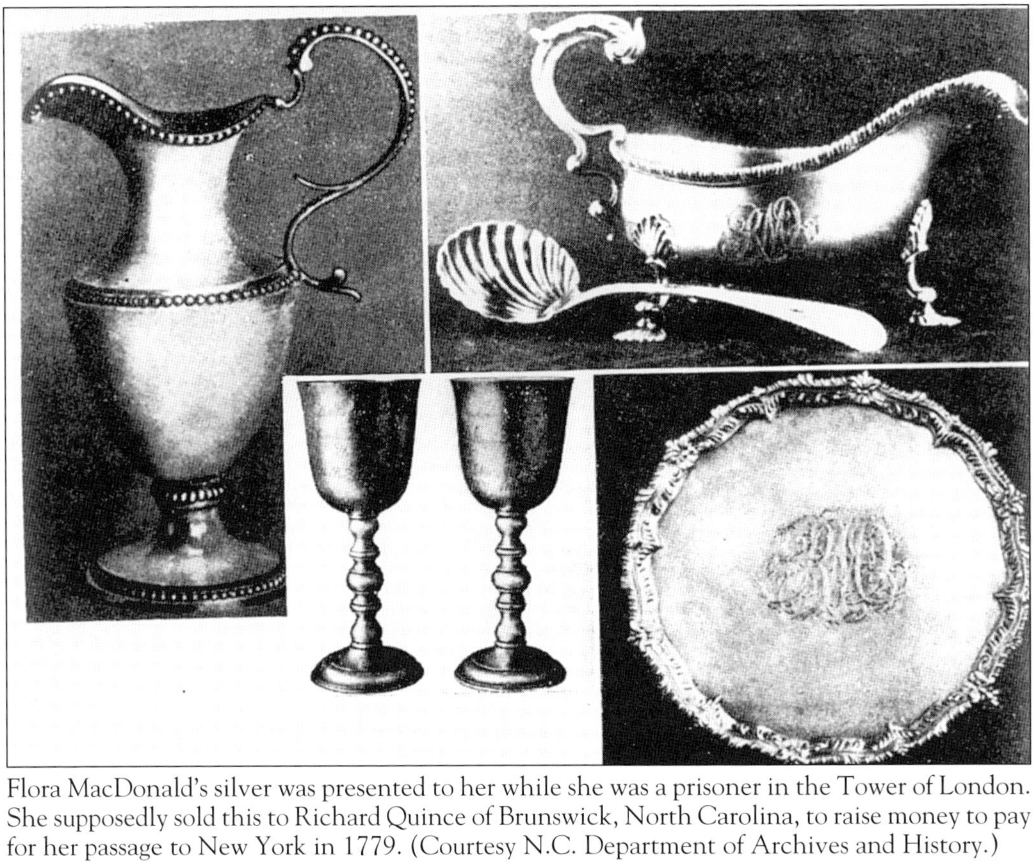

Flora MacDonald's silver was presented to her while she was a prisoner in the Tower of London. She supposedly sold this to Richard Quince of Brunswick, North Carolina, to raise money to pay for her passage to New York in 1779. (Courtesy N.C. Department of Archives and History.)

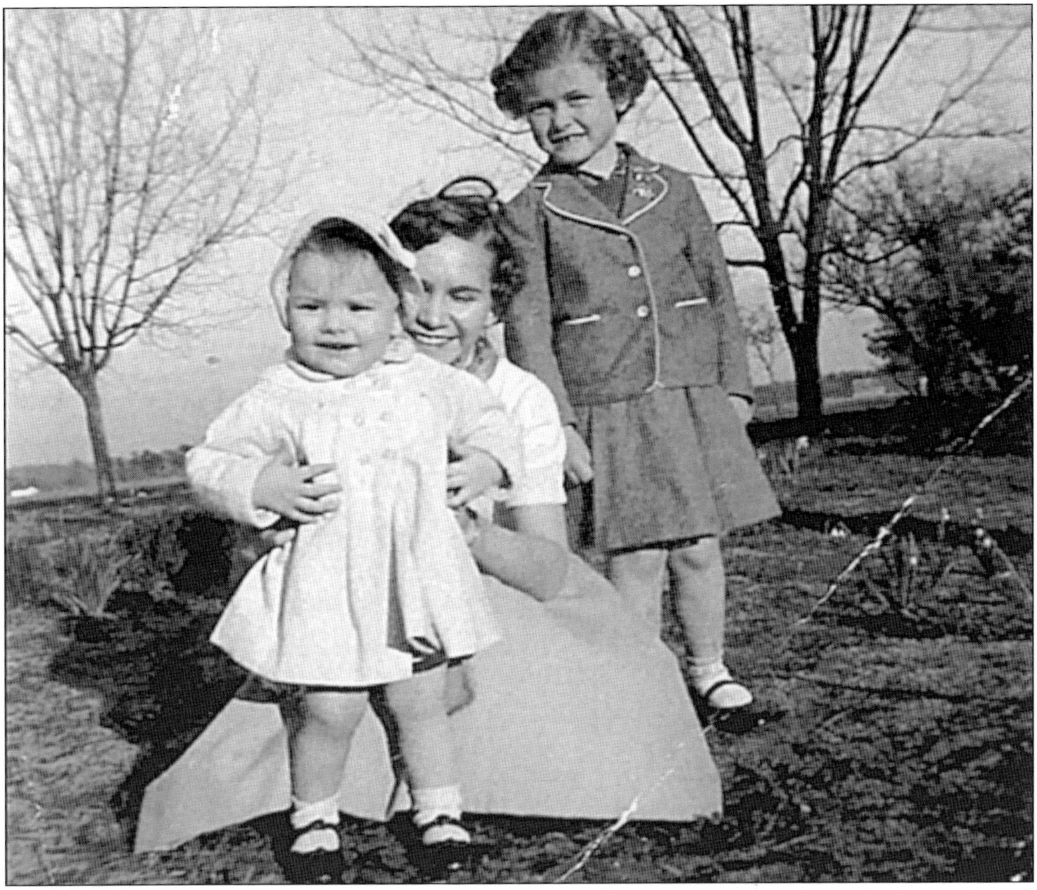

Debbie Powell, Mary Fuller Autry, and Mary Jo Williams are pictured in Wade on Easter Sunday, 1955.

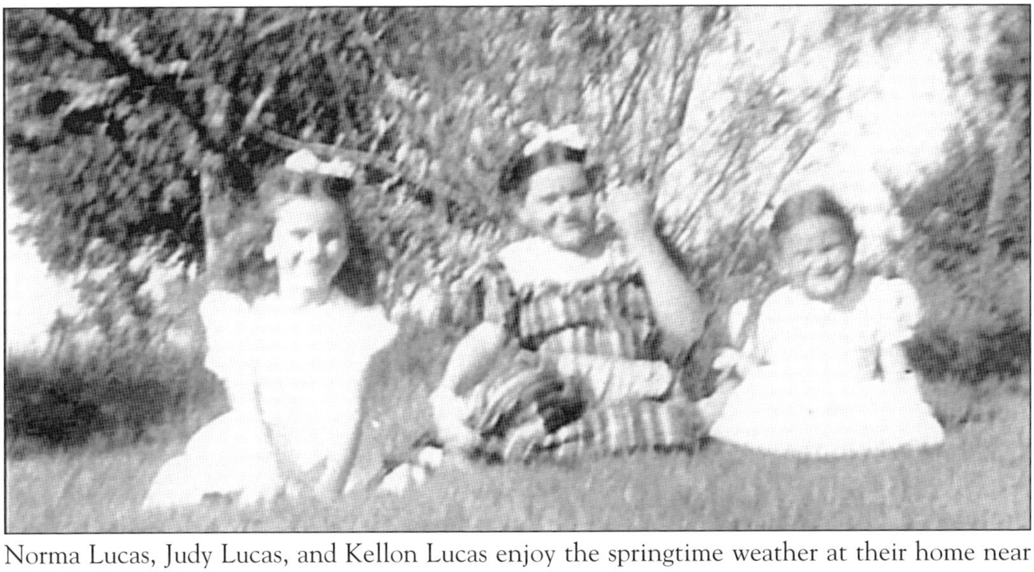

Norma Lucas, Judy Lucas, and Kellon Lucas enjoy the springtime weather at their home near Godwin in 1950.

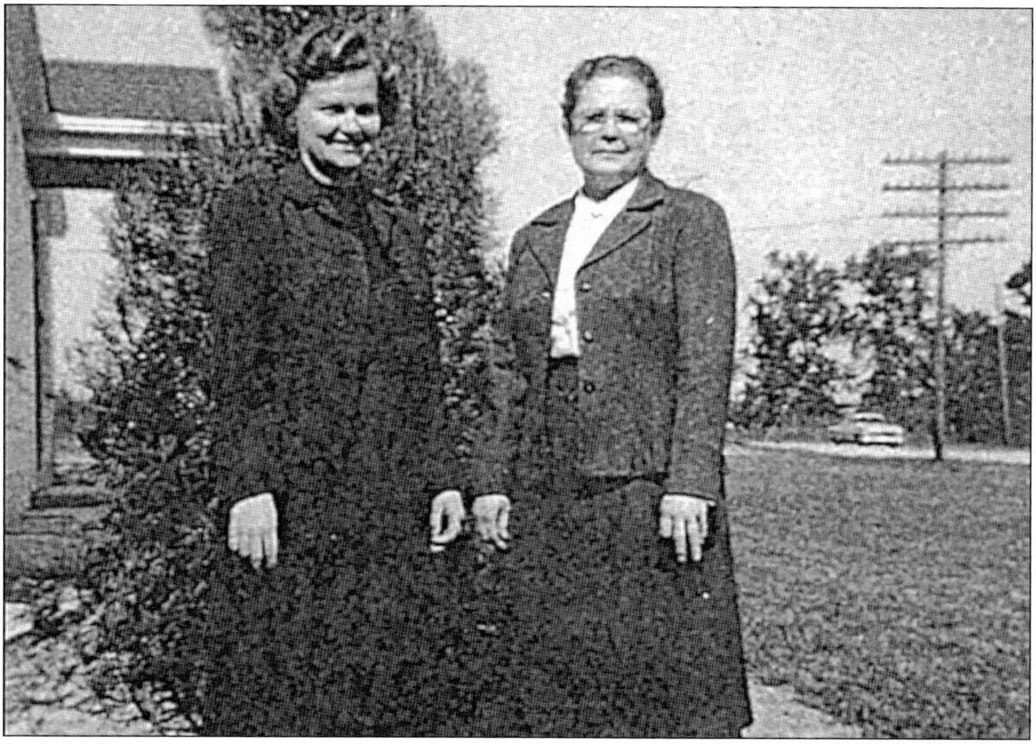

Doris Williams and Louise Strickland are pictured in Godwin in 1957.

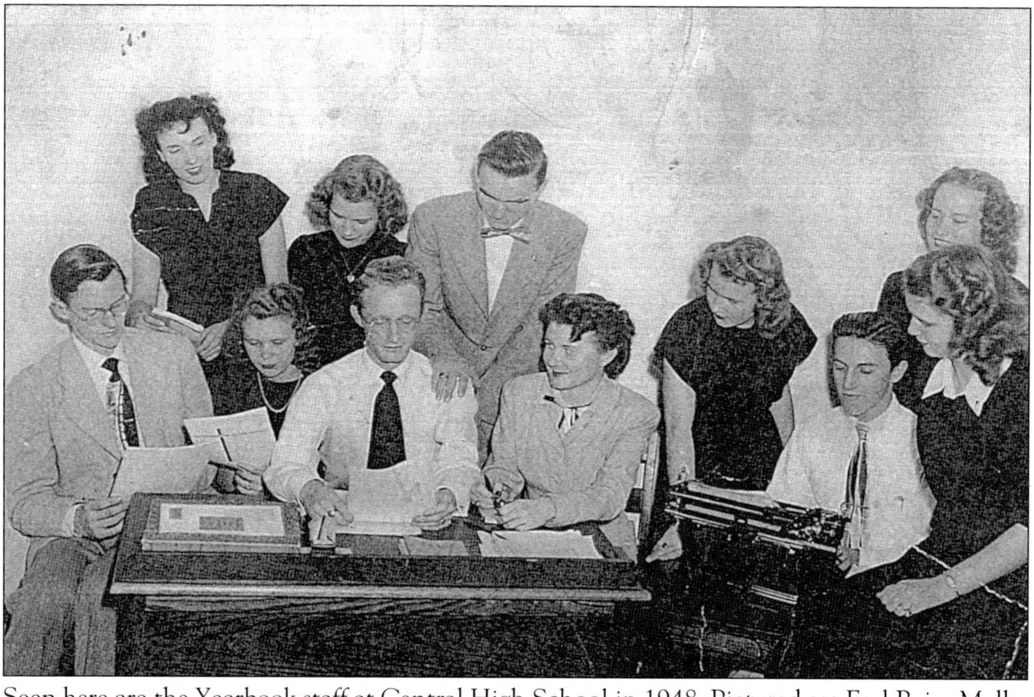

Seen here are the Yearbook staff at Central High School in 1948. Pictured are Earl Bain, Melba Williams, Bob Williams, Iretice Holland, Mackie Holmes, Violet Lovick, Odell Parker, Maxine Williams, Mattie Bunce, Peggy Lucas, and faculty advisor Dell Sweat.

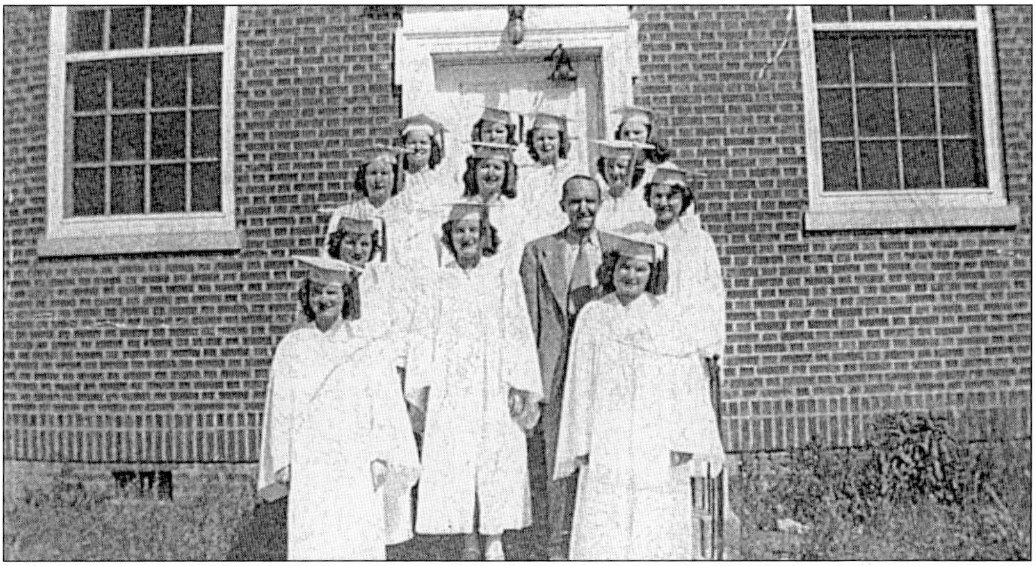

Female members of the Central High School senior class of 1949 pose before graduation along with class sponsor S. Rhodes Moffitt.

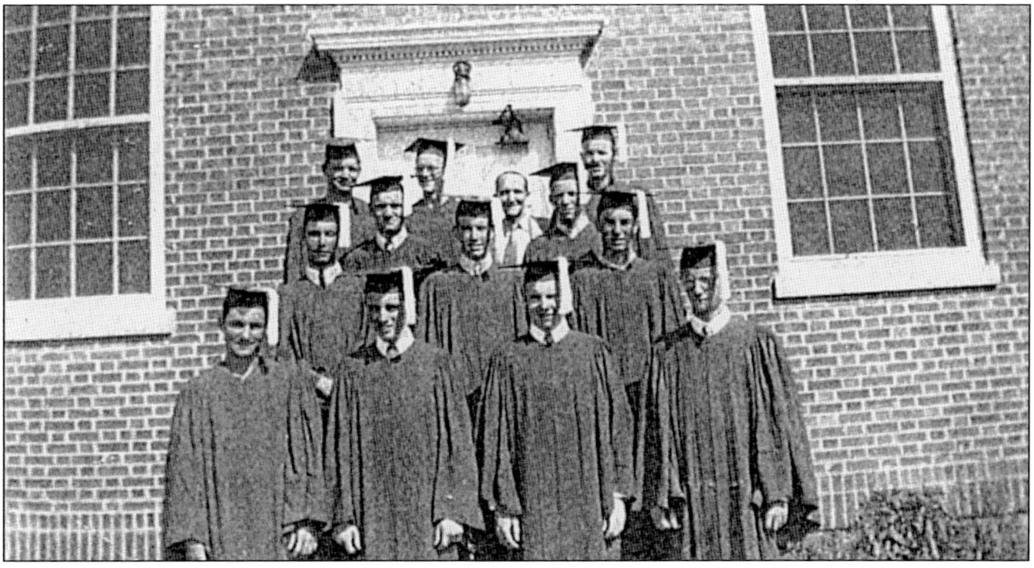

Seen here are male members of the Central High School senior class of 1949.

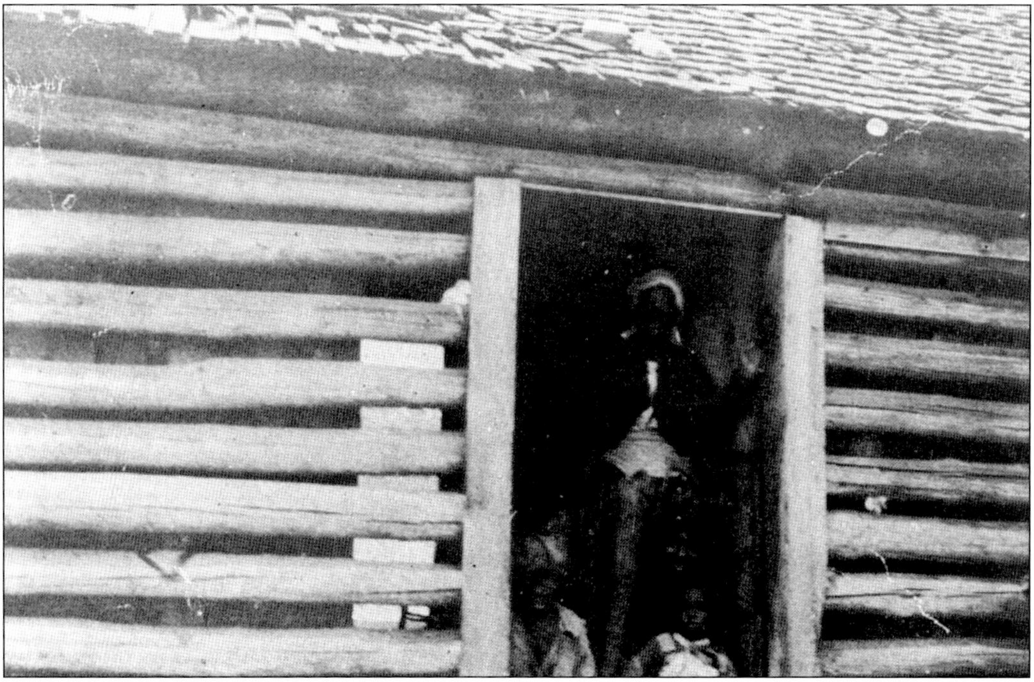

A tenant farmer's cabin is pictured in 1918. (Courtesy N.C. Department of Archives and History.)

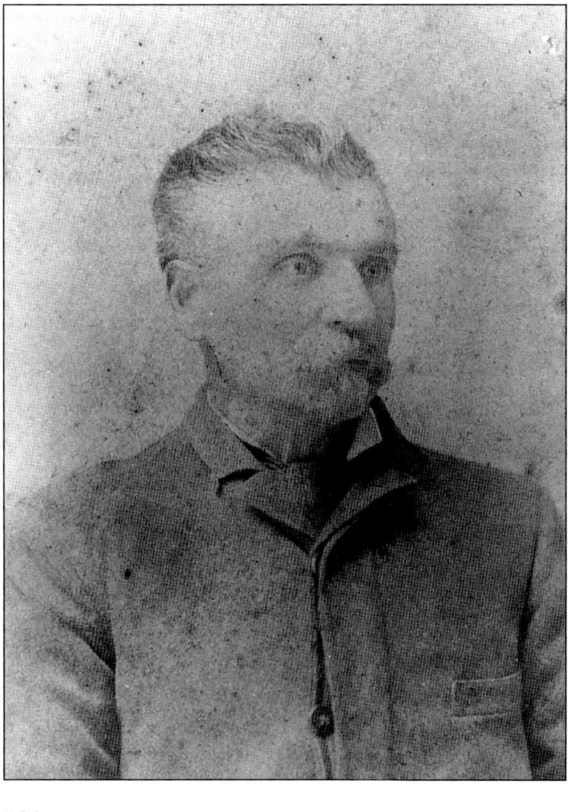

Walter Watson, born in 1836, was a British immigrant who taught rifle making at the Fayetteville Arsenal. (Courtesy N.C. Department of Archives and History.)

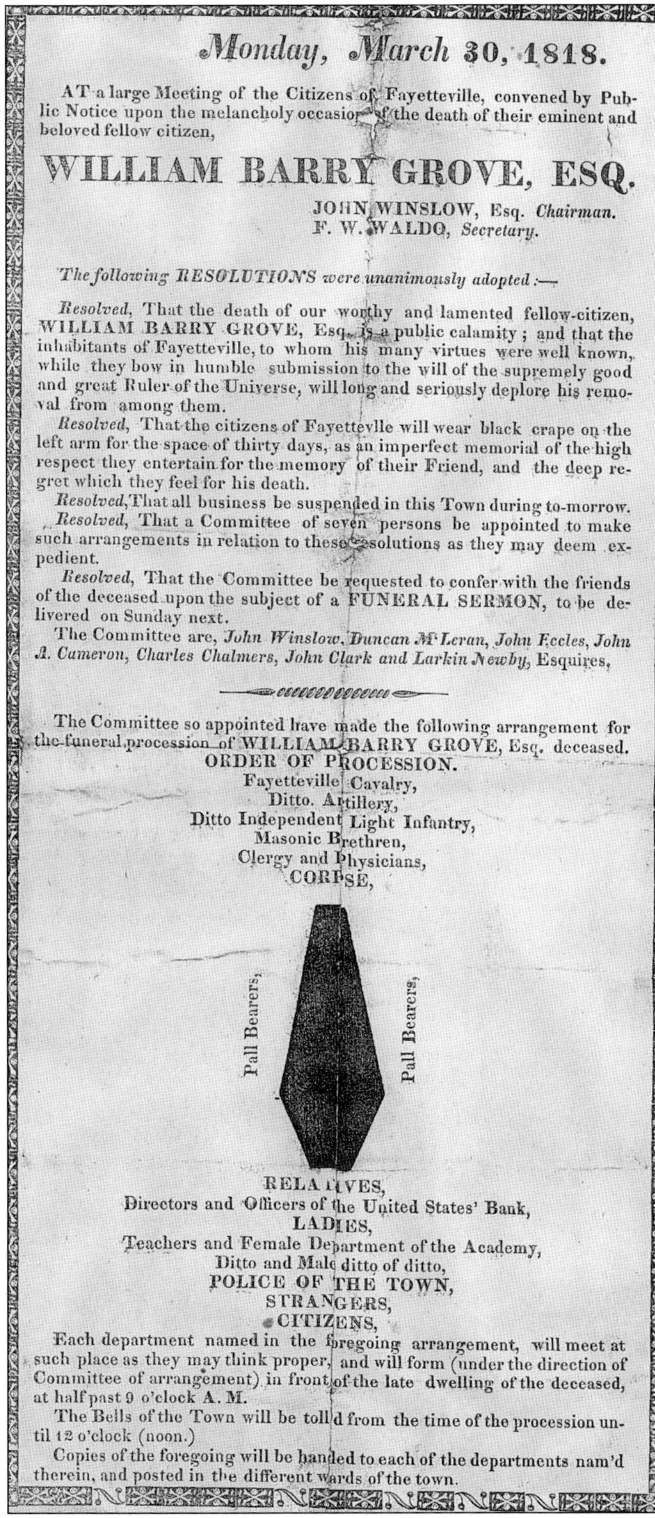

Monday, March 30, 1818.

AT a large Meeting of the Citizens of Fayetteville, convened by Public Notice upon the melancholy occasion of the death of their eminent and beloved fellow citizen,

WILLIAM BARRY GROVE, ESQ.

JOHN WINSLOW, Esq. *Chairman.*
F. W. WALDO, *Secretary.*

The following RESOLUTIONS were unanimously adopted:—

Resolved, That the death of our worthy and lamented fellow-citizen, WILLIAM BARRY GROVE, Esq. is a public calamity; and that the inhabitants of Fayetteville, to whom his many virtues were well known, while they bow in humble submission to the will of the supremely good and great Ruler of the Universe, will long and seriously deplore his removal from among them.

Resolved, That the citizens of Fayettevlle will wear black crape on the left arm for the space of thirty days, as an imperfect memorial of the high respect they entertain for the memory of their Friend, and the deep regret which they feel for his death.

Resolved, That all business be suspended in this Town during to-morrow.

Resolved, That a Committee of seven persons be appointed to make such arrangements in relation to these resolutions as they may deem expedient.

Resolved, That the Committee be requested to confer with the friends of the deceased upon the subject of a FUNERAL SERMON, to be delivered on Sunday next.

The Committee are, *John Winslow, Duncan M'Leran, John Eccles, John A. Cameron, Charles Chalmers, John Clark and Larkin Newby,* Esquires.

The Committee so appointed have made the following arrangement for the funeral procession of WILLIAM BARRY GROVE, Esq. deceased.

ORDER OF PROCESSION.

Fayetteville Cavalry,
Ditto. Artillery,
Ditto Independent Light Infantry,
Masonic Brethren,
Clergy and Physicians,
CORPSE,

Pall Bearers, Pall Bearers,

RELATIVES,
Directors and Officers of the United States' Bank,
LADIES,
Teachers and Female Department of the Academy,
Ditto and Male ditto of ditto,
POLICE OF THE TOWN,
STRANGERS,
CITIZENS,

Each department named in the foregoing arrangement, will meet at such place as they may think proper, and will form (under the direction of Committee of arrangement) in front of the late dwelling of the deceased, at half past 9 o'clock A. M.

The Bells of the Town will be toll'd from the time of the procession until 12 o'clock (noon.)

Copies of the foregoing will be handed to each of the departments nam'd therein, and posted in the different wards of the town.

Broadside announces the death and funeral plans of William Barry Grove in 1818. Grove was a congressman and served as an original trustee of the University of North Carolina. Grove Street in Fayetteville is named in his honor.

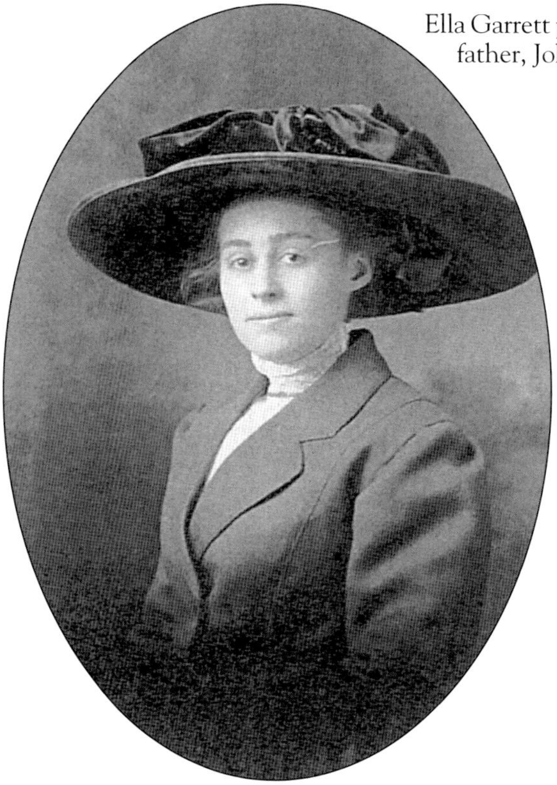

Ella Garrett poses for her graduation portrait in 1910. Her father, John E. Garrett, was a Fayetteville alderman.

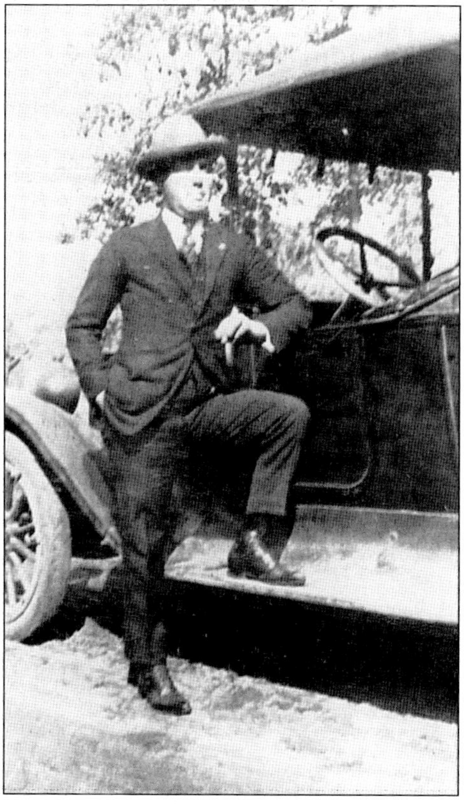

John Edgar Garrett, twin brother of Ella Garrett, is seen standing by his Model T in 1912.

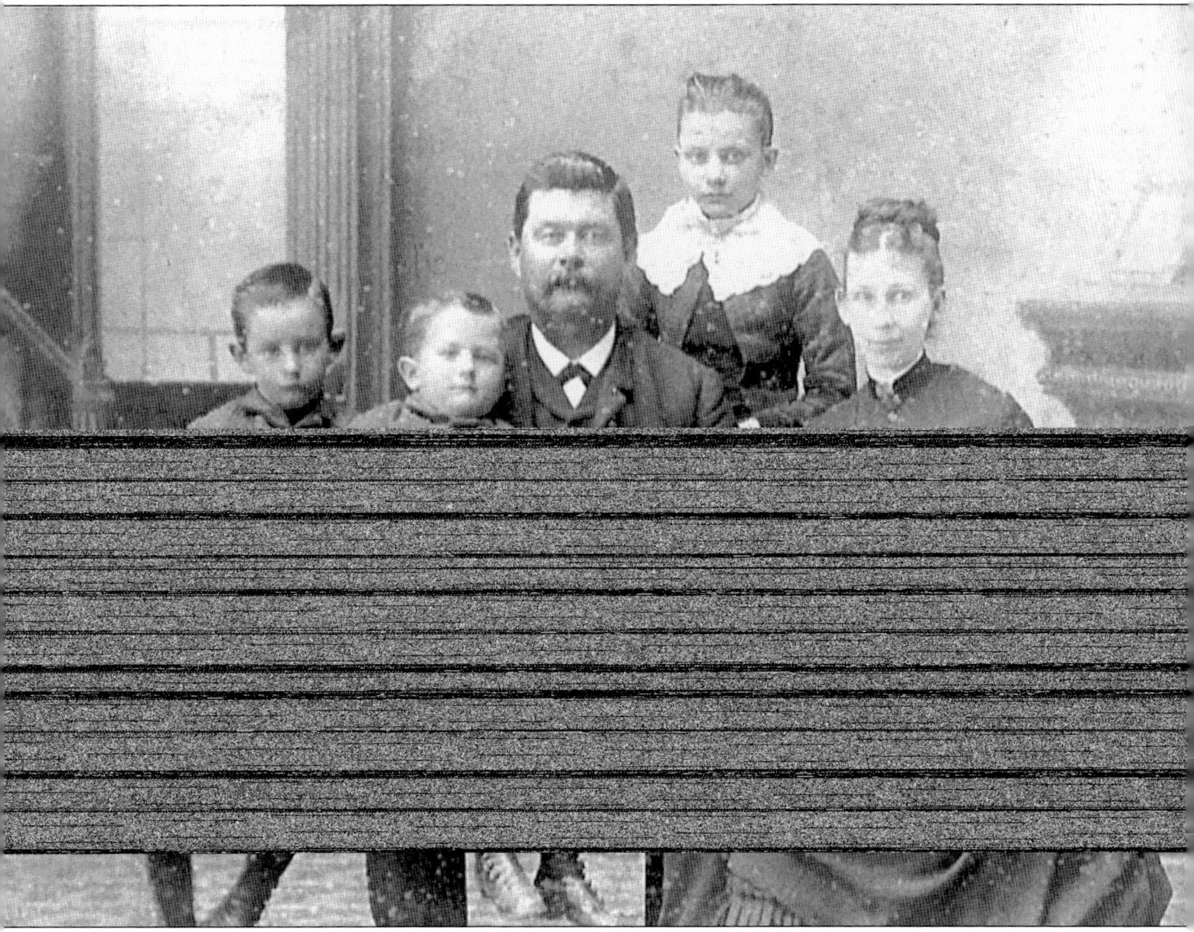

The Danny Pate family sits for a photograph in the living room of their Fayetteville home.

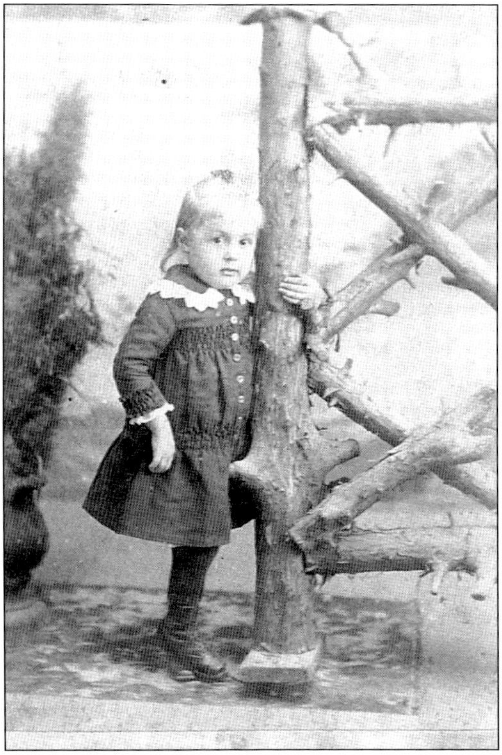

Ida Garrett, daughter of John E. Garrett, is pictured in 1880.

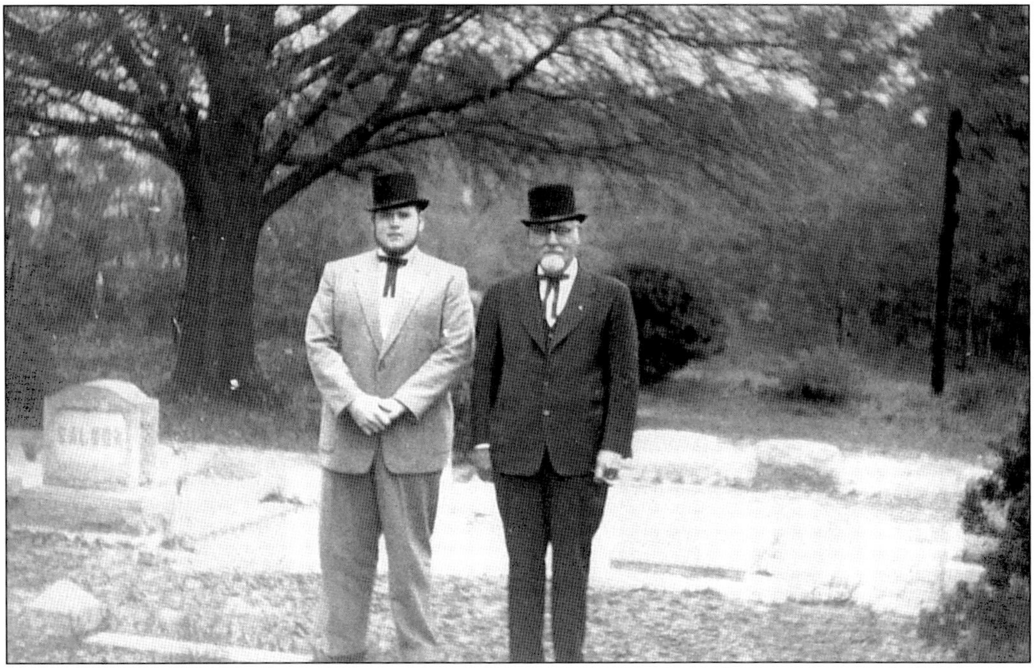

Linwood Rivenbark and alderman Joseph Beard are photographed at Cross Creek cemetery in the early 1950s.

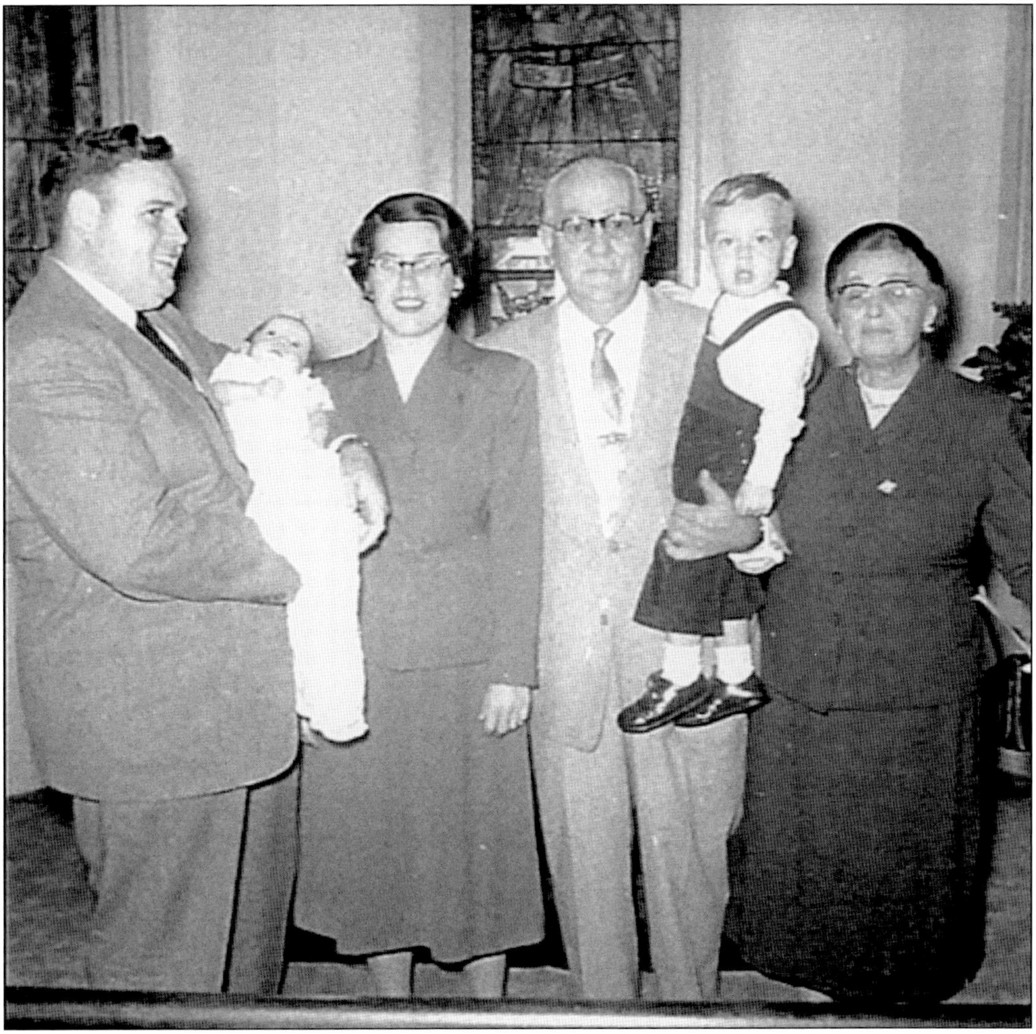

Joella Rivenbark, daughter of Peggy and Linwood Rivenbark, is shown following her infant baptism service at Hay Street Methodist Church in Fayetteville on December 23, 1956. Pictured from left to right are: Linwood Rivenbark holding Joella, Peggy Rivenbark, grandfather Joseph Beard holding Russ Rivenbark, and grandmother Ella Garrett Beard.